# RED FEMINISM

Kate Weigand

# RED
# FEMINISM

American Communism

and the Making

of Women's Liberation

The Johns Hopkins University Press
Baltimore and London

The Johns Hopkins University Press
2715 North Charles Street
Baltimore, Maryland 21218-4363
www.press.jhu.edu

A catalog record for this book is available from the British Library.

Library of Congress Cataloging-in-Publication Data

Weigand, Kate, 1965–
   Red feminism : American communism and the making of women's
liberation / Kate Weigand.
      p.   cm.—(Reconfiguring American political history) Includes
bibliographical references and index.
   ISBN 0-8018-6489-5 (hardcover : acid-free paper)
   1. Women and communism—United States—History—20th
century.   2. Women in politics—United States—History—20th
century.   3. Women's rights—United States—History—20th century.
4. United States—Politics and government—20th century.   5. United
States—Social conditions—20th century.   I. Title.   II. Series.
   HX546 .W35 2001
   324.273′75′082—dc21

00-008874

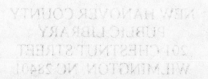

To Nancy and Jonah

# Contents

# List of Illustrations

# Preface and Acknowledgments

LIKE MANY HISTORICAL MONOGRAPHS, this book grew out of a doctoral dissertation. I began the dissertation in 1991 and sent off the final version of the book in 1999, so the entire process of research and writing took place after the supposed end of the Cold War. Nevertheless, for all those years, whenever I told people about my work, they would look at me strangely and ask, "How did you ever get interested in that?" It was clear to me then, as it is now, that even in this post–Cold War period of U.S. history, most people still think of American Communists as pawns of the Soviet Union—naïve at best, at worst, evil.

Because they realize that scholars' research interests often grow from their personal experiences, the second question people have asked me over the years is whether I am a Communist or whether my parents or grandparents were. I suspect that some other people have also wondered whether I might be trying to follow in the footsteps of J. Edgar Hoover, aiming to discredit the women's movement by proving that it was actually a Communist plot. In fact, none of these things are true. My grandparents were ethnic working-class Catholics who probably cheered for Joe McCarthy. My parents were good liberal Democrats but a little too conventional to participate in the movements of the 1960s. I was born in the mid-1960s and, although my parents' lessons about peace and civil rights and equality ultimately made me more radical than they, growing up in the 1970s and 1980s made it clear to me that Soviet-style Communism was not the solution to problems I wanted to solve. And by the 1980s, the Communist Party in the United States was so small and embattled that I probably would have had trouble finding it, had I wanted to join.

The real reason I became interested in American Communism in the period of the 1940s and 1950s is that I became politically active in the 1980s. As an enthusiastic but isolated left-leaning feminist who spent three years on a conservative college campus at the height of the Reagan years, I was desperate to find some historical role models, some other women who remained committed to radical politics in conservative and demoralizing periods. In 1987 I began graduate school in women's history with a vague and undefined interest in what I thought of as "radical women in the McCarthy era." In 1988 I began research on the radical women—most of them Communists—who testified before the Ohio Un-American Activities Commission in the early 1950s. In the course of that process I found what I expected to find—that Communist women posed a challenge to the feminine mystique simply by the unconventional ways they lived their lives. But I also found evidence that took me quite by surprise: the contents of Communist Party newspapers, magazines, and pamphlets made it clear that between 1945 and 1956 at least some Communist and progressive women were writing and talking a great deal about the sources of women's oppression and struggling against male supremacy in the Communist Party as well as in their families, their workplaces, and U.S. society at large. That material convinced me that despite their shortcomings, progressive and Communist women were the most radical feminists of the antifeminist 1950s, and it made me wonder whether or not they had had any impact on the women's movement of the 1960s and 1970s. Now, ten years later, I have concluded that they did. Here I tell their story.

IN THE LONG COURSE of completing this book, I have benefited from the help of many people. First and foremost my appreciation and admiration for Leila Rupp are boundless. I have gained immeasurably from her advice, her brilliant insights, and her encouragement and reassurance throughout every stage of this project. Even after I was no longer officially her student, she made time in her busy life to read nearly every version of this manuscript. In the twelve years I have known her, she has been an excellent dissertation director, an important personal and professional role model, and a generous colleague and friend. I also thank Susan Hartmann and Warren Van Tine for their support, helpful comments, and suggestions.

Thanks to the Johns Hopkins University Press, especially Joan Cashin for her interest in the manuscript, Ronald Walters, and an anonymous reviewer for their valuable comments, and Robert Brugger for his patience and editorial assistance. Thanks also to Jean Eckenfels for her efficient and elegant copyediting of the manuscript.

I thank the following people for reading and responding to sections of the dissertation or suggesting useful ideas and directions: Sara Evans, Dorothy Healey, Daniel Horowitz, Maurice Isserman, Paula Schwartz, Linn Shapiro, and Gerald Zahavi. Linn Shapiro and Kathy Campbell both aided my efforts by lending me important primary source documents that I could not have located elsewhere. I am also extremely grateful to the women I interviewed who were very generous with both their time and their memories. Finally, I thank Paul Mishler, Kathleen Nutter, Eleanor Trawick, and Nancy Whittier for reading and responding to the entire manuscript. All of these people are responsible for much of what is good about this book, but of course any errors it contains are solely mine.

The staffs of several libraries and manuscript repositories provided critical assistance. Irene Still Meyer and Kristie French in the Special Collections Department of the California State University–Long Beach Library granted me access to the Dorothy Healey Collection even though the building was in the midst of renovation. Peter Filardo at the Tamiment Library at New York University provided important information about sources and arranged for me to borrow a large number of taped oral history interviews through interlibrary loan. Eva Moseley at the Schlesinger Library arranged to have the Mary Inman papers processed so that they would be available for my use. Elizabeth Swain at the Wesleyan University Library located a full run of the *Worker* in library storage and moved them into the main reading room so that I would not have to go to Washington and read them in the Library of Congress. The staff of the Sophia Smith Collection and the College Archives at Smith College, especially Amy Hague and Margery Sly, was particularly helpful in the research phase of this project. They took great interest in my topic and went above and beyond my expectations, providing expert assistance at locating relevant source materials. The reference staff and interlibrary loan staff at the Neilson Library at Smith College also provided much appreciated assistance.

My research was funded by a Women's Studies Small Grant from the Center for Women's Studies and a Graduate School Alumni Research Award, both from Ohio State University. A Presidential Fellowship awarded by the Graduate School at Ohio State provided me with a year free from teaching responsibilities to devote to the dissertation. That funding allowed me to complete my research and initial writing for this project more quickly and easily than I would have otherwise. The Five College Women's Studies Research Center at Mount Holyoke College provided a forum for my ideas at an important time in the formative stages of this process, and my colleagues there provided valuable support and feedback.

Last but by no means least, I am indebted to my friends and family for the roles they played in the completion of the book. My parents Maureen and Dick Weigand nurtured in me the values and persistence that enabled me to pursue these ideas for as long as I have. My friend Tarin Weiss listened empathetically to my grumblings about the difficulties of combining work and parenthood. Tarin, along with the wonderful teachers at the Smith College Infant and Toddler Program and the Campus School preschool, also nurtured and entertained my son for many hours in order to give me the time to write.

Jonah Weigand-Whittier's impending arrival provided the ultimate incentive for finishing my dissertation. His infancy and very early childhood coincided with the manuscript's transformation from dissertation to book. While his compelling needs and antics often distracted me from my work, his extraordinary presence also served as a constant reminder about why feminist and progressive activism continues to be important.

Finally, I will always be grateful to Nancy Whittier for the seemingly limitless emotional and intellectual support she generously gave over the whole course of this project. Our long late-night conversations about social movement continuity, the origins of everything in the Communist Party, and the importance of culture and consciousness were critical to the formation of my ideas. Without her enthusiasm and patience—not to mention her willingness to earn more than her share of money, cook more than her share of dinners, and occasionally do more than her share of parenting—I would not have been able to write this book. Most of all I thank Nancy and Jonah for their timely reminders that there was life away from the computer keyboard, and especially for their enduring love and companionship.

# RED FEMINISM

# Introduction: Old Left Women,

# the U.S. Women's Movement,

# and the Legacy of Anti-Communism

IN 1946, THIRTY-YEAR-OLD SUSAN B. ANTHONY II, grand-niece and namesake of the famous nineteenth-century suffragist and feminist, offered her assessment of gender relations in the United States at the time. "Just as the white race likes to raise its own prestige by detracting from and minimizing the abilities of the Negro race," she wrote, "so men in general like to build up their superiority by minimizing all women." They did so, she suggested, by presenting "women as frivolous, superficial, flighty, catty, stupid and weak." Anthony argued that "this process begins in the home, and is nurtured by textbooks, press, movies, radio and theater" and that "these prevalent attitudes result in giving women a sex inferiority complex, second only to the racial inferiority complex of many Negroes." Ultimately, Anthony concluded that this process perpetuated women's oppression by making women "feel that they do not deserve and therefore should not ask for a better place in the world."[1]

Anthony's outspoken feminist analysis was remarkable given the magnitude of antifeminism in the post–World War II decade. She demonstrated a degree of race consciousness surprising in a young white woman writing well before dramatic events like the Montgomery Bus boycott made civil rights a national political issue. Her attention to the similarities between sexism and racism and to their effects on self-esteem was something that one would expect to see in a document from the late 1960s, not the late 1940s.[2]

Susan Anthony did not develop her ideas as an isolated individual in the conservative and antifeminist 1940s, nor was she motivated solely by a desire to carry on her famous great aunt's work. Rather, Anthony was just one participant in a small but significant group of women activists that included Eleanor Flexner, Gerda Lerner, and Eve Merriam, all of whom would emerge as influential feminist writers in the 1960s and later. These women, along with many others who are less well-known, worked for women's liberation within their own political circles and in the United States at large during the hostile years of 1945–56. The group consisted primarily of women who had cut their political teeth in the Left and labor struggles of the 1930s.

1

The circles in which these women did their most important work in the 1940s and 1950s centered around the American Communist Party (CP).

Anthony and her comrades shared with their contemporaries in the Old Left a vision for a new American society. Along with most others who participated in and joined such coalitions and movements in the 1930s and 1940s, these women worked toward the creation of a socialist world that could guarantee economic, social, and political equality for everyone regardless of class, race, or ethnicity. Moreover, this group made women's liberation a priority. The Old Left in general and the Communist Party in particular, they believed, did not take women's oppression or the much-discussed "woman question" seriously enough.[3]

The mid-1940s was not an easy time for any woman—Communist or not—to become a feminist. Throughout the "decades of discontent" that came between the suffrage victory of 1920 and the publication of *The Feminine Mystique* in 1963, the lack of a visible women's movement allowed most people to believe that disgruntled women were simply neurotic malcontents.[4] Without the support of a broad-based women's movement Anthony, Lerner, Merriam, Flexner, and others turned instead to the tradition of feminist writing and activism that had flourished during the 1910s. They used the ideas pioneered by earlier activists such as Charlotte Perkins Gilman, Henrietta Rodman, Crystal Eastman, and others to nurture a new radical women's movement. In doing so, they sought to expand the typically narrow Marxist understanding of women's oppression, which focused on economic structures to explain women's inferior status around the world. Most important, they argued that male supremacy impaired both individual and structural relations between men and women, and they pushed the Communists to put their theoretical commitment to women's liberation into practice at every level of the progressive movement.

Though their efforts met with limited success, progressive women's accomplishments were quite significant given the cultural and economic norms of the postwar period. In response to their pressure, Communist publications dramatically expanded their coverage of women's issues. By the late 1940s, many Communist leaders and rank-and-file members alike agreed that women's oppression had social and cultural as well as economic components and discussed the distinctive problems faced by African American women and other women of color. Party leaders also encouraged women and men active on the Left to identify and resist sexism in their organized political activities, their family lives, and their personal relationships.

It goes without saying that progressive women's struggles of the 1940s and 1950s did not even come close to eradicating gender inequality among

American Communists and their supporters. Throughout those decades the Communist Party and the progressive Left continued to perpetuate many of the discriminatory attitudes and policies toward women that Anthony and the others set out to change. Nevertheless, progressive women's work is particularly significant because its influence ultimately reached far beyond the Old Left. Anthony and the others did not simply resurrect the radical feminist thinking of the 1910s. They revolutionized it by conceptualizing the dynamics of women's oppression and liberation within a framework that made race and class central. They sustained a small but vibrant women's movement through the 1940s and 1950s and transmitted influential terminology, tactics, and concepts to the next generation of feminists. Their bold new thinking about the interdependence of gender, race, and class, and about the personal and cultural aspects of sexism, shaped modern feminism—both directly and indirectly—and laid absolutely crucial groundwork for the second wave. Since its emergence in the 1960s the modern women's movement has transformed gender relations and women's status in the United States. The issues Communist and progressive feminists raised in the decade after World War II still reverberate throughout American society as we enter the twenty-first century.

THE STORY OF SUSAN B. ANTHONY II and her comrades is a central episode in the history of the U.S. women's movement and gender relations in the second half of the twentieth century. Why, then, has their story been almost completely overlooked? How have feminists and the general public come to believe that the critique of male chauvinism in personal and family relations emerged for the first time in the mid-1960s? The powerful legacy of anticommunism in the United States is largely responsible for their obscurity. By the time progressive women brought an awareness of gender issues to the Party's agenda, the anti-Communism wrought by Joseph McCarthy and many others had already begun to devastate the Old Left by identifying progressive groups and their constituents as agents of the Soviet Union.[5] In the short term McCarthyism convinced many people that the Left was a large and influential force in American life and that Communists and Communism posed a dangerous threat to the United States. In the long term it forced countless progressive activists to retreat from organized activity and to deny or conceal their political pasts. By the time the New Left appeared on the scene the Old Left looked small, ineffective, and insignificant.

Although it was largely discredited as a political movement by the mid-1960s, McCarthyism has continued over the last forty years to shape Americans' thinking about the role Communists and Communism have played in the United States. Long after the political tide had turned, conservative writers perpetuated the Cold War view of Communists as uncritical and irrational followers of the aggressively expansionist and antidemocratic Soviet Union. Similarly, even many radicals emphasized the Old Left's orthodox Stalinism and suppression of dissent and downplayed actions at the grassroots, its links to other progressive movements of the time, and its contributions to the movements of the 1960s and later.[6]

Ironically, feminists have also played a role in obscuring this important chapter of their own history. Feminism emerged in the United States in the 1910s, when radical young middle- and working-class women sought to redefine the meaning of womanhood and to transform women's status through their work in the suffrage movement and their participation in groups such as Heterodoxy and the National Woman's Party (NWP). Before 1919 many of these early feminists also advocated socialism but, as Nancy Cott suggests, feminism and socialism both became "more organizationally and ideologically specific—the former in the NWP and the latter in the newly formed U.S. Communist Party," and it became less possible for such women to maintain their dual commitments.[7] According to this standard view, radical women had to choose sides as the NWP repudiated every goal but equal rights for women and the Communist Party rejected "reformist" tendencies, such as women's rights, in favor of revolutionary class consciousness.[8] Those women who chose the Left and joined the Communist Party, the story goes, had little choice but to abandon feminism because the Party consistently emphasized the primacy of class over gender, celebrated the heterosexual nuclear family, and refused to support the Equal Rights Amendment. This view suggests that, because of the Communist Party's social and cultural conservatism, individual Communists accepted traditional notions about women's natural submissiveness and subordination.[9] In short, the Old Left seemed insignificant for the history of feminism. Instead, as they searched for their foremothers and reconstructed a "canon" of feminist texts, activists and writers credited the NWP, the YWCA, the American Friends Service Committee, and the United Auto Workers with sustaining feminist ideology and activism through the doldrums of the 1940s and 1950s until a new generation politicized by the Civil Rights movement and the New Left revived the women's movement in the 1960s.[10]

It would be naïve to suggest that such conclusions about the Communist Left and the position of women within it have no basis in reality. It is true, for example, that Party leaders in the United States often repressed dissent within the organization and all too frequently followed Soviet directives that were ill suited to American social and political contexts. This rigidity, in combination with Communists' belated acknowledgment of Stalin's crimes and the impact of McCarthyism, shattered the Old Left and sharply diminished its long-term impact on social protest in later decades. But although a significant number of Communists and progressives abandoned the Left in the 1950s for these reasons, many continued to define themselves as radical political activists of one kind or another. Rather than simply vanishing from politics, some put their years of experience to work in the Civil Rights movement, the anti–Vietnam War movement, the New Left, the antinuclear movement, and the gay and lesbian movement even if they were not always open about their political pasts.[11]

It is also true that for many years Communists tended to glorify aspects of traditional womanhood, to follow conventional patterns of male-female interaction, and to rely on purely economic explanations for women's oppression. This was especially true in the 1930s, the heyday of American Communism and the period most research has focused on. Many progressive women defined themselves and their interests around motherhood and the family and adopted a maternalist style of activism that valorized features of traditional femininity. On its surface, progressives' "women's work" definitely looks somewhat old fashioned and very different from contemporary conceptions of feminist activism.

For all these reasons, many have discounted the possibility that any Communist or progressive women embraced feminist politics or influenced later feminists. But Anthony's 1946 statement suggests that it is too simple to dismiss all Old Leftists as nonfeminist and irrelevant for the history of the U.S. women's movement. The sum of the efforts led by women such as Anthony, Flexner, Claudia Jones, and others demonstrate the Left's real challenges to hegemonic notions about women. They built an ideological and organizational base for a much more visible and successful women's movement twenty years later. They contributed their most valuable feminist work not during the 1930s, when American Communism was a fairly large and influential movement, but during the 1945–56 period, when Communists and their supporters were increasingly marginal and isolated from the masses of U.S. women. *Red Feminism* tells their story. In doing so, it challenges the powerful legacy of McCarthyism by altering the ways we think about the history of Communism and the progressive Left, the history of American feminism, and the relationship between the two.

Although it has been more than ten years since politicians and the media proclaimed the official end of the Cold War, it would be naïve to think that documenting links between the Communist Left and the women's movement in the United States is no longer controversial. On the contrary, even at the very end of the twentieth century, the terms *communism* and *feminism* still evoke strong reactions in most people, especially among those who have some stake in the telling of this story. For related but different reasons many readers will find this argument troubling.

Feminists are understandably suspicious of any effort to uncover a relationship between the current women's movement and the Communist Left. For although anti-Communism obscured the Left's real contributions to feminism, anti-Communists also repeatedly linked Communism with feminism in order to discredit the women's movement. In the 1920s, for example, right-wing groups red-baited American women's organizations (including the National Woman's Party and the Women's International League for Peace and Freedom, among others) by circulating "spider web charts" that supposedly documented "Bolshevik" control of those organizations.[12] In 1947 psychologists Ferdinand Lundberg and Marynia Farnham argued in their best-selling book *Modern Woman: The Lost Sex* that "the political agents of the Kremlin abroad continue to beat the feminist drums in full awareness of its disruptive influence among the potential enemies of the Soviet Union."[13] And from 1969 to 1972 FBI director J. Edgar Hoover ordered agents to infiltrate feminist organizations, presumably with the hope that they would discover Communist "outside agitators" whose presence would undermine the movement.[14]

Ironically, this book provides evidence to support the belief that at least some Communists regarded the subversion of the gender system as an integral part of the larger fight to overturn capitalism. Nevertheless, it is not another attempt to show that feminism was a Communist plot. For although it is true that after 1945 Communist and progressive women and modern feminists are similar in many ways, there are also stark differences between the gender politics of the post–World War II Communist Party and those of the second wave of the women's movement. Communists saw gender and race oppression as derived from class-based economic exploitation, whereas many feminists pointed to the existence of male domination in precapitalist and so-called socialist societies as evidence that gender superseded class. These divergent views went along with opposing strategies for dealing with sexism. The Party insisted that the common interests of women and men required them to work side by side to oppose all the exploitative consequences of capitalism, including male supremacy, which they often made secondary to larger social and economic reform. A large number of feminists, on the other hand, argued that traditional political organizations favored "male" issues over female ones and that sexism made it difficult if not impossible for women to work for their own liberation within mixed-sex groups. Furthermore, although Communist activists recognized the personal implications of their political beliefs, they tended to focus primarily on larger social and economic institutions as sites of struggle against male domination and, by and large, to neglect questions about sex and sexuality. Due in part to the context of the sexual revolution out of which 1960s feminism emerged, 1960s feminists made issues of sexuality central and emphasized the need to transform themselves and their surroundings, even though they also worked to change economic and social structures.

These differences—along with many others—mitigate any suggestion that Communist women incited the women's movement or that 1960s feminists adopted the gender politics of the Old Left wholesale. But although the women's movement of the 1960s and 1970s differed in many ways from what came before it, the movement did not emerge as a fully developed entity in the mid-1960s. Rather, second-wave feminists built upon the work of various groups that preceded them, including the work of women who inspired and were inspired by the Old Left's efforts to take women's issues seriously after 1945.

As feminists are reluctant to be associated with Communism, so are many former Communists and other Old Leftists hesitant to be identified with feminism. Their objection stems not from any opposition to the larger goal of women's liberation, which they generally supported, but from Communists' long tradition of antagonism to the distinct and historically specific meaning of "feminism" as a term. In a conversation with German revolutionary Klara Zetkin, Lenin established the official Communist point of view in 1920, when he declared that feminism was a dangerous right-wing deviation invented by a misguided segment of the bourgeoisie. American Communists naturally adopted this position because it came from Lenin himself, but also because their experiences with organized feminism in the United States consistently bore out his conclusion.

From the 1920s until the early 1960s "feminism" was the domain of National Woman's Party members and supporters.[15] These self-defined feminists spent forty years lobbying elected officials to improve women's status and campaigning for the passage of various reforms, especially the Equal Rights Amendment. But while the NWP worked actively to win formal legal equality for women, it had strong ties to the traditional political system. Its members were in many cases conservative and even reactionary when it came to other struggles for social change. Political progressives knew Alice Paul, the founder and leader of the NWP through the forties and fifties for her anti-Communism, her opposition to the labor movement, and her racism and anti-Semitism. Because the NWP claimed the terms *feminist* and *feminism*, Communists understandably wanted nothing to do with them. In the minds of most progressive women in the United States, to be a feminist meant not only that one supported the ERA rather than protective legislation for women workers, thereby privileging white middle-class women's interests, but also, as numerous articles in the Party press suggested, that one was probably racist and anti-Semitic as well.

Consequently, progressive and Communist women went to great lengths to avoid calling themselves feminists. When Anthony wrote to a Communist friend in the early 1940s, for example, she specified that she "was so conscious of being a subject sex" that she saw "everything from the non-feminist woman angle," meaning that she interpreted her life from a point of view that we would call feminist, even though she did not want to call herself one. Recognizing the need for a concise term to define their complicated perspective on gender these women searched for a reasonable alternative. Anthony was not the only progressive woman to suggest that "We are going to have to coin a word to describe our platform on the woman question." Unfortunately, neither Anthony nor her fellow progressives ever came up with a concise term that embraced both their Marxism and their commitment to women's liberation. Throughout the forties and fifties they searched for "a good descriptive word for those of us who believe that the ending of discrimination against women is fully as vital a problem today as the ending of discrimination against Negroes, foreign born and Jews."[16] Even at the height of their feminist efforts these women were still simply calling themselves Communists or progressives or sometimes "good Communists" and "good progressives." As late as 1968, even many New Left women who supported women's liberation continued to refer to feminism as "the F-word."[17] Despite their conscious rejection of the terms, however, the contemporary meanings of the words *feminist* and *feminism* best describe these women's ideology and political work. I call them progressive feminists, not because I want to minimize or disrespect the important distinctions these women made in the 1940s and 1950s, but because they were feminists according to our current understanding of the term and because it seems the best way to make their sophisticated consciousness about women's position in the United States completely clear.

Not only are Old Left activists sometimes still averse to calling themselves feminists, but some of them—particularly those who have long been quiet about their political pasts—will undoubtedly feel threatened when they are identified here as participants in the Communist movement of the 1940s and 1950s. Indeed this issue of public identification of Communists and their supporters is a difficult one. Some would argue that my efforts to name progressives and Communists mentioned in American Communist and feminist documents in the 1990s are little different from HUAC's efforts to do the same thing fifty years ago. In reality, however, there are crucial distinctions between the two. First of all, the current context is very different from that of the late 1940s and 1950s. Whereas American Communists seemed ubiquitous and threatening during the first decades of the Cold War, in the post-Soviet world many people see them as humorously marginal and almost completely insignificant. Naming former participants in the Communist movement is a far less dangerous prospect in the twenty-first century than it was even twenty years ago. Second, intention and interpretation are important. Joseph McCarthy and other anti-Communists "named names" in order to disgrace individuals and to discredit the Old Left as a whole. My intention is to acknowledge the important contributions that Communists and their allies made to the women's movement and to recognize the significant role they played in shaping late-twentieth-century politics. Far from attempting to defame or malign women who did not publicly disclose their progressive pasts, this book aims to acknowledge their accomplishments and to recast their political histories as a source of pride and dignity, not shame or embarrassment.

For my purposes, whether or not an individual was actually a member of the Communist Party is not particularly important. The Communist Party was the center of a large progressive movement that encompassed many organizations, and it profoundly influenced thousands of women and men. Many of them read the Party press and participated in formal and informal Party activities without officially joining the organization.[18] Their exposure to and support for Old Left ideas about women's oppression and male supremacy are what really matter. Both—some progressive women who joined the Party and some who did not—learned from Party writings and classes about the woman question and, inspired by their new knowledge, continued to champion women's issues throughout the 1950s and into the 1960s. Ultimately, it was their tenacious commitment to women's liberation, not the degree of their commitment to the Communist Party itself, that created a framework upon which 1960s feminists could build.

Finally, those who continue to believe that the American Communist Party was simply a "conspiracy financed by a hostile foreign power" and assume that every rank-and-file Communist pledged "both unconditional and unwavering loyalty to the dictates of Soviet policy" will undoubtedly be appalled by the suggestion that Communist and progressive women influenced second-wave feminism.[19] These conservative commentators cite evidence from recently opened Soviet archives that shows some American Communists participated in Soviet espionage activities and suggest it confirms McCarthy's assumption that the Soviet Union exercised substantial power over the Party in America. Such documents do, in fact, reveal the American Party's dependence on "Moscow gold" and show that some American Communists worked as foot soldiers for the Comintern. They do not, however, prove that either the American or the Soviet Communist

Party controlled every individual U.S. Communist or that American Communists and progressives toed the Soviet Party line assiduously. On the contrary, progressive rank-and-filers in the United States could sometimes take advantage of the Soviet Union's failure to dictate policy on a particular issue and, with hard work, gradually challenge and even change the Party's stance on that issue. Old Left women did so when they mobilized their movement for women's liberation within the infrastructure of the Party. Although the American Communist Party was a rigid and hierarchical organization partially controlled by the Soviet Union, it was also the institutional center of a large, influential, and uniquely American radical political movement. As such, it regularly channeled thousands of grassroots activists into a whole range of respected political causes including the civil rights and union movements and, occasionally, learned from them in turn.[20]

In spite of such potential for controversy, it is important to tell this previously little-known story of women's liberation within the Communist movement in the 1940s and 1950s and its impact on second-wave feminism. Progressive women faced disadvantages that ranged from the paralyzing effects of McCarthyism to the lack of a mass-based women's movement and the prevailing cultural assumption that American women were primarily domestic beings. Yet they developed a new approach to women's liberation in this decade after World War II that combined existing Marxist and feminist ideology in new ways, challenged the Old Left's complacency on the woman question, and created an atmosphere within which discussions about women's oppression and liberation became routine. In this environment feminist ideology could survive into the 1960s.

In addition to its intrinsic importance, however, the story of progressive women's struggles against male supremacy inside and outside the Old Left sheds new light on U.S. politics since 1945. Without Anthony, Flexner, Jones, Merriam, and their supporters, the immediate postwar period appears quite bleak. Stalinism and McCarthyism together combined, in effect, to destroy the remains of the American progressive movement during the 1940s and 1950s and made conformity, conservatism, and antifeminism the order of the day. Restoring progressive women to the historical record and recognizing their feminist achievements changes this view considerably. It reveals that beneath the political repression that dominated the post–World War II period was a struggling but spirited feminist movement composed of black and white, working- and middle-class women who expanded upon early-twentieth-century feminism and developed new approaches to women's liberation even though they also accepted some elements of traditional female roles.

That Anthony and her comrades could successfully organize to address the Left's longstanding neglect of the woman question—and that they could convey important elements of their approach to 1960s feminists—suggests that neither Communist authoritarianism nor anti-Communist repression completely stifled 1950s radical rank-and-file activism. These women's opposition to sexism, their interest in personal transformation, and their efforts to create a progressive culture through which they could live out their politics suggests that the late 1940s and 1950s were not nearly as distinct from the 1960s as people have assumed. By persisting in their struggles against male supremacy, striving for gender equality in their personal and political lives, and working to improve women's status politically, economically, and culturally, Communist and progressive women and men forged a foundation upon which the second wave could build. In all these ways, Susan Anthony and her comrades quietly ushered women's liberation into the late twentieth century. Despite the devastating impact of McCarthyism, Communist feminists set in motion a powerful movement to transform women's status and gender relations that continues to shape American politics and culture as we enter the new millennium.

# I
# FOUNDATIONS

# 1 Building Unity amidst Diversity:

## Ethnicity, Race, and Gender in the Early Years

## of American Communism

THE EARLY HISTORY of the Communist Party in the United States is complicated and tumultuous and does not, on the surface, appear to suggest an environment likely to generate activism around the issues of ethnic identity, race, or gender. Starting in 1919, when U.S. Communists severed their ties with the more moderate Socialist Party, competing groups engaged in intense and frequent sectarian battles over a variety of issues, each attempting to win official and exclusive recognition and legitimacy from the highest Communist authority, the Soviet-led international Communist Party, or Comintern. Even after the rival factions finally merged in 1922, they continued to wage internecine war with one another.[1] These struggles, combined with the effects of the red scare of the 1920s, drove the infant Communist movement underground, reduced its original membership by more than half, and limited its ability to carry out "mass work." Given such circumstances, it seems highly unlikely that any Communist—whatever his or her stance on revolutionary ideology and strategy—could consider any issue beyond short-term survival.

Despite their preoccupation with the pressing question of how to sustain and build a revolutionary movement within the world's preeminent capitalist nation, American Communists could not ignore the issues of ethnicity and race in the 1920s and 1930s. On the contrary, Communists' desire to build an effective and unified Party in the increasingly multicultural United States compelled them to pay close attention to these issues.[2] The lessons Communists learned from their early work toward resolving the Party's ethnic and racial conflicts influenced their later strategies for liberating oppressed groups. Specifically, CP leaders became increasingly aware throughout the twenties and thirties that some members held chauvinistic beliefs about others and that the oppressive attitudes and behaviors of even a few individual Communists could hinder the whole group's efforts to create a working model of ethnic and racial integration. This knowledge, combined with a large influx of women members late in the 1930s, built the foundation for Communists' eventual approach to gender issues. Their regard for the "woman question" in the 1920s was minimal and tokenistic

15

compared with their attention to the "ethnic question" and the "Negro question," but by the late 1930s Communists began using the lessons they had learned from their campaigns against ethnic fragmentation and racism between 1919 and 1936 to make gender issues a more central part of their program. This activity, flawed though it was, laid important groundwork for the pioneering "women's work" they would undertake after World War II.

## 1919–1929

During the CP's formative years ethnicity was the root of both solidarity and cleavage among Communists. Certainly native-born Americans participated in both the Socialist Party and the Communist factions that emerged from it. But because immigrants were more likely than the native-born to embrace radical politics in the 1920s, foreign-born and often non-English-speaking members dominated many of the early Communist groups, including the Workers' Communist Party and its successor the CPUSA.[3] Until 1925 the CP's local divisions consisted of language federations that united those who shared the same ethnicity, language, and political outlook. In addition to serving as local governing units, the federations also worked to maintain important elements of each one's particular ethnic, social, and cultural practices by sponsoring choral and theatrical groups, dances, clubhouses, and language schools for children.

As early as 1919 Communists' disagreements with one another often broke down along ethnic lines. The Russian federation, for example, wanted to emulate Bolshevism as closely as possible; Russian émigrés saw themselves as the natural leaders of the Communist movement in the United States. The Finnish federation, on the other hand, promoted consumer cooperatives as a primary weapon in the class struggle. Native-born American Communists saw a slow and cautious takeover of indigenous working-class institutions such as the American Federation of Labor as the best way to achieve an American Communist state.

After the creation of the newly unified organization called the Workers Communist Party in 1922, rival Communists' disagreements continued to focus around these ethnic divisions and ultimately boiled down to three related issues: First, ethnic factions disagreed about the means by which an American Communist Party could most effectively work toward a Bolshevik-style revolution in the hostile atmosphere of the United States. Second, they argued over who was in the best position—Americans, who were most familiar with the U.S. political situation, or Russians, who saw themselves as the natural champions of Bolshevism—to lead a unified American Communist Party. Third, and most important, there was considerable debate over whether every member of the American CP needed to unite around an identical theoretical and practical approach to Communism, regardless of his or her ethnic identity and political traditions. In other words, the primary question was whether or not it was acceptable—even desirable for the sake of recruiting and retaining members—to permit the CP's ethnic divisions or language federations to retain their various identities and practices and the assorted approaches to Communism that came with them?

Communists were divided by their positions on these complex issues and by the ethnic allegiances and traditions that shaped their diverse cultures and organizing contexts. Throughout the first half of the 1920s Communists in the United States could not agree on either a theoretical approach to revolution-building or a plan for mass action. In 1925, with American Communists still unable to resolve these sectarian problems by themselves, the Communist international stepped in and directed the American CP to accept a new policy it called Bolshevization as the solution. From 1925 to 1928 the American CP adopted Bolshevization by defining ethnic solidarity among Communists as an impediment to Party unity and reorganizing itself to duplicate the structure of the Soviet Communist Party. The Party's new Central Committee stripped the language federations of their autonomy and reorganized them into multiethnic street- and shop-based units that brought together Communists who lived in the same neighborhoods or worked in the same factories.[4] Because Communists who spoke many different languages comprised these new units, the CP implemented a policy they called Americanization to work hand-in-hand with Bolshevization. That process required immigrant Communists to learn English and cooperate with members from other ethnic backgrounds, whether they wanted to or not.

The joint processes of Bolshevization and Americanization discouraged ethnic insularity, but predictably they did not immediately make the Communist Party a more effective force in the United States. In the short term, Americanization and Bolshevization weakened the movement by driving many ethnic groups out of the Party and limiting its ability to recruit members in immigrant working-class communities. Ethnic radicals who found the Communist Party appealing before 1925 frequently regarded it as confused and misled afterwards. Italians, Finns, and Jews, among others, left Bolshevized and Americanized Communism in large numbers and retreated into the radical community institutions they found familiar. In early 1925 CP membership stood at 16,325 and by October of that year the Party counted only 7,213 members. Between 1927 and 1930 membership rebounded somewhat but remained about one-third smaller than in the early 1920s, averaging between 9,000 and 10,000 members.[5]

Bolshevization eroded the American CP's membership in the short run, but by the end of the decade the policy actually strengthened the CP considerably because it unified the organization's leadership and ended the worst of Communists' political and cultural infighting. Furthermore, the newly Bolshevized CP increased its appeal to African Americans in this period.[6] As long as the language federations, many of which had a well-deserved reputation for exclusivity and racism, dominated the Communist Party, it was difficult for the few African Americans who had joined the Party in the 1920s to recruit others.[7] With Bolshevization and Americanization, however, not only did the language federations lose power, but the new Soviet-influenced leadership asserted that African Americans constituted an oppressed nation within the United States and confirmed that "Negro rights" should be a major component of the CPUSA's agenda.[8] In 1928 the American Communist Party adopted a resolution, commonly known as the Black Belt theory, which declared that African Americans had the right to self-determination in the southern states, where they formed a majority.[9] Though somewhat convoluted and ambiguous, these new policies made it clear that "Negro work" was one of the major priorities of American Communism. Consequently, by 1929 the U.S. Communist Party had successfully recruited several hundred black members and made a solid commitment to training black leaders.[10]

Bolshevization, which discouraged white ethnic exclusivity, along with the Black Belt theory, which emphasized the vital importance of black struggle, attracted increasing numbers of African Americans to the Communist Party, but the two policies in tandem also created considerable tension among Communists in cities such as Chicago and New York, where a significant percentage of the membership was black. Since slavery African Americans had frequently formed their own religious and cultural organizations, separate from whites, and they did not, as a group, usually work toward either physical or cultural assimilation. Historically, black churches, schools, and fraternal institutions were a source of strength for African American community organizing. Because the Bolshevization policy discouraged ethnic solidarity, however, the Communist Party had to direct African Americans away from black organizations—even though Communists emphasized the concept of black nationhood—and into integrated Party units. Integration was not an easy matter for African Americans, in part because of their long tradition of separate organizing. Certainly the legacy of residential, religious, educational, and social segregation in the United States meant that whites found integration difficult as well. Despite what were often their best intentions, cultural differences and the damage done by years of myths and stereotypes on both sides made mixed-race events perplexing and awkward for nearly everyone involved. Not surprisingly prospective African American Communists distrusted the motives of whites, and white Communists often resented blacks and frequently evaded the Party's directives to fight for Negro rights.

Despite these challenges, CP leaders upheld their commitment to interracial organizing in Party branches and soon expanded it by announcing that "the closest association of the white with the Negro comrades in social life inside and outside the Party is imperative."[11] Several instances of white hostility toward black members in social settings and much generalized confusion about how far whites were supposed to go in making black members feel comfortable soon compelled CP leaders to initiate a campaign to combat racism at the individual level as well as in society at large. They began with a "thorough educational campaign . . . to stamp out all forms of antagonism, or even indifference among our white comrades towards Negro work" and, soon afterwards, launched a second campaign of self-criticism and discussion intended to help Communists stamp out white chauvinism "branch and root."[12]

As larger numbers of African Americans began to join in Party activities and racial conflicts persisted, black and white CP officials joined together to rethink their earlier approach. According to the historian Mark Solomon, in 1930, after much debate and discussion, leading Communists rejected the assumption that white chauvinism grew simply from white ignorance and refuted the idea that it could be remedied with education alone. Their new approach to the Negro question redefined white chauvinism as a manifestation of ruling-class ideology that "polluted the white workers in America" and prevented the interracial unity that was necessary to achieve a revolutionary social transformation.[13] In other words, they fully embraced the notion that white chauvinism impeded the interests of both white and black workers, that it betrayed revolutionary theory and practice by advancing the interests of the class enemy, and that it must be purged from the Party's ranks. In December 1930 black Party leader Ben Amis wrote in the *Daily Worker* that any Communist guilty of chauvinist behavior would be exposed in the Party press, placed on trial, and "ruthlessly prosecuted" before integrated workers' courts.[14] The Party actually made good on this threat more than once in this period. In Seattle, Washington, for example, "several comrades who objected to the presence of Negro workers at Party dances were expelled," and the CP Central Committee then intervened and expelled twelve more who had opposed the expulsion of the original group.[15]

The anti–white chauvinism campaigns, which grew out of the earlier policies of Bolshevization and Americanization, effectively politicized African Americans' personal experiences, personalized race politics for many white Communists, and led the American Communist Party to adopt a more complicated explanation of racial oppression than the one offered by a strict class-based analysis. Communists became aware, in other words, that personal attitudes and behaviors had political origins and consequences and that Communists had to struggle to enact their political values at the personal level. This insight set in motion changes that would ultimately make it possible for radical women to emulate African American Communists and to organize on their own behalf. Nevertheless, organizing by women for women did not happen immediately. During most of the 1920s the CPUSA's record on women's issues was far from stellar. Although numerous women who had been militant feminists in the 1910s joined the emerging Communist movement in the 1920s, the Party did very little to organize women and its female memberships remained quite small.[16]

The CP's neglect of the woman question in the 1920s undoubtedly reflected the decline of feminist activism in the United States after suffrage, but other factors also shaped Communists' indifference to women's issues. Marxist classics such as *The Communist Manifesto,* Engels's *Origin of the Family, Private Property and the State,* August Bebel's *Women and Socialism,* and Lenin's *Women and Society* justified Communists' tendency to make gender secondary to class by defining women's oppression as an economic phenomenon reversible only through socialist revolution.[17] Intense sectarianism and the persistent strength of traditional notions about proper male and female roles among American Communists also limited the U.S. Communist Party's ability to articulate feminist positions early on. In 1922, when the Communist International urged all Communist parties to set up women's departments and to argue for the incorporation of women into public life and the socialization of household tasks, the American CP complied only minimally. It adopted the position that women should be allowed to participate fully in the workforce and politics but abandoned support for the reorganization of the private sphere. Furthermore, though it followed orders and established a Women's Bureau, the Party gave the new department no power to create a program for women's liberation or put one into practice.[18] Not until the mid-1930s would Communists even begin to think about the woman question in earnest.

## 1929–1939

The 1930s was a decade of dramatic changes for the Communist Party. By 1929 the Party had finally resolved many of the conflicts that had divided and weakened it during its first ten years, built a membership of approximately 18,000, and organized many of its important internal institutions such as its newspaper, the *Daily Worker.*[19] When the Great Depression began in the same year, the CPUSA found itself in a good position to begin recruiting thousands of workers and intellectuals who were losing confidence in capitalism. By 1934 the CPUSA had grown to more than 26,000 members and included such intellectual luminaries as John Dos Passos, Sidney Hook, Matthew Josephson, Granville Hicks, Edmund Wilson, Sherwood Anderson, Theodore Dreiser, and Lincoln Steffens.[20]

As white ethnic influence in the CP declined and ethnic conflicts lost their intensity over the course of the 1930s, race and gender issues took on increasing importance.[21] Race, in particular, moved to the forefront of American Communists' agenda as more African Americans joined the CPUSA and integrated a larger number of previously all-white Party units and events. In the early 1930s Communist leaders intensified the campaign against "white chauvinism" and prosecuted white rank-and-filers in several high-profile cases for "serving the capitalists and endangering the Communist Party" by exhibiting racist attitudes and behavior.[22] This continuing commitment to fighting racism at the individual level, combined with the Communists' heroic efforts in Scottsboro to defend the nine black men sentenced to death for the alleged rape of a white woman and to organize the interracial Sharecroppers Union in Alabama, won the CP a great deal of credibility in black communities in the North and the South.[23] By the mid-1930s African Americans constituted about 9 percent of the CPUSA's total membership. Many others who never joined the Party still supported it as the only predominantly white organization in the United States with a genuine interest in racial equality.

From 1935 to 1939 the CPUSA joined the Russian and European Communist parties in adopting the Popular Front against fascism as its new strategy for organizing. As a part of the Popular Front strategy, Communists backed away from the pursuit of sweeping revolution, emphasized democracy, and embraced Franklin D. Roosevelt's New Deal and other more typically American forms of political activity, including electoral politics. These developments, in turn, made it possible for the CP to attract large numbers of new members and to attain a wide following in many sectors of American life. By the later 1930s the CP "provided national, regional and local leadership to many important industrial unions as well as liberal, student and cultural organizations," and "Communists and 'fellow travelers' served as a dynamic wedge of radicalism within the dominant New Deal liberalism."[24] Because of the success of Popular Front recruiting efforts in the late 1930s, the CP emerged as the core of a mass progressive movement that provided leadership to diverse activist efforts, including union organizing and eviction protests in the North, civil rights struggles in Harlem and in the South, and the Spanish Civil War in Europe.

Elizabeth Gurley Flynn and Ella Reeve Bloor with a group of women at an International Women's Day Celebration, circa 1950. Courtesy of the Sophia Smith Collection, Smith College.

In the period of the Popular Front, Communists sought to enter the political mainstream by deemphasizing revolution, declaring that "Communism is twentieth-century Americanism," and joining with Socialists and liberals to fight for the New Deal and other progressive reforms. The Popular Front also brought the emergence of a new and more fundamentally American approach to organizing African Americans. The new policy that the Party announced along with the Popular Front in 1935 rejected the CP's earlier view of black religious and fraternal organizations as "agents of the bourgeoisie" and proposed instead that Communists should work within such black organizations to build support for Communist programs.[25] The recognition that they could not just replace African American cultural traditions and organizations with Communist ones was more respectful of black history and culture and made it possible for the CP to expand its sphere of influence in the black community and to increase its black membership even more significantly. Instead of focusing primarily on recruiting black workers, the new approach induced Communists to consider middle-class intellectual and professional African Americans as potential comrades as well. Most important, however, this policy recognized that, despite Communists' acceptance of Bolshevization, there was some value in permitting black members to work within black organizations. Separate organizing by one group, Communist leaders conceded, did not always interfere with Party unity. In this case African Americans could maintain race solidarity *and* work for black liberation and still not lose sight of the larger issues of class exploitation and Communist revolution.

At the same time that Communists encouraged African Americans to begin working within black organizations, the high percentage of black unemployment during the depression also induced Communists to move away from their strict emphasis on union and workplace issues and to turn their energies toward the domestic realm. By the middle of the 1930s black and white Communists alike focused a great deal of effort on campaigns for lower rents and prices and equal access for African Americans to relief programs and public housing. Communists also developed a new commitment to promoting African American history and culture in books, theatrical performances, and music. This work consolidated the CP's position as one of the foremost organizations working for civil rights in the United States before World War II.

The depression and the emergence of the Popular Front transformed the CPUSA's position on the Negro question. These developments also revolutionized the Party's approach to organizing women in some of the same ways. The CP's new emphasis on the broad social and economic problems of the working class meant that the Party could no longer dismiss domestic issues as irrelevant to the class struggle. Consequently, in the early 1930s the Communist Party actively encouraged rank-and-file women's efforts to organize women's councils and neighborhood committees and by 1936 the number of women in the CP had increased to 25 percent. By the end of the decade women composed between 30 and 40 percent of the CP's rapidly increasing membership, and they participated in a limited way in both national and local Party leadership, wrote for party publications, organized and joined workplace and neighborhood struggles, and pushed the Communist Party to take their problems more seriously.[26]

In part because of the larger number of women participating in Communist activities in the mid-1930s, the CP was considerably more committed to women's issues than it had been in the 1920s. During the Popular Front period the Central Committee finally empowered the previously nonoperative CP Women's Commission to centralize planning and supervision of Communist women's work and increased the circulation of its progressive women's magazine from 2,000 to 7,000. It also supported women's access to free and legal birth control and abortion and urged women to challenge male domination in the workplace.

Furthermore, as Communists had begun to reach out to professional and intellectual African American political activists in this period, they also began to make alliances with middle-class professional and intellectual women. The CP had long opposed the Equal Rights Amendment first proposed in 1923 by the National Woman's Party on the grounds that by stressing the total sameness and equality of women and men it threatened the hard-won protective legislation that codified essentialist notions of women's difference from men and prevented employers from requiring women to work excessively long hours and during the night. This opposition had proved a barrier to the recruitment of middle-class and professional women who, because they did not benefit from protective laws, were more likely to support the ERA. In 1936 Communist and other progressive women decided to try to strike a compromise between middle- and working-class women by endorsing a new proposal they called the Woman's Charter, which proposed to codify women's equality in every area of life and to recognize gender differences and the need to shield working women from the most exploitative employer practices.[27] Finally, as they did with African Americans, Communist leaders began to recognize that women could organize as women and still fully support the CP's larger goals.

Despite these gains, however, the CP still resisted change in some areas of women's work. For although the Popular Front strategy forced Communists to take women more seriously, in practice the Party's desire to appeal to the masses in the late 1930s limited its will to oppose traditional gender arrangements in the family and in society at large. This became especially clear when some of the most radical women in the Communist Party such as the pioneering Communist feminist Mary Inman followed African American Communists' opposition to white chauvinism and denounced "male chauvinism" in Party ranks and in their own families and relationships. Instead of responding with extensive educational campaigns or male chauvinism trials, like the white chauvinism trials of the 1920s and the early 1930s, many Communist men still dismissed women's complaints and called the protesters "bourgeois feminists." Similarly, when progressive women declared that cultural as well as economic factors contributed to women's oppression, they often met with resistance from the upper levels of Party leadership.[28] By the end of the 1930s the Communist Party had 55,000 members, approximately 22,000 of whom were women. But, although it supported women's liberation in theory, the CP still would not, in this period, fully embrace a practical program for resisting male chauvinism in the family, in Party settings, or in American society at large.[29]

1939–1945

Except for the brief period between August 1939, when Stalin and Hitler signed a nonaggression pact, and June 1941, when Germany invaded the U.S.S.R., American Communists continued during the first half of the 1940s to pursue the Popular Front strategies of embracing reformist politics and portraying themselves as regular and patriotic American citizens. The Nazi-Soviet pact had an understandably negative effect on Communist organizing, particularly among African Americans, many of whom joined the Party in the 1930s because of its strong antifascist and antiimperialist orientation. Between late 1939 and mid-1941 the CP lost many black members and allies, including such prominent activists as A. Philip Randolph, who later excluded Communists from his March on Washington movement, the most important civil rights event of the 1940s.

The Communist Party's return to Popular Front tactics in June 1941 rebuilt its political base. By the time the Japanese attacked Pearl Harbor, the Party had 65,000 members, about 10 percent of whom were African Americans. Although the CP's national chairman, Earl Browder, did away with the Black Belt theory during World War II, the CP continued to pay significant attention to civil rights and racism, and its recruitment drives among African Americans were even more successful than they had been before the war. In 1943, for example, the *Daily Worker* reported that African Americans were joining the Party in "growing numbers": 44 out of 94 new recruits in Michigan, 14 out of 34 in Maryland, 8 out of 52 in Wisconsin, and 8 out of 64 in New England were African Americans. Later that year, after a recruiting competition between the Upper Harlem and the Chicago Southside sections of the Party, the Upper Harlem branch reported that it had recruited five hundred members in the spring alone.[30] By the end of World War II, when race issues began to supersede class issues in national politics, the American Communist Party already had a long history of concern for and attention to the problems of African Americans in both the South and the North. When civil rights emerged as a highly visible national movement in the 1950s, numerous black and white activists with ties to the Communist movement of the 1930s and 1940s helped to chart its course.

For women active in the Communist movement, the World War II years, like the 1930s, were simultaneously progressive and regressive. As the wartime mobilization of men into the armed forces created labor shortages in traditionally male-dominated industries, progressive women accompanied their more mainstream counterparts into the industrial workforce. Similarly, as thousands of progressive men left the country to fight in Europe and Japan, Communists and other progressive women also moved into the leadership positions of many Left organizations, including state and local Communist Party clubs. By 1943, women finally achieved numerical parity with men in the organization.[31]

Despite those gains in all sectors of the Party, however, the Popular Front emphasis on appealing to mainstream America still prevented the CP from expanding its conception of women's oppression to include cultural and personal factors. At the same time that women gained more influence in the CP leadership, national Communist Party leaders instructed their supporters to work within the mainstream political system to assist the United States in its fight against fascism. This strong belief in the need for a united American front led the Party as a whole to abandon temporarily many of its radical demands and to support such wartime policies as the no-strike pledge for American labor.

In 1944 CP National Chairman Earl Browder decided that an oppositional political party was no longer necessary. Deepening the Communist commitment to Popular Front politics, Browder took reformism to the next level by dissolving the Communist Party USA and replacing it with the explicitly nonrevolutionary Communist Political Association.[32] Although Communists maintained a theoretical commitment to gender equality throughout the war years, women leaders emphasized the issues of women's oppression and women's liberation far less between 1940 and 1945 than they had during the late 1930s.[33] Even those Communist women who had been most dedicated to women's issues in the 1930s put their efforts on hold. Instead of working to broaden women's roles in the progressive movement and in society at large, Communist women, like many women working with more conventional organizations, focused on fighting fascism by organizing neighborhood scrap-metal drives, volunteering for the Red Cross, working in munitions plants, and demanding federally funded nurseries for children of working mothers.[34]

In late 1945, following the Allied powers' victory in Europe and Asia, the context for Communist and progressive activism began to shift dramatically once again. In the immediate postwar period national liberation struggles erupted in Africa and Asia, Communists and other leftists gained political influence all over Europe, American workers launched an unprecedented strike wave, and U.S. president Harry Truman proposed a program of reforms that included national health insurance and civil rights for African Americans. In part because of the opportunities for revolutionary change the postwar environment seemed to offer Communists around the world in 1945, the Comintern engineered the expulsion of the Party's Popular Front leader Earl Browder and condemned his support for reformist politics.

When the new Party chairman, William Z. Foster, reconstituted the CPUSA in 1945, American Communists resumed public criticism of the Party's position on the woman question. Citing women's vital contributions to the Allied victory, progressive women began organizing to take advantage of the widespread political upheaval that characterized the immediate postwar period and returned to the gender-based struggles they had set aside in 1940. Between 1946, when the Communist Party began to lend its support to progressive women's attempts to organize independently, and 1956, when Kruschev's revelations about the crimes of Stalin finally destroyed what little was left of the Communist Party's mass base after years of anticommunist intimidation, Communist women and their allies did their most important work on the woman question. Using the Party's approach to African Americans and racism as a model, they revived much of the analysis of women's oppression originated by Communist Mary Inman in her book *In Woman's Defense*, published in 1940, and, through their new women's organization, the Congress of American Women, strengthened and refined their earlier efforts. By engaging in separate women's organizing, theorizing about the role of culture in women's oppression, and protesting against male chauvinism in both personal and political settings, progressive women forced the Communist Party to rethink its narrowly economic understanding of women's oppression, to clarify the relationship of gender oppression to race and class oppression, and to acknowledge that women's so-called personal problems had political solutions. Much more than the Communist Party's problematic position on the woman question in the 1930s, these activities sustained the U.S. women's movement through the doldrums of the McCarthy era and laid vital practical and theoretical groundwork for the women's liberation movement of the 1960s and 1970s.

## 2  The Mary Inman Controversy and the (Re)Construction of the Woman Question, 1936–1945

IN 1941, MARY INMAN, a long-time Marxist from Long Beach, California, launched a one-woman battle with national leaders of the American Communist Party over their response to her book *In Woman's Defense*.[1] Inman's fight, provoked by Communist leaders' resistance to her suggestion that housework, like factory work, is productive labor, lasted more than forty years, until her death in 1985. Clearly, Inman did not back down easily. Despite the CP's often well-deserved reputation for inflexibility, Inman turned out hundreds of pages of argumentation aimed at convincing Communists and anyone else who would listen that she was right and the Party's leaders wrong. Her tracts not only condemned Communist leaders for refusing to redefine the economic nature of housework but also lambasted them for "purposefully liquidating the Party's work for women."[2]

For many years few people took notice of Mary Inman's campaign, and her story might have been just an interesting footnote to the history of the Communist Party, except that she ultimately played a critical role in interpreting the Party's position on women. After two decades of obscurity, Inman finally got some recognition when feminists, inspired by the women's liberation movement to seek out their foremothers, rediscovered her work. Still reeling from their own fight for the recognition of male chauvinism in the New Left, the organizers of the first national Women's Liberation Conference wrote to Inman in 1968 asking for copies of her books. Throughout the 1970s Inman talked publicly about the ways she perceived her situation and sent feminist researchers copies of her work. In 1978, Inman, still hoping to win support for her position, sent copies of her "Program for Women" to various scholars including Ellen DuBois, Amy Swerdlow, Madeline Davis, and Nancy Gabin, and her "Two Forms of Production under Capitalism," to Meredith Tax. In 1979 she sent copies of several of her writings to Joan Kelly. In the last years of Inman's life, historian Sherna Gluck won her trust and interviewed her extensively. Although Inman insisted that their conversations not be tape-recorded, Gluck was later able to share what she learned with others.[3]

Since 1980 Inman's version of her story has been cited over and over

28

again as the shining example of what happened to Communist women who were interested in the issue of women's liberation. Scholars represent Inman as one of only a few women who dared to suggest that women, as a group, are oppressed, and they conclude from her experiences and writings that the Party opposed any discussion of or organization around the problems of women's oppression before World War II, and in the late 1940s and 1950s as well.[4]

Certainly U.S. Communists had numerous limitations in this area, but Mary Inman was never an isolated critic of male chauvinism in the Party and at no time was it the thoroughly sexist organization that she described in the 1940s and later. On the contrary, Mary Inman was able to write and sell many copies of *In Woman's Defense* precisely because the Communist movement in the 1930s provided an atmosphere that encouraged progressive women and men to take women's oppression seriously; some Party leaders criticized Inman's work, not because she wanted to organize women but because they were worried that her equation of domestic work with productive labor glorified housework and could be used to reinforce the reactionary notion that women's place was in the home. But while the CP dismissed Inman's arguments about housework, it also adopted many of her other views. Even as she was denouncing Communists for neglecting women's problems after 1945, the documentary evidence proves without a doubt that they were incorporating many of her points about the causes and effects of women's oppression into their analysis, thereby strengthening it significantly.

Mary Inman's efforts to establish the correctness of her theory became her life's work. Although *In Woman's Defense* contained important insights and made vital contributions to Communists' understanding of women's oppression, her subsequent works became increasingly dogmatic and removed from the reality of many women's experiences in the Communist Party. By the time historians made contact with Inman in the 1970s, her isolation, her singleminded focus on the events of 1940-43, and her sense that she was the victim of a Communist conspiracy against women had taken a toll on her; she was not a reliable source of information about the controversy that developed around her book or about women's status in the Communist movement more generally. This chapter relies on Mary Inman's personal papers to reconstruct the story of her life and work, to describe how *In Woman's Defense* both reflected and enhanced Communists' work for women's liberation in the 1930s and 1940s, and to reexamine the controversy over the book from both sides to show how the events actually unfolded. These sources show how Inman's ordeal has been misinterpreted and her version of events mythologized by those who mistook her accounts of the past as statements of objective truth. As the records demonstrate, Mary Inman's significance comes *not* from her parting with the Communist Party but from her contributions to the organization's analysis of and programs for women and, ironically, from her ability to convince scholars that the Communist Party resisted women's efforts to organize on their own behalf.

IDA MARY INMAN WAS THE YOUNGEST of nine children (five boys and four girls), born to Mildred Taylor Inman and James Jett Inman in Kentucky on June 11, 1894. At age six she moved with her family to Creek Nation Indian Territory in Oklahoma, where she lived for the next seventeen years. The other details of Inman's personal history are sketchy, and most come from her own incomplete autobiography, a document written clearly to show her early development as a pioneering Marxist and feminist and to help redeem the place in history she thought she had been denied. According to Inman's account, her mother died in 1905 and, when her older sister died two years later, she had no choice but to become the "woman of the house" and to take care of her father and older brothers for the next ten years.

Despite her heavy responsibilities at home, Inman wrote that she became a socialist, joined Eugene Debs's Socialist Party in 1910 at age sixteen, and, "on fire with zeal for . . . politics," played "an active role in the political movement" that included work for woman's suffrage. That same year she met her future husband, twenty-five-year-old J. Frank Ryan, secretary for the Oil Workers Union of the IWW in Tulsa. She was drawn to him because "he listened to me attentively and even encouraged me to talk about my vision of a future world without war, poverty and crime."[5] After a long courtship the two were married, in July 1917. When they moved to Kansas City, Missouri, in late 1917 to escape anti-Wobbly vigilantes, they began to live and work under the name Inman and continued to do so for the rest of their lives.[6] There is no record of when or why the Inmans moved to Southern California or when Mary Inman began her associations with the Communist Party, but by the late 1930s Frank was working for Pacific Telephone and Telegraphic Company, and Mary was writing *In Woman's Defense* in a rented office in a downtown Los Angeles office-building. Inman finished the manuscript in 1936 and, by 1939, was a lively and enthusiastic participant in the Communist Party, especially active in women's work.[7]

## Communist "Women's Work" in the 1930s

Despite the Communist Party's numerous shortcomings regarding women in the 1930s, it also had some real strengths.[8] Gender-conscious women who encountered the CP in this period would undoubtedly have criticized its male-dominated national leadership and opposed the sexist representations of women that appeared in the CP press. But for most women who supported or joined the Communist Party during the 1930s, the benefits of doing so outweighed such problems. Like many men who participated in the CP's political, social, and cultural life, progressive women gained opportunities, education, and self-confidence they probably could not have found elsewhere.[9] In addition to training them to make speeches, write leaflets, and argue with those who disagreed with them, the Communist Party also taught black and white women specifically about the distinctive and common obstacles they faced in American society. Furthermore it encouraged them to confront those obstacles head on. Communist leaders never argued that women's concerns would have to wait until after the revolution when socialism could guarantee women's emancipation. Even as the Party often idealized women's roles as wives, mothers, and sex objects, it also pushed them to transcend those roles and to work alongside men in political activities that would ultimately lead to their complete liberation.

During the Popular Front period, some Communist women engaged quite seriously in activity that they hoped would improve their status. In the absence of a unified women's movement, Communist women appointed themselves as the heirs of Lucy Stone and Sojourner Truth and attempted to forge ties with women in organizations such as the YWCA, the League of Women Voters, the Parent Teacher Association, and the Women's Trade Union League. Within these coalitions Communists worked to oppose Nazism, but they also fought for women's rights and access to birth control.[10] In 1936 and 1937, Communists won the support of women union members and some middle-class women's rights advocates (including Mary Anderson and Mary Elizabeth Pidgeon, from the Women's Bureau of the Department of Labor; Mary van Kleeck, of the Russell Sage Foundation; Dorothy Kenyon, of the Consumers' League and the American Civil Liberties Union; and Charl Williams, of the National Federation of Business and Professional Women's Clubs) in their campaign for the "Women's Charter," an alternative to the Equal Rights Amendment intended to guarantee equal rights for women without undermining protective legislation for women workers.[11] When the Women's Charter coalition dissolved in 1938, Communists continued to urge women to "celebrate" the ninetieth anniversary of the birth of the American women's movement by advocating the passage of federal laws to safeguard women's health in employment, to cover maternal and child health services under the Social Security Act, and to guarantee equal rights for black women.[12]

In addition to broad-based campaigns for legal and political reforms, some Communist women took their work a step further in the mid-to-late

1930s as they began to elucidate the concept of male supremacy and to criticize its manifestations within the Party. In 1935 the Sunday edition of the Party's newspaper, the *Worker,* sponsored a "Dear Mr. Husband" contest and published letters women wrote "telling him in what ways he treats you as an inferior, why he does it, and in what ways he is harming himself by doing so." The editor also encouraged women to write to the paper at other times with similar complaints.[13] One woman wrote, "I'd like to bring to the attention of your readers the narrow-mindedness of some of the members where their wives and daughters are concerned. Apparently meetings, parades, dances, and picnics and other Party activities are reserved only for the male sex, while mother and daughter are supposed to sit quietly at home and knit." These men beam and approve of the work of other girls and women "when they see them selling *Daily Workers,* distributing leaflets, or carrying on the work of the party," she explained, "but it is different, should they confront their own wife or daughter mingling with others and helping the Party. Make this question clear to these men comrades. It would benefit the Party as well as these wives and daughters."[14]

Other complaints the paper published at various times focused on husbands who would not help with housework and child care, male Party organizers who intimidated or ignored women members, Communist men who made fun of the suffrage movement, and husbands who encouraged their wives to go to Party meetings but clamped down when they expressed interest in becoming Communist speakers or leaders.[15] The Party's National Women's Commission and its state and district women's commissions took complaints like these seriously and made a valiant if not always successful effort to legitimize and address such problems.

### In Woman's Defense and Inman's Reconstruction of the Woman Question

Mary Inman was an active participant in the California Communist Party's somewhat gender conscious social and political environment during the years she researched and wrote *In Woman's Defense.* Her experiences keeping house for her father and brothers as an adolescent and her exposure to the struggle for women's rights waged by Socialist women before 1919 probably influenced her work to some extent, but many of the views she presented in the book grew directly from the Party's Popular Front perspective on women.[16] Serialized in the West Coast Communist newspaper, the *Daily People's World* in 1939 and published as a book in 1940, *In Woman's Defense* incorporated much of the Party's interwar approach to the woman question. Building on the assertion made by Communist leader Margaret Cowl that "all women are in an unequal position with men in all countries,"

Inman argued that despite their class differences women are subjugated as a group.[17] She suggested that although male supremacist attitudes emanate from the ruling class, they permeate every level of society, right down to the working class where working men became the buffers between women and their real oppressors. The solution to women's problems, she reasoned, would not be found in the feminist "battle of the sexes" but in the progressive movement, which—as the rightful heir of the nineteenth-century woman's rights movement—could overcome women's "ideological backwardness" by drawing them out of their isolated households and into active struggles for a variety of causes, including women's rights. Inman also recognized the need to change "the backward attitude" of some progressive organizations and "their reluctance to effectively take up the task of organizing women."[18] Like other Communists who wanted to combat male chauvinist attitudes and behavior in the Party, she repeatedly compared discrimination against women to discrimination against African Americans.[19]

*In Woman's Defense* reflected these important elements of the CP's analysis of women's status in the 1930s, but it also contributed several important new insights that would ultimately refine and strengthen the Party's approach to women in the 1940s. Before the appearance of Inman's work discussions of women's oppression in the Party press rarely, if ever, moved beyond economic explanations of women's problems. Although they recognized that the ideology of male supremacy played some part in keeping women down, Communists toed the traditional Marxist line and cited women's exclusion from the workforce and their isolation as domestic laborers in the home as the fundamental sources of their subordination. Mary Inman added to this view by suggesting that, although women's oppression has economic origins, like black oppression it is largely perpetuated through cultural norms and practices. She argued convincingly that conventional child-rearing methods "manufacture femininity" by training little boys to be "confident and independent" and "little girls to be cautious and dependent." She demonstrated the degree to which sexism pervades American culture by listing ninety-nine derogatory names for women and challenging her readers to think of more than one or two such names for men. She also pointed out the absurdity of admonishing women not to beat their husbands and wrote at length about how the "overemphasis of beauty" is used to keep women in subjection.[20] Inman devoted three chapters of the book to prostitution, documenting its control by big business and its role in the sexual objectification of women, and linking it to the double standard and the notion that women require men's protection. Inman suggested that progressives needed to fight these manifestations of male supremacy as well as pushing for larger social and economic change. By 1948 these ideas would all become central to Communists' conceptualization of women's oppression.

The second major argument Mary Inman developed related to two questions that had troubled Marxists for the better part of the previous century. After she had laid out her ideas about the vital role played by male supremacist ideology in the oppression of women, Inman turned to the issues of domestic labor, its economic function under capitalism, its role in the oppression of women, and the consequent place of housewives in the class struggle. Marx and Engels had each touched on these questions in their respective books *Capital* and *The Origins of the Family, Private Property, and the State* nearly one hundred years earlier. Although Marx did not devote significant attention to an economic analysis of domestic labor, in *Capital* he refuted the essentialist notion that women's place was in the home and stated clearly that the tendency of capitalism to "draw women out of the social isolation and patriarchal oppression in the peasant family" and into "the great work of social production" was a "progressive, sound and legitimate tendency." But Marx's own Victorian notions about the superiority of women's morals and the innate weakness of their bodies also led him to suggest that the exploitative conditions in industrial workplaces under capitalism harmed women even more than they did men. In a capitalist economy, he argued, the freeing potential of productive labor for women "was distorted into an abomination." Despite his belief that women needed protection, however, Marx also acknowledged that "woman has ... become an active agent in our social production" and that "major social transformations are impossible without ferment among the women." In order to put these ideas into practice in the 1860s, Marx pushed the English International Working Men's Association to establish female branches. In doing so, according to socialist-feminist scholar Lise Vogel, Marx not only offered "the rudiments of a theoretical foundation for analyzing women from the point of view of social reproduction" but "established the principle and legitimacy of autonomous women's organizations within the mass working-class movement."[21]

After Marx's death in 1883, Friedrich Engels attempted to use Marx's underdeveloped ideas to examine women's social and economic position more thoroughly. His book *Origin of the Family, Private Property, and the State*, hastily written over a two-month period in 1884, ultimately became the work most Marxists used to formulate and justify their various practical approaches to the woman question (even though Engels himself regarded it as a "meagre substitute for what my departed friend no longer had the time to do").[22] Engels asserted that the development of private property and the subsequent emergence of class society led to the institutionalization of patriarchal monogamous marriage, which, in turn, required women's confinement and isolation in the home. He saw this system of marriage as the mechanism that excluded women from participation in social production, made them dependent, and created their oppression. Consequently, he proposed that large-scale capitalist industry created the conditions through which women could begin to liberate themselves by breaking out of their isolated households and joining in the process of social production. Only then, he suggested, could they counteract the supremacy of their husbands, organize to fight for their legal equality, and join in the class struggle that would eventually, through revolutionary transformation, free them completely.

From the beginning the Communist Party, like every other Marxist political organization from the German Social Democratic Party of the 1890s to the American Socialist Party of the 1910s, based its official analysis of the woman question on this earlier work and defined women's exclusion from equal participation with men in the process of social production as a major source of their subordination. Mary Inman dared in *In Woman's Defense* to suggest something different. Inman proposed that it was the widespread denigration of housework and child rearing—not the economic function of the work itself—that was actually the cause of women's subordination. Probably emboldened by the Party's depression-era recognition that domestic issues could be political and its efforts to recruit housewives, she argued that women, by keeping house and bearing and raising children, did participate in the process of social production by producing the labor power of present and future generations of workers. In other words, she suggested, domestic or "reproductive" labor was productive labor. Housewives did not work for their husbands and children, but for capitalists who paid them through their husbands' wages. They were not, as Engles suggested, parasites who were dependent on their husbands for survival, but workers who contributed directly to the process of production and earned its benefits.

Despite her apparent efforts to elevate the role of domestic labor in Marxist economic terms, Inman understood and agreed with Communists' conviction that housework was a terrible burden on women. Alongside her discussion of its merits, she detailed the problems that came from performing hours of housework every day in isolated homes by outmoded means. She assured her readers that these problems could be solved by socialism, under which families would live communally with the benefits of round-the-clock nurseries, socialized house-cleaning systems, and centralized laundry and cooking facilities. But until socialism was achieved, Inman wrote, housewives, like industrial workers, could fight for better wages and working conditions in specially organized housewives' unions that would simultaneously change people's attitudes about women's inferiority, educate women about the real sources of their oppression, and give them a decisive role to play in the larger struggle for social change. The crux of Inman's second point, then, was that it was not absolutely necessary for progressives to draw women into the workforce so they could fight for justice alongside workers because they were already workers themselves. Inspired by the examples of Communist women who were organizing in their communities to fight for better housing and against high prices, Inman declared that housework could be defined as a source of strength for women and that housewives could play a central role, as producers, in the fight against capitalism.[23]

*In Woman's Defense* was very popular among progressives all around the United States, and it went through three printings in 1940. In a letter to Barbara Giles of the *New Masses,* a representative of Mercury Printing Company, the printer and distributor of the book, wrote that "The book has had a good reception here on the West Coast. The Frontier Book Shop in Seattle has sent us an order each week for the past six weeks, and each week's order was larger than the previous one. They say it promises to be a best seller." The company also reported that "the YWCA and other women's organizations have reviewed it and stimulated sales from their members. The other day we received our third order from the Educational Committee of the Steel Workers' Organizing Committee of the C.I.O. at San Francisco."[24]

The *Daily Worker* reviewed *In Woman's Defense* favorably in 1940, and Communist Party schools around the country began to adopt it as a textbook in their courses on the woman question.[25] Enthusiastic readers from around the United States wrote to Inman to express their appreciation for the book and to ask further questions. Most correspondents did not mention her arguments about the productive nature of housework but instead expressed excitement over her explanations of the widespread existence of male chauvinist attitudes and behavior. In 1941, for example, she received a letter from a woman who wanted to know "whether the little courtesies on the part of men, such as opening doors, helping one off street cars and others of that sort amount to sex chauvinism."[26] In late 1940, Inman received a letter from Susan B. Anthony II, the grandniece of the famous suffragist, who confided that "prior to reading your book I had always thought my name and relationship with Susan B. Anthony an unfortunate burden to be ignored rather than cherished. Since your book, however, I am very happy that I have a label that should help in the work for women you have outlined as such a necessity."[27]

As a consequence of her popularity, Mary Inman began to teach a course at Workers' School in Los Angeles entitled "Woman's Status under

Capitalism and Its Relation to the Labor Movement" and to speak and lecture at other progressive events around Southern California. By late 1940 many in the Communist movement regarded Inman, who was by then a CP member, as the leading progressive expert on the sources of women's oppression and the struggles necessary to overcome it.[28]

## The Controversy

While many Communists cheered Inman's efforts to show the pervasiveness of women's oppression, some Party members criticized her book. No one objected to her suggestion that sex oppression affected all women or criticized her arguments about the cultural causes and effects of women's subordination or suggested that organizing women to fight male supremacy would hurt the class struggle. Rather, the emerging critique of Inman's work focused on her assertions about the economic value of housework and her suggestion that progressives could organize housewives as workers. "Glorifying" housework, her critics suggested, could have dangerous and reactionary implications; people could use Inman's argument to justify keeping women in the home and, in that way, impair existing efforts to win them to the progressive movement. Their difference with Inman was both theoretical and tactical: Should Communists work to improve women's status by accepting the sexual division of labor as a given, promoting housewives as workers, and pushing for better working conditions within their homes? Or should they oppose housewifery as part of an oppressive sexual division of labor and encourage women instead to join the workforce so they could fight sex and class oppressions on an equal basis with men?

In 1940, as now, there were no clear answers to these questions, and numerous people debated the implications in the Party press in late 1940 and early 1941.[29] This debate led local Party leaders in the Los Angeles area to examine Mary Inman's argument about housework more closely. On Monday night, March 24, 1941, after teachers at the Workers' School concluded that the theory was problematic, California Party leaders Eva Shafran and Al Bryan came to Inman's classroom and explained to her students that, despite what their teacher had told them, housework is not productive labor. Inman argued with Shafran in the classroom and continued to defend her work in the weeks that followed. She attempted to clarify her argument and insisted that she did not want to limit women to domestic work but only to organize those housewives who could not find jobs in industry. At the end of the term each woman was frustrated by the other's refusal to see her point. Shafran, exasperated by Inman's unwillingness to concede that there might be problems with her analysis, canceled Inman's course permanently.[30]

Inman was understandably upset by this turn of events. As much as she was unable to see that the implications of her analysis could have negative consequences for women, so was Shafran unwavering in her insistence that Inman's arguments had no merit. Inman defined herself as a writer, theorist, and teacher and apparently drew much of her self-esteem and sense of purpose from these activities; Shafran's influence in California threatened Inman's status as the foremost progressive thinker on the woman question. In order to preserve her prominence and popularity—and to preserve her perception of herself as an important progressive intellectual figure—Inman was willing to go to great lengths. She appealed her case to Party leaders in California. When those efforts failed, Inman and her husband requested a meeting with representatives of the CP's National Committee. In August 1941, they traveled to New York City to meet with Party leaders Elizabeth Gurley Flynn, Ella Reeve (Mother) Bloor, Avram Landy, and Johnny Williamson, hoping to win a reversal of the California decision so that Inman could resume her work and protect her good name.

Although several people on the committee were sympathetic to Inman's views, the meeting with representatives of the CP's national leadership did not go the way she hoped it would. Inman was defensive from the start and refused to answer many of the questions Party leaders asked in order to understand what had taken place over the preceding months. Mother Bloor wrote to a friend afterwards that she "had a clean understanding heart" in the early phase of the meetings but that "Mary Inman became intensely personal to any one of us who offered any disagreement in theory" and that "she left us with the feeling that she considered us enemies."[31] Flynn reported that initially she "felt considerable sympathy with Mary and thought she had been dealt with rather severely" but that after more than two days of Inman's "determined argumentation," sectarian name-calling, and personal attacks she decided that Inman could not be satisfied with anything less than total vindication and "that the Party in California—State, County, and at the Workers' School in Los Angeles—acted correctly and did the only thing that could be done in relation to her." Her "one track minded-ness [sic]; her lack of a sense of proportion and her fanatical assumption of a messianic role," Flynn said, made it impossible for the National Committee to compromise with her. After more than three days of meetings they arrived at an impasse: Landy, Bloor and Flynn were "convinced by [the Inmans'] attitude that further discussion would be futile." According to Flynn, Mary "went back to California convinced that everyone here is wrong."[32]

In the wake of the August meetings, Party leaders decided that, because of its potentially conservative implications, Inman's theory about housework should not be represented as the CP's position. On the basis of

Mary Inman at home in Long Beach, California, on her 86th birthday. Courtesy of the Schlesinger Library, Radcliffe Institute, Harvard University.

Inman's behavior in the meetings, Bloor and Flynn both worried that she would try to create a faction around the housework issue and, because of her popularity, present a real danger to Party unity. In a letter dated August 4, 1941, Bloor asked a friend to "show Mary Inman that we are sincere honest comrades and really tried to get at the 'common denominator' of the proposals and not to have her go home bitter and resentful."[33] Flynn wrote at length to Harrison George, editor of the *People's Daily World* and promoter of Inman's work, describing her perception of the situation and asking him to help teach Inman how to be "useful and happy in our Party," to do his best "to stop the prolongation of this controversy," and to explain to Inman that "she isn't discredited as she believes, but she will be by her actions."[34] But Inman could not be consoled. When she continued to press her point in communications with Communists around the country, the National Committee asked Avram Landy to write an article for the CP's theoretical journal, the *Communist*, outlining the official Marxist-Leninist line on housework in order to make the Party's position clear and visible. If Mary Inman was not willing to accept Landy's interpretations, the National Committee instructed, she would have to refrain from public activity on the woman question for one year.[35] Landy's article appeared in September 1941; it did not refer to Inman or her book by name, but outlined her analysis and proposed alternately that since housework was useful but not productive, women should be organized as workers and in trade union auxiliaries, not in housewives' unions.[36] In October 1941, Inman wrote to Susan B. Anthony II that "things had reached such an impossible situation that life was unbearable under existing conditions" and that "reluctantly and painfully" she had decided to resign from the Communist Party.[37]

Mary Inman's rendering of her conflict with the Communist Party differed significantly from the one outlined above.[38] In her version, the Party attacked her for analyzing the issue of women's oppression from a Marxist perspective, banned her works, and expelled her in 1942.[39] The male leaders of the Communist Party, she argued, were unwilling to debate the woman question openly and freely because they thought it would be heretical for women to organize separately around their unique oppression. Even discussing women's special oppression, Inman concluded, "proved too threatening for the Party to handle."[40]

This interpretation does not mesh with the one suggested by documentary sources from the other side of the conflict. What accounts for the discrepancy? One could argue that Communist leaders had an interest in placing the blame for the intensity of the conflict, and the impossibility of compromise, on Mary Inman herself; that they wanted to protect themselves and the Party and that they could only do so by discrediting her as obsessed, fanatical, and personally difficult. It appears instead as if it was the combination of her extreme single-mindedness, belligerence, and tenacity that finally provoked Communist leaders to attack Inman and her theory explicitly in 1943 and that led Inman to produce the volume of documents that made her an obvious source for historians working in the 1970s and 1980s. Inman's postcontroversy writings provide much evidence to support Communist leaders' assessments of her as bitter and angry and even as obsessed and fanatical. Historians' dependence on the documents Inman produced after 1940, and their uncritical acceptance of her appraisal of Communists' work on women after World War II, led them to write a history of women in the Communist Party in the 1940s and 1950s that mythologizes the views of one hostile person and erases the experiences of many who built on Inman's analysis and continued to fight against male supremacy inside and outside the Party.

## Inman's (Re)Construction of the CP's Approach to Women

Mary Inman's departure from the Communist Party in the fall of 1941 did not signal the end of her conflict with its national leaders. No longer subject to Party discipline, Inman criticized the leadership more severely as a reluctant former Communist than she ever had as a Party member. After her resignation from the CP, Inman's goal was not primarily to organize women but to win the recognition she thought she deserved from Communist leaders for her theory about the productive nature of housework. In August 1942, she published *Woman Power,* in which she accused the Communist Party and Landy (to whom she referred as "Professor X") of attacking housewives by denying the importance of their work by organizing them as consumers rather than as producers. When Party leaders responded by publishing Landy's pamphlet, "Marxism and the Woman Question," and reviewing it prominently in the *Daily Worker* in July 1943, they abandoned the restraint they had exercised up to that point.[41] Since summer 1941, when the Nazis invaded the Soviet Union, the Party had actively supported a U.S. victory in World War II and by this time Party leaders, like mainstream corporations and politicians, were actively encouraging women to leave their homes and enter the wartime labor force.

In part because of their wartime emphasis on women's place in the workforce and in part because leading Communists were completely fed up with Inman's attacks on the Party, Landy challenged Inman much more directly.[42] His pamphlet and his review of her book reiterated the Party's views on the backwardness of housework and denigrated Inman's theory explicitly, calling it "false and deceptive," and "a weird distortion of economics and biology."[43] But these efforts to end the conflict once and for all only made Inman more determined. She published a four-page newsletter, *Facts for Women,* ostensibly for the purpose of educating and organizing women, from 1943 until 1946. In reality, however, the newsletter carried articles with titles such as "Marxism on Woman Question Outlawed in California in 1941" and publicized her "Program for Women" as her "alternative" to the Communist Party's nearly identical list of demands.[44] After ceasing publication of *Facts* in 1946, Inman turned her attention entirely away from organizing women and instead devoted her time to writing documents and letters that condemned the Communist Party for its "anti Marxist-Leninist distortion of the woman question" and presented her theory as the one true basis for Marxist women's work.

Inman made her most scathing attacks on the Communist Party and its leaders between 1949, when she produced "Thirteen Years of CPUSA Mis-leadership on the Woman Question," and 1972, when she sent a 66-page typewritten letter detailing "Browderism on the Woman Question Today" to CP National Chairman Gus Hall and three progressive magazine editors.[45] In these manuscripts Inman claimed that she documented how the wartime CP chairman, Earl Browder, "wrecked the woman question" and demonstrated the Party's failure to "correct these liquidatory practices affecting women as was done in the case of other issues and groups" after the change in leadership in 1945.[46] There was a grain of truth to Inman's appraisal of Browder—he did dismantle the Party's National Women's Commission in 1940 in an attempt to integrate women's work and general Party work—but Communists also maintained at least a partial commitment to women's issues all through the war and initiated a new phase of serious work on the woman question after the CP expelled Browder in 1945. Inman's emphasis on the notion that Communist leaders continued to carry out their liquidation of Communist work among women after 1945, despite reams of evidence to the contrary, shows how far she was willing to go to prove her point. Her insistence that this "liquidation" was carried out "in a secret and semi-secret manner" verges on conspiracy theory, and her assertions that the Party's work on women's issues was really intended to create conflict between men and women Communists makes little sense. In Inman's mind, the Party's liquidation of women's work explained why CP leaders rejected her theory in 1940; their secret perpetuation of that liquidation and purposeful distortion of the woman question after 1945 explained why she was not invited back into the Party to lead its work in the area. Because Mary Inman believed that her theory was the only true basis for effective work on women's issues, she had to insist that until the CP adopted her idea it was forsaking women's work completely.

In order to "prove" her analysis, Inman resorted to blatant distortions of the truth and personal attacks on Party leaders. She argued, for example, that Landy's 1941 article "branded such work [as] raising children . . . as socially unnecessary" and purposely "killed the nursery movement," even though, in reality, Communists and others associated with the progressive movement worked at the forefront of the fight for day-care centers in major cities throughout World War II and for several years afterwards.[47] When Party Chairman William Z. Foster called for a "persistent struggle ideologically against all manifestations of masculine superiority" and an effort to overcome "a pronounced reticence in dealing with questions of sex" in 1948, Inman could not concede that Communist leaders were doing something right, even though these suggestions resembled those she had made in her book eight years earlier.[48] Instead she was forced into a strange sort of double-think that attributed positive-sounding plans to deceptive ulterior motives. In this case Inman reasoned that Foster was a "double-dealing hypocrite" who directed Party members "into the blind alley of bourgeois feminism" and consciously presented a "diversion [that] detracts from more important and more pressing phases of work amongst women," such as organizing housewives.[49] Her analysis grew even more bizarre when she went on to suggest that the Communist Party's neglect of women's issues began when organizations set up by Herbert Hoover in the 1920s influenced N. I. Bukharin in the 1930s, who later influenced Browder and Landy and others.

By 1972, when Inman wrote a lengthy letter to Gus Hall and the editors of the *Nation*, the *Progressive*, and the *New Republic*, the Communist Party was no longer a significant force on the American political landscape. Its role as the primary left-wing proponent of radical change in the United States had been assumed by the broad-based civil rights, antiwar, and student movements that began in the 1960s. Women's status in the United States had also changed dramatically by this time as millions of women joined the paid labor force and participated in the resurgent women's movement. But despite these new opportunities for radical and feminist activism, Inman remained interested only in calling attention to the "Browder revisionism" of the 1940s and 1950s.[50] In 1973 she was still focused on the past. Although she was certainly aware of the women's movement, she was unable or unwilling to shift her attention to the new political context. American women were actively advocating equal pay, free day care, and nonsexist child-rearing practices, but Inman continued to spend her time lobbying the Communist Party to renounce Landy's "shoddy writing," to reverse its position on domestic work as productive labor, and to take up her program for organizing women instead.[51]

Mary Inman was by no means the only progressive in the 1930s and 1940s calling for more attention to women's issues in and around the Communist Party, and, although her early work broadened Communists' understanding of women's oppression, it appears that her later work served only to isolate her from Left progressives and post–World War II feminists alike. When Communist women—motivated in part by ideas presented in *In Woman's Defense*—resumed their struggles to fight for women's liberation in the newly formed Congress of American Women and in the Communist Party in 1946, they did so without Inman. Her narrow focus after 1941 on the issue of housework as productive labor prevented Inman from seeing how many of her other ideas Communists had adopted and required her to deny that anyone in the Communist movement was doing useful and constructive work on women's issues. Her essays that "document" the absence of Communist work among women bear little relation to reality. They were written not by a pioneering feminist trying to continue her work in isolation after her expulsion from the Communist Party, but by a hostile and resentful woman, desperate to regain the prominence she believed she was denied by a Communist plot against women. As sources about what really happened to women who fought against sexism in the Communist Party they are of very little value.

By the time historians corresponded with and interviewed Inman in the late 1970s and 1980s, her anger, isolation, and long-standing belief that she was the victim of a conspiracy against women had taken a severe toll on her stability. Mary Inman was not only still consumed by the desire to win the recognition she thought she deserved, but she was troubled by fears of harassment and even persecution. She continued to write letters to various people, including officials in the Soviet Union, trying to win support for her theory.[52] She read a variety of documents from the women's movement, carefully underlining and checking the parts that corresponded to her theory and indicating "not true" and "no" where they disagreed.[53] Following her usual pattern, she suggested that because most feminists were not proceeding according to her prescriptions for organizing women, they were not proceeding correctly. Inman kept a file of "notes on homosexuals" to "document" the CIA's recruitment of lesbians whom it could use to "discredit and weaken" the women's movement as it gained influence. She also kept a file of notes documenting her neighbors' alleged efforts to persecute her by making strange phone calls, throwing garbage in her yard, and spraying "odorless poisons" into her garage.[54] It is no wonder that Inman was reluctant to grant interviews and that she was reluctant to allow Sherna Gluck to tape-record their conversations. It seems clear that, given her state of mind, Inman's account of her associations with the Communist Party was neither a reliable indicator of the way the organization dealt with women's issues nor a credible source of information about her own significance. Her determination to discredit Communist leaders and promote her theory not only clouded her interpretation of the past but made her more rigid and dogmatic than the Communist Party itself. Despite these problems, Inman got some of the recognition she had worked for when historians wrote about her ordeal and, following her lead, condemned the CP for quashing debate on the woman question. Because she was prolific and completely unwilling to concede defeat, her 40-year obsession became the myth upon which the history of women in the Communist Party was written.

MARY INMAN'S STORY—her report about how she was driven from the Communist Party in 1941 and her analysis of the Party's abandonment of women's issues in the succeeding decades—has served as compelling evidence for those who have inquired about women's experiences in the Old Left. But the way her story has been used illustrates the potential problems presented when oral histories and autobiographical documents alone are used as primary sources. It is a good example of the pitfall of generalizing from one person's experiences to write the history of an entire group or subject. Inman's story also shows the power that one person's interpretations can command when they have been written down and published. Without context and evidence from opposing perspectives, Inman's illusions and rationalizations, along with her grains of truth, became facts. Once these "facts" were established, they were cited and passed from one publication to the next and Inman's myth quickly became history. By 1990 it seemed, the verdict was in: organizing and discussion around the issue of women's oppression was incompatible with class struggle, and women who displayed gender consciousness before 1956, if they were noticed at all, were treated with disdain by the Communist Party.

Mary Inman is an extremely significant figure in the history of the CP's work on women's issues, but not because her story actually supports scholars' conclusions about Communists' failure to address gender oppression before and after World War II. Rather, Inman is important because her work after 1942, despite its inaccuracies and distortions, convinced many that the Communist Party had little concern about women's oppression and little interest in women's liberation. It is most ironic that by disparaging Communists' efforts to combat male supremacy and denying their significance for the later women's movement, Inman also effectively obscured the vital contributions she made to the CP's program for women's liberation and concealed her own significance for the history of feminism. Her book, *In Woman's Defense,* informed many progressives' views on the woman question. By 1945 numerous Communist women had actually adopted Inman's assertions about the pervasiveness of women's oppression and the cultural manifestations of male supremacy, and a few of them began to implement her ideas for a cross-class women's congress devoted to women's issues. Their efforts began to pay off in 1946 when the Congress of American Women, a newly created organization based on plans Inman helped to lay out in 1940, raised the consciousness of hundreds of progressive women who, in turn, demanded that the CP address their concerns about male supremacy inside and outside the Party. It is to the story of the Congress of American Women that we now turn.

# 3    The Congress of American Women: Catalyst for Progressive Feminism

THE YEAR 1945 was a watershed for American women. At the beginning of that year, with World War II still raging in Europe and Asia, many believed that women's participation in the war effort had permanently altered their role in U.S. society. Inspired by images like that of the popular "Rosie the Riveter," six million women who had never before worked outside the home had joined the labor force. The War Labor Board's ruling on equal pay for equal work led many to assume that sex discrimination in industry was waning. In addition to all those women who served as army and navy nurses, three hundred fifty thousand women had joined the army's WACs, the navy's WAVES, the Coast Guard's SPARS, and the Marines's MCWR. Even women's traditional domestic work had acquired political and nationalistic meaning, for they recycled metal, rationed food, cultivated "victory gardens," and governed families without the input of their absent husbands. The sum of such changes led one editorialist to write, "It is hard to foresee, after the boys come marching home and they marry these emancipated young women, who is going to tend the babies in the next generation?"[1]

By summer 1945, however, it was increasingly clear that most of these changes had been only temporary. As men left the armed forces and returned home, employers and political leaders made it clear that they expected women to leave their jobs and resume their exclusively domestic roles. In order to ensure that the transition back to a predominantly male workforce was a smooth one, social commentators and popular magazines both emphasized that women's true job was the one they did at home. Just as the muscular and self-sufficient Rosie the Riveter image had drawn many women into the industrial workforce in 1942, the romantic and idealized image of the devoted wife and mother pulled some of them out again three years later. By 1946 mainstream American culture was once again saturated by the notion that "marriage and sensible motherhood are probably the most useful and satisfying of all the jobs that women can do."[2]

Although many women voluntarily left their wartime jobs in order to nurture their families, a significant number also fought back. Those who liked their jobs and depended on the wages that came with them staged picket lines and petitioned their unions to protest their forced withdrawal from the skilled industrial workforce. Some women, particularly those who were members of such left-leaning unions as the United Auto Workers and the United Electrical Workers, made explicitly feminist arguments as they pressed their male bosses and co-workers to abandon traditional sex-based job classifications.[3] But although the UAW women's postwar efforts succeeded in winning permanent status for their Women's Bureau within the union's Fair Practices and Anti-Discrimination Department, it would be years before they made any significant progress in their quest for gender equality. By the end of 1945 it was clear to most women who had pinned their hopes on the war to bring about a transformation of women's role in U.S. society that, in fact, very little had changed.

Like so many working women, most feminists within women's rights organizations also found that the immediate postwar period bred disappointment, dashed hopes, and forced retreat.[4] The antifeminism of the post–World War II period was both intense and widespread, but it did not impede every segment of the American women's movement to the same degree. Mainstream feminists lost ground after 1945, but progressive women, who were accustomed to defining themselves in opposition to dominant political and cultural ideologies, continued to see the postwar period as an opportunity for new beginnings.[5] Inspired by women's mass participation in the war and in reconstruction efforts internationally, and still undaunted by increasing anti-Communism and antifeminism at home, progressive and Communist women saw 1945 as the ideal time to resume and improve upon the women's work they had abandoned at the start of the war. Beginning late that year a core group of these women, including Susan Anthony and Mary van Kleeck among others, worked with the Communist Party's support to create a new cross-class, multiethnic and racially integrated women's organization that they hoped could revive the struggles of the nineteenth-century woman's movement and attract women radicalized by their wartime experiences into the larger progressive movement.

The Congress of American Women (CAW), launched in 1946, lasted only four years.[6] Throughout its short life the organization's membership remained relatively small and, despite efforts to expand, limited to no more than twenty cities. But although the CAW never became the mass organization its founders envisioned, the group's failure to achieve its original objectives does not diminish its significance for the history of feminism in the United States. Between 1946 and 1950 CAW leaders were able to build on the CP's discussions of women from the 1930s and, using insights from Mary Inman's work, to develop a sophisticated analysis of women's oppression that recognized both the importance of women's race and class differences and the need for women to unite on the basis of gender to fight for their own emancipation. Armed with this broad understanding of the factors that limited women in American society, CAW activists also created a program for women's liberation that valued women's roles as housewives and mothers, challenged the social and cultural structures that excluded them from work and politics, and insisted that women could be different from but still equal to men.

By the time the CAW disbanded in 1950 the organization had, in the words of one participant, "resurrected from the dead an earlier movement and [taken] it forward to something that was very current."[7] In doing so, the CAW also raised the consciousness of hundreds of Communist and progressive women who subsequently used their new-found knowledge and confidence to demand that the Communist Party take their problems and its own male supremacy more seriously. Although Communist leaders never intended it to, the Congress of American Women moved the Party's program for women's liberation far beyond the one it endorsed in the 1930s. Ultimately, the CAW defined the terms for Communists' discussions about women's issues over the next decade and, by making women's liberation a more legitimate focus for Communist women's activism, mobilized the activities that would sustain the radical segment of the U.S. women's movement during the hostile years from 1945 to 1960.

THE CONGRESS OF AMERICAN WOMEN held its founding convention at the City Center Casino in New York City on International Women's Day, March 8, 1946.[8] After months of preparations CAW founders established the group as the official American branch of the Women's International Democratic Federation (WIDF), a pro-Soviet and antifascist international women's organization founded in Paris in November 1945 by Communist resistance leaders Eugenie Cotton and Marie-Claude Vaillant-Couturier.[9] Following the lead of their European counterparts the American women, guided primarily by Susan Anthony and Mary van Kleeck, organized their group around three major concerns: international peace, child welfare, and the status of women. They also created three national committees, the Commission for Action on Peace and Democracy, the Commission on Child Care and Education, and the Commission on the Status of Women, each one responsible for planning and coordinating activities related to its own area of concern.[10] In addition to these three committees the original members of the CAW also appointed a slate of officers to oversee the organization's national activities as a whole. In 1946 the group's national leadership consisted of long-time progressives Dr. Gene Weltfish, an anthropologist on the faculty at Columbia University; Muriel Draper, of the Committee for

American-Soviet Friendship; Mary van Kleeck, of the Industrial Department of the Russell Sage Foundation; journalist Susan Anthony II; and a number of well-known Communists including CP National Committee member Elizabeth Gurley Flynn.[11]

In the first two years of its existence the CAW closely resembled the typical progressive Popular Front organizations of the 1930s and early 1940s. Although it made no secret of its connection with the pro-Soviet WIDF, the CAW attracted a broad constituency including middle-class women who had been active in the suffrage movement, trade union women, and liberal supporters of women's rights as well as Communists and other progressives. The organization's early promotional materials claimed a membership of "hundreds of thousands" with chapters in at least twelve cities around the country.[12] But while the CAW presented itself as a fully independent organization supported by politically mainstream women such as Cornelia Bryce Pinchot, the wife of a former governor of Pennsylvania, it is clear that the Communist Party had a hand in charting its course from the very beginning. Not only did the organization's leadership include such nationally known Communists as Flynn and, later, Claudia Jones, but Eleanor Flexner, author of the pioneering work of women's history *Century of Struggle*, has written that while she was a member of the CP she "was drafted by the Communist Party . . . to be the Executive Secretary of . . . the Congress of American Women," and that "the main strength or guidance of the organization and its efforts were leading figures in the American Communist Party."[13]

In addition to supplying leadership and direction to the fledgling CAW, the Communist Party also publicly endorsed the organization in 1946 and, for the next three years, devoted considerable space in the *Worker* and the *Daily Worker* to articles that publicized its goals, analyses, and activities.[14] Communist Party support for a separatist women's organization with an explicitly feminist agenda was, as historian Amy Swerdlow has also suggested, something new.[15] In the 1930s and early 1940s Communists viewed both separatist organizing and feminist politics as bourgeois strategies to divert working-class women from class struggle. In general, however, though they might have dismissed them five years earlier, Communists and progressives accepted the CAW's outspoken feminist ideas in 1946 and 1947 as part of an important new analysis of the vastly changed postwar world in which they believed women were destined to play a central part.[16] What few people realized, however, was that neither the CAW's analysis of women's oppression nor its strategies for women's liberation were entirely new. The ideas that formed the basis for the CAW's program to liberate women originated in the late 1930s and, ironically, many of them came from Mary Inman's work.

BY 1946, MARY INMAN's fight with the Communist Party was already five years old. Although she knew about progressive women's attempt to revive the U.S. women's movement by creating the CAW she was extremely critical of their efforts precisely because the Communist Party supported them. Despite all evidence to the contrary, Inman insisted that as far as Communist women were concerned, "Browder revisionism" remained the order of the day.[17] She could not acknowledge that the progressive women's movement was proceeding without her. She attended the first two meetings of the CAW in Los Angeles in 1946, but when she found out that the group's structure and leadership were already in place, she dismissed it as an organization controlled by "a machine" that publicized meetings only among a "small, select list, carefully screened to eliminate anyone critical of the leadership." Using her strange and contradictory logic, Inman concluded that the Communist Party decided to promote the CAW in 1946 in order to appear as if it were organizing women, but that because it had been "liquidating" women's work since 1940, the Party also repressed the organization and kept it secret from the very women to whom it was supposed to appeal.[18]

Inman refused to recognize it, but she actually played a crucial role in inspiring the Congress of American Women and developing the major points of its program. Her book, *In Woman's Defense*, suggested that women's emancipation could come only after mainstream middle- and working-class women joined with progressives to fight for it. Between December 1940 and February 1942 she corresponded extensively with Susan B. Anthony II and together the two women expanded and developed her ideas for a cross-class women's congress through which progressives could lead the fight against women's oppression.[19] When Anthony joined Mary van Kleeck to organize the CAW in 1945, she implemented many of the ideas that she and Inman developed together four years earlier; as the driving force behind the organization's Commission on the Status of Women in 1946, she presented Inman's analysis of women's status as her own. Mary Inman and the Communist Party were arch enemies after 1941, but through Susan Anthony, Inman's ideas became the cornerstone for the CAW's work, indirectly transformed Communists' analysis of women's position in capitalist society, and sparked a new phase of women's struggles to free themselves from the bonds of oppression inside and outside the Communist movement.

## Inman, Anthony, and the Roots of the CAW

Susan Anthony became active in the progressive movement when she was in her early twenties, but, before she read *In Woman's Defense* at the age twenty-four, she was not involved in activities devoted exclusively to women or women's equality.[20] Although she was active in a number of other progressive causes before 1940, Anthony did not then realize that her difficulties balancing her personal and political commitments also troubled most other women in her political circles.[21] Only after reading *In Woman's Defense* did she begin to understand the ways that male supremacy affected her. She readily accepted Inman's ideas about the economic origins of women's oppression and its cultural and psychological manifestations in the twentieth-century United States. Shortly after reading the book, she wrote to Inman about how it changed her life. "Your book came at an auspicious time," she wrote. "I had been married only a few months and was getting restive under the role that even my very progressive husband expected of women—that of the docile servant of detail, whose main thoughts should be concentrated on buying a new chair cover and fascinating menus." But, Anthony went on, "your book crystallized the vague ideas that had been wandering around in my brain. . . . [It] has made clear to me the necessity of working for the economic and political and moral emancipation of women."[22]

Anthony's new awareness made her see that "even most of the progressives are partially blind on the subject" of women's oppression. In order to remedy this problem, Anthony informed Inman that, from then on, she intended to "devote most of [her] time and effort to the woman movement." Anxious to expand her knowledge, Anthony wrote, "I thought that I should have the benefit of your further thinking on this so that we might start action on bringing American women into the economic and political life of the nation," and asked Inman for her "advice on method and plans for a new down-to-earth woman's organization with a solid platform that can be backed by all working people." Mary Inman, flattered by Anthony's letter, replied, "It is so utterly fitting that you should be interested in the woman's movement, and that there should be a continuation of the name and line of Susan B. Anthony in this field." She communicated her pleasure at having enlisted Anthony in glowing terms. "Your grasp of basic issues, your enthusiasm for the organizational tasks that lie ahead, and your great and beautiful name with all that name stands for in the minds of oppressed women—and men—," Inman gushed, "you offer to throw into the struggle on woman's side." Inman ended her letter by declaring, "Susan, we accept your offer with love and admiration."

In the months that followed the two women wrote to one another frequently and in summer 1941, Mary Inman visited Anthony and her husband Clifford McAvoy in Washington, D.C. As their personal relationship developed, so did their political partnership. Anthony wrote, "I am eager to hear your plans for organizing women for action—the more I think about and discuss this problem the more I feel that I want to get started doing some active work on the question," and Inman began to spell out her ideas. "I believe we must have three things as a minimum of tools with which to construct a women's movement in this country," she wrote, "a Woman's Congress, a national nursery movement, and a woman's newspaper with national circulation. . . . [A Woman's Congress] would serve the same purpose as the Negro Congress now serves in relation to the Negro People's struggle. . . . It would be a powerful force for peace and would weld together existing women's organizations, trade union auxiliaries, the most progressive of the women's social clubs, etc."

By late January 1941, Susan Anthony was pushing Mary Inman to put these ideas into practice; she wanted Inman's help launching a progressive woman's congress that could combat the NWP's proposed Equal Rights Amendment, which both liberals and progressives opposed because of its potential to overturn laws that protected working-class women from extreme exploitation, and could facilitate alliances between progressives and moderate groups such as the General Federation of Women's Clubs and the League of Women Voters. Tempting Inman with the suggestion that she could enlist her friends Pearl Buck and Mary Beard to help with the effort once she had "definite ideas as to the program," Anthony asked her to "jot down a few ideas for a program around which to rally women for a woman's congress," and promised, "I will do likewise." One month later Inman and Anthony put their ideas together, creating a basic platform for their proposed congress that outlined the causes of women's oppression and, building on ideas from *In Woman's Defense,* presented various suggestions for eradicating them.

In creating their plan for the congress, Inman and Anthony had several unstated goals. They wanted to try to bridge the gap between the progressive/labor tradition of women's activism from the 1910s and the equal rights tradition that came out of the nineteenth-century woman movement. They also wanted to popularize Inman's ideas about the social and economic importance of women's labor in the home and her analysis of the role of culture in perpetuating women's oppression. The result of their efforts was a program that incorporated many proposals that were by this time standard for women's emancipation while it also presented bold new thinking on the question. They saw no contradiction in accepting special treatment for women in some cases and rejecting it in others and promised that the woman's congress would fight to maintain protective legislation and maternal and infant welfare programs and to reverse discrimination against women in the labor force, politics, and the legal and educational systems.[23] Although they anticipated that the congress could win greater respect for housekeeping and motherhood and give housewives more political credibility, Inman and Anthony also argued that publicly funded twenty-four-hour nurseries, communal kitchens and laundries, and socialized housecleaning services were necessary to liberate women from confinement in the home.[24] In order to guarantee women's equality they proposed an alternative to the Equal Rights Amendment—an improved version of the Woman's Charter of the mid-1930s—that would abolish discrimination against women without invalidating legislation that protected women workers from long hours and unhealthy conditions. Such an amendment, they suggested, would allow the congress to fight the National Woman's Party effectively by appropriating the good parts of the ERA and doing away with the bad.

These ideas were not particularly original; they integrated the diverse perspectives of women such as Elizabeth Cady Stanton, the original Susan B. Anthony, Florence Kelley, Charlotte Perkins Gilman, and Mary van Kleeck and showed that Inman and Anthony were well versed in the history of American feminism. But although they relied heavily on contributions from women's struggles past and present to form their program, Inman and Anthony also developed two new demands. First, they built on Inman's ideas about the cultural and ideological elements of women's oppression and resolved that the congress would oppose the slander and degradation of women and resist society's efforts to make them feel inferior and submissive. Second, they acknowledged that not all women were oppressed alike and determined that the congress should protect minority women by fighting discrimination based on race, religion, and political affiliation. These additions, particularly the latter one, made Inman's and Anthony's program substantially different from any other articulated by feminists since the turn of the century. Their concern with race and their interest in the cultural sources of women's oppression gave their proposed congress the potential to transform women's struggles and to carry the U.S. women's movement into the postwar world.

Unfortunately, Inman's and Anthony's joint project never got beyond the planning phase. By spring 1941 progressives became increasingly engrossed in issues and activities related to the war in Europe, and Mary Inman was beginning her long battle with the CP National Commission. When Inman left the Party in October 1941, Anthony told her not to get dis-

*Ten Women Anywhere Can Start Anything,* Congress of American Women organizing pamphlet, circa 1947. Photo by Barney Stein; courtesy of the Sophia Smith Collection, Smith College.

couraged and continued to push their ideas for a woman's congress at events
such as the National Conference of CIO Auxiliaries.[25] But when Mary
Inman wrote to Anthony in January 1942 asking her to become co-editor of
her new newsletter *Facts for Women,* Anthony refused, stating that although
a women's paper was needed, "such a newspaper must be at least approved
by the most progressive forces in the nation, or else it will be ineffective."[26]
Inman apparently regarded Anthony's refusal as evidence that she had
joined the Communist "conspiracy" to repress the woman question. Probably feeling hurt and betrayed, Inman wrote to Anthony one last time on
February 3, 1942, to explain, "with apologies to no one," that her paper

would avoid the "platitudinous, narrowed-down, choked-to-death approach which now passes for Marxism." After February 1942 there was no more correspondence between them; in "Thirteen Years of CPUSA Misleadership on the Woman Question," Inman referred to Susan Anthony's "Woman's Status Amendment" as "confused and inadequate" and dismissed her as bourgeois and deceitful. Although it was clear that Anthony continued to support Inman's theories, her refusal to join Inman's fight against the Communist movement brought their friendship and collaboration to a sudden and bitter end.

Susan Anthony probably regretted losing Mary Inman as a friend and mentor, but she must have realized that by dissociating herself from Inman she was also preserving her credibility in Communist circles. With her reputation intact, Susan Anthony was able to take what she had learned from Mary Inman between 1940 and 1942 and to continue working to implement their joint ideas even though the two women were estranged from one another. In 1943 and 1944, when Communists were absorbed in various wartime activities, Anthony worked to maintain some public awareness of women's problems. Her 1943 book, *Out of the Kitchen—Into the War: Woman's Winning Role in the Nation's Drama*, borrowed heavily from Inman's program as it made a case for nationalizing nurseries and cafeterias in order to free women for work in war industries.[27] At the end of the Second World War Anthony's long struggle to garner support for a national woman's congress began to pay off. When the Congress of American Women finally got off the ground in spring 1946, it was due in large part to her efforts.

## Foundations

Susan Anthony played an indispensable role in the planning and organizational phases of the CAW in 1945 and 1946. With Mary van Kleeck she cochaired the committee that gathered the data the American delegation presented to the founding convention of the Women's International Democratic Federation in Paris in November 1945.[28] Although Anthony did not attend the Paris convention herself, she co-authored with van Kleeck and Elinor Gimbel the "Report on the Problems and Status of Women in the United States," which the American delegation presented at the convention, and she continued to lead the CAW's organizational efforts between December 1945, when the delegates returned home from Paris, and March 1946, when the group was officially launched in the United States.[29] At the first working conference of the Congress of American Women, held at the Essex House in New York City on May 25, 1946, a group of six hundred delegates heard and approved the report of the Paris conference and rewarded the chief organizers of the CAW with official leadership positions: they elected Gene Weltfish as chairman [sic], Muriel Draper as vice chairman, and Susan Anthony as head of the group's Commission on the Status of Women.[30]

In her work as an officer for the CAW in 1946 and 1947 Anthony helped to formulate the group's structure and agenda and, in doing so, drew very heavily on the conversations she had had with Mary Inman between 1940 and 1942. As Inman and Anthony had planned for their woman's congress to continue the struggles of earlier generations of American feminists, Anthony and the other founders of the CAW consciously presented themselves as the bearers of the nineteenth-century woman's rights tradition and even called the group "the first women's political-action organization [in the United States] since the suffrage movement."[31] In keeping with that tradition—and with Inman's desire to "recognize the social value of the work performed in the home"—the CAW embraced a program for women's activism that celebrated women's roles as housekeepers and mothers at the same time that it sought to change them.[32]

The CAW's Peace and Child-Care commissions asserted that because women bear and rear children, they are the best, most committed fighters for peace. The CAW, like the Communist Party in the Popular Front period, proposed that women needed a stronger voice in American politics so that they could be more effective in their efforts to improve their homes and their cities' schools and playgrounds. Mothers' efforts to defend their families against nuclear weapons, high prices, and urban crime, they suggested, were the struggles that could deliver the world from the looming threats of poverty, destruction, and moral decay.[33]

While the Congress of American Women's approach to the issues of peace and child-welfare tended to reinforce traditional assumptions about women's "natural" roles, its desire to lead the struggle to raise women's status economically, politically, and socially also required the organization to challenge assumptions that women were fit only to keep house and bear children.[34] From its earliest days the organization tried to convince women that they could be political actors and, if they joined together nationally and internationally, wield considerable political power. As the chairman of the Commission on the Status of Women and the author of the "Report of the Commission on the Status of Women," Susan Anthony documented the ways that discrimination, not personal preference or biology, kept American women from participating fully in the workforce, politics, and social life and formulated the CAW's strategies for stopping it. In this capacity Anthony brought her collaboration with Mary Inman to bear on the CAW. Although she could not include *In Woman's Defense* in the bibliography of the

"Report of the Commission on the Status of Women" for pragmatic reasons, Anthony adopted many features of Inman's analysis within it.[35] Ultimately, *In Woman's Defense,* combined with Anthony's 1940-42 correspondence with Inman, served as the foundation for the CAW's analysis of women's oppression and its strategies for women's liberation.

Anthony began her report by analyzing the economic position of women in the United States. Still influenced by Inman's focus on the importance of housework, Anthony not only outlined the often-described problem of sex discrimination in the workforce but also described the problems of women who endured the burden of a "double job" if they worked outside the home and of housewives who performed outmoded work without pay in the isolated environment of their homes.[36] In order to remedy the problems of working women, Anthony drew on the progressive tradition and suggested that the CAW support the same kinds of struggles that Communists and other radical activists had been recommending for years. Based on Anthony's suggestions, the CAW called for equal pay for similar work, the addition of the word "sex" to the Fair Employment Practices Bill, the extension of the Fair Labor Standards Act and the Social Security Act to agricultural and domestic workers, equal access to education for women, the admission of both white and black women to the professions, and the entrance of all unorganized women workers into democratic trade unions.

What made Anthony's report particularly interesting, however, were the remedies she suggested for the "double job" and the difficulties of housewives and paid domestic workers—problems that Communists were only just beginning to recognize. Just as Inman suggested that collectivized housekeeping in the form of "large, new, well-built apartment houses," with "centrally arranged housecleaning units . . . central places for dining, [and] centrally situated nurseries for children" would solve the problems of both working women and housewives, Susan Anthony argued that "to free women from housekeeping, America must have a vast network of Government, community and commercial services" including "Government housing projects [with] community facilities such as laundries, child care centers, infirmaries and cafeterias . . . [and] large-scale housekeeping services [with] specialized chambermaids, window washers, and house cleaners, operating from a central agency, to which families would pay their share of the cost."[37] Consequently, the CAW endorsed the notion that for women to achieve equal economic status with men they needed relief from their domestic and maternal burdens and resolved to push for a national housing program, government-funded twenty-four-hour child care, and socialized cooking and housekeeping arrangements.

The second focus of the Commission on the Status of Women was U.S.

women's relationship to the political system. Anthony's discussion of American women's political status, like her analysis of their economic status, suggested that they had a lot to gain. She argued that, although the suffrage movement achieved "the 19th Amendment to the Constitution, which finally raised women to the status of white men, Negro men and foreign born men," after 1920 women were diverted away from party politics and excluded from state- and national-level political offices. Even in 1946, she asserted, women in some states remained legally subordinated to men by old laws that prevented them from making contracts, owning property, or sitting on juries. In order to improve women's participation in the political system, Anthony suggested that year-round electoral activity was necessary to win the support of the masses of women. In response the CAW promoted a political action campaign organized around Anthony's slogan "Forty-eight Congresswomen in 1948" with the hope that women could eventually achieve gender parity not only in the U.S. Congress, but in the Cabinet and the Supreme Court as well.[38]

Anthony's recommendations for improving women's subordinate legal status came directly out of the plans she made with Mary Inman before the war. Like Inman and the supporters of the Woman's Charter of the 1930s, she argued that the elimination of antiwoman laws could be most easily achieved with an amendment to the U.S. Constitution that would read, "There shall be no discrimination against women because of sex or marital status, economically, legally, politically or socially in the United States of America and in the territories subject to its jurisdiction. Nothing in this article shall be so construed to invalidate or prevent the passage of legislation improving the condition of women in their work or in their family status." Such an amendment, Anthony suggested, would guarantee women's equality without threatening protective labor legislation and maternity benefits and, by creating common ground for all true supporters of women's equality, make the CAW the dominant women's organization in the United States in the postwar period. The ratification of this amendment, which came to be known as Anthony's Woman's Status Amendment, quickly became one of the CAW's primary objectives.

Anthony's last task as the head of the Commission on the Status of Women was to examine the inferior social status of U.S. women and to suggest ways to improve it. This was relatively uncharted territory among progressives, and although she made no mention of it in the text of the report, Anthony relied almost exclusively on *In Woman's Defense* for the analysis of women's social subordination she put forth in the document. As Mary Inman described the ways that "Jim Crowing women along sex lines" isolated them from men, made men and women "unnaturally sex conscious just as Negroes and whites are made unnaturally race and color conscious," and built "walls of strangeness between them," Anthony's discussion of "Jim Crow Customs and Laws against Women" concluded that "women's second-class status is manifested in bans on women in public places, bans against their admission to certain all-male inner sanctums, curfews on their public unescorted appearances and of course in the double standard of morals which duplicates socially the double standard in wages."[39] And as Inman analyzed the "manufacturing of femininity" in the home and the perpetuation of a "culture of women's subjugation" through literature and movies, women's clothing styles, language, and stereotypes, Anthony argued that women are raised to feel inferior to men, that the differences between the sexes are further exaggerated by women's "curves, high heels and elaborate clothes," and that the process of minimizing all women is "nurtured by textbooks, movies, radio and theater" that belittle women's work, intelligence, appearance, and interests.

Anthony's analysis left little doubt in CAW leaders' minds that women were subordinated socially and culturally as well as economically and politically, and as a result of her arguments the CAW resolved to "collect and analyze the main Jim Crow customs and laws against women and recommend concerted action to remove them," to act as "watchdogs" against misrepresentations of women and take proper action against them, and to "establish a permanent sub-committee of the Commission on the Status of Women to coordinate this work."[40]

By summer 1946, the CAW's agenda was set and the group was ready to move forward and to recruit members, set up chapters around the country, and begin working toward its goals. Using two informational pamphlets, one entitled "What Is the Congress of American Women" and the other "Ten Women Anywhere Can Start Anything," the group explained its brief history, laid out its program, listed its officers, and invited "all women who wish to act together with other women for a secure future and a better world for all of us," to join. The CAW founded its first chapters, composed largely of Communists and other progressive women, in New York City and Los Angeles. Within a year the group expanded to include branches in Chicago, Detroit, Milwaukee, Seattle, Kansas City, Washington, D.C., Portland, Cleveland, and Pittsburgh.[41] More than any other women's organization that existed in this period, the CAW made a strong effort to recruit women from a variety of racial and ethnic groups. In addition to forming strong working relationships with groups such as the Croatian Women's Council, the American-Serbian Democratic Women's Committee, and the Emma Lazarus Division of the Jewish People's Fraternal Order, the CAW also established affiliations with the National Association of Colored

Women and the Illinois Association for Colored Women.[42] In keeping with their goal of fighting all forms of discrimination in the United States, including racial discrimination, the founders of the CAW worked especially hard to recruit African American women and to promote them into leadership positions. Harriet Magil, national treasurer of the organization in 1947, stressed that the CAW had trouble organizing black women because they "weren't ready for it . . . they were too busy making ends meet."[43] Nevertheless, in its early years the organization successfully formed a Harlem chapter and claimed at least five African American women leaders including progressives Dr. Charlotte Hawkins Brown, Thelma Dale, Vivian Carter Mason, Halois Morehead, and Ada B. Jackson.[44]

During its first year, things looked promising for the CAW. The organization grew fairly rapidly and succeeded in attracting attention from both progressive and more mainstream women. Even high-profile feminists such as Dorothy Kenyon, who had served on the League of Nations Commission to Study the Status of Women and who would, in 1947, become the U.S. delegate to the United Nations Commission on the Status of Women, attended the group's opening convention and spoke at a forum supporting Anthony's Women's Status Amendment later that year.[45] In order to facilitate organizational unity, the CAW national office appointed an editorial board and in 1946 began to publish a national newsletter, the *Congress of American Women Bulletin* (later renamed *Around the World*).[46] As the national organization grew stronger, so did its local chapters. Both the Los Angeles and Chicago chapters published their own newsletters, and those and other chapters organized neighborhood activities and babysitting cooperatives and orchestrated successful political actions including a citywide consumer protest against high meat prices in Detroit, a campaign to save wartime child-care centers in Chicago, and a drive to support striking packinghouse workers in Kansas City.[47]

Women inside the CAW also stirred up considerable grassroots support for civil rights in some communities in the immediate postwar period. Various CAW chapters around the country worked for such causes as the integration of public swimming pools.[48] Following in the footsteps of both African American and white women's organizations that had been fighting against lynching in the United States since the end of the nineteenth century, in September 1946 the group cosponsored a nationwide campaign to end lynching in the South, participated in a march on Washington to oppose lynching, established its own national antilynching committee, and circulated a list of recent lynchings in the United States and the actions women should take against them.[49] Beginning in spring 1948, the CAW also led a campaign to defend Rosa Lee Ingram, a poor African American share-

cropper from Ellaville, Georgia, who became the group's symbol of the oppression of black women in the South after she and her two teenaged sons
were sentenced to death for accidentally killing the white farmer who tried
to rape her.[50]

The CAW never gained as much ground on women's rights issues as it
did on peace and community issues, but it was not for lack of trying. Once
she had established the CAW's agenda for improving women's status, Susan
Anthony struggled to keep women's liberation at the center of the group's
mission. She worked tirelessly in 1947 in an effort to win consultative status
for the CAW with the UN Commission on the Status of Women.[51] She also
led the push to organize broad-based campaigns to fight discrimination
against women in employment, politics, legal codes, and social customs. Although she did manage to win broad support for her Women's Status
Amendment as an alternative to the ERA, Anthony had less success with the
other areas of her program.[52] Despite her revelations about the social and
cultural sources of women's oppression in the "Report of the Commission
on the Status of Women," Anthony was never able to mobilize any mass opposition to misrepresentations of women in the media or sexist social customs that kept women down.[53] Anthony's attempt to wage war against the
cultural oppression of women and to redefine women's images of themselves consisted of a series of small efforts, such as commissioning a cantata
called "Women Are Dangerous" to be performed on International Women's
Day at the Hotel Capitol in New York.[54]

When Susan Anthony resigned her position with the CAW in order to
become the WIDF representative at the United Nations in spring 1948, Betty
Millard, a Communist and former editor of *New Masses,* replaced her as the
head of the Commission on the Status of Women.[55] Millard, educated at
Barnard College, the Geneva School of Industrial Studies, and the University of London, was clearly influenced by Anthony's assessment of women's
inferior status in the United States, and she took up Anthony's campaign to
promote the importance of women's rights within the CAW with renewed
energy. Millard's first column in *Around the World* reminded readers to
"watch all state and national legislation concerning women very carefully
and to have CAW reps at all hearings in your state" and urged them for the
first time since Anthony's report appeared in 1946 to "protest to editors all
magazine articles and stories slandering women."[56]

Aware that the knowledge of women's past struggles had the potential
to mobilize them in the present, Millard also sent educational material on
the Seneca Falls convention of 1848 to all CAW chapters and planned a rally
to commemorate the hundredth anniversary of the convention to take place
at Elizabeth Cady Stanton's grave in Woodlawn Cemetery in the Bronx on

July 19, 1948. Among the fifty participants at the rally were Stanton's grand-daughter Nora Stanton Barney, Frederick Douglass's nephew Haley Douglass, and Susan B. Anthony II. Barney, herself a new member of the CAW, reminded the assembled audience that her grandmother had "wanted far more for women than the right to vote" and reaffirmed Stanton's 1898 declaration that "it is time for agitation on the broader question of philosophical socialism."[57] In the wake of the rally Millard continued to tie the CAW's women's rights platform to the history of women's suffrage and labor struggles with the hope that she could convince the masses of American women of the need to fight for their emancipation. Millard's efforts inspired the Los Angeles chapter of the CAW (which counted pioneering women's historian Gerda Lerner as one of its members) to organize and teach two classes on American women's history and status, but because of the increasingly conservative political context of the late 1940s her desire to recruit average housewives to the movement went unfulfilled.[58]

Anthony, Millard, and the other CAW leaders were no doubt disappointed when American women failed to heed their call for a grassroots struggle to raise women's status domestically and internationally. But despite their failure to mobilize a mass base for work on women's liberation, neither Anthony's nor Millard's efforts went completely unrewarded. At least some women who were active in and around the Communist Party, unlike their more mainstream counterparts, were ripe for conversion to the CAW's position on the need for women's emancipation. In 1946, when the *Worker* serialized Susan Anthony's "Report of the Commission on the Status of Women" in its newly revived women's pages, her "new" ideas, adopted in large part from Mary Inman's work, made many progressive women aware that they constituted an oppressed group and aroused their interest in fighting male supremacy along with racism and capitalism. According to one woman, "It heightened my awareness and changed my way of seeing my own life, my own relationships, and so on."[59] In the weeks and months after Anthony's work appeared in the paper, numerous women and a few men wrote to the women's page and, using Anthony's analysis, reinforced the importance of the woman question, criticized male supremacist practices in Communist circles, described their desire to work on the issue at the local level, and called for more support for women's liberation from the Party's national leaders.[60] In 1948, the publication of Betty Millard's article "Woman against Myth" in *New Masses* sparked a new and even more intense round of debate and activity on women's issues in Communist circles all around the country. By this time, the CP national leadership was forced to take a strong stand in support of Communist women's demands, to condemn male supremacist thinking and behavior inside and outside Communist settings, and to initiate new policies and activities that aimed to combat sexist practices in laws and workplaces, in mainstream politics and social customs, and in the Party's own theory, activity, and culture.

In the volatile political context of the immediate postwar period the CAW, with the support of the Communist Party, might have had the potential to spark the resurgence of a mass women's movement in the United States. But, as we shall see, by the time the Communist Party fully embraced the CAW's arguments about the need for women's liberation in 1948, the domestic policies that accompanied the Cold War put both organizations on the defensive. Whereas in 1946 and 1947 the CAW supported a broad range of women's issues, by late 1948 the group was expending most of its limited resources on only two causes. The group's foreign policy emphasized opposition to the Truman Doctrine and the Marshall Plan, and its domestic policy criticized anti-Communist deportation proceedings and supported American Communist Party leaders who were under attack by the U.S. government.[61] As a result of these activities, and the frequent trips made by CAW members to WIDF meetings in Communist countries, Truman's Justice Department investigated the group and, in May 1948, added the CAW to its list of subversive organizations. This tactic served its intended purpose: the subversive label scared many of the group's supporters, drastically reduced the CAW's membership, and exacerbated the group's financial difficulties.[62] In May 1949 the remaining CAW leaders organized the group's first Constitutional Convention in order to analyze and assess the organization's problems and to begin anew, but the damage had already been done. Only three hundred members attended. By this time it seemed clear that the CAW's days were numbered.[63]

## The End of the Beginning

The U.S. government dealt the final blow to the Congress of American Women when the House Un-American Activities Committee published its scathing *Report on the Congress of American Women* in October 1949. HUAC's report concluded that the purpose of the organization was "not to deal primarily with women's problems, as such, but rather to serve as a specialized arm of Soviet political warfare in the current 'peace' campaign to disarm and demobilize the United States and democratic nations generally, in order to render them helpless in the face of the Communist drive for world conquest."[64] In a last-ditch effort to counter HUAC's charge that the group functioned "behind a suffrage camouflage" as a tool of the Soviet Union, the CAW disaffiliated with the WIDF in December 1949. Despite this effort, in January 1950 the Justice Department demanded that CAW officers and board members register under the Foreign Agents Registration

Act.[65] Muriel Draper and other CAW leaders sought legal advice from sympathetic attorneys John Abt and O. John Rogge with the hope that they could find a way to keep the organization alive, but when it became clear that a legal battle would be very expensive and that the Communist Party was already too burdened by its own defense to assist the group financially, they decided to disband rather than risk imprisonment.[66]

The Congress of American Women, which had begun with such great promise in 1946, looked like a failure when its members voted to disband in 1950. The group started out with the goal of mobilizing the masses of American women for political activity in alliance with their sisters overseas, but although it had sometimes claimed as many as a quarter of a million members, it had probably never recruited more than a few thousand women, many of whom already had ties to the Left.[67] It sponsored a grand plan for improving the status of American women and had only managed to convince a minority of its members to embrace the cause of women's emancipation. In light of that evidence Katherine Campbell has argued that the organization is little more than "an intriguing 'might have been'" and Amy Swerdlow has suggested that along with the CAW's demise "went the connection between the suffrage generation, the Old Left, and women's peace activism."[68]

But although the CAW never achieved a mass base for any of its work, much less its women's rights agenda, neither the group's principles nor its influence died along with it in 1950. And whereas some have suggested that the CAW's close ties to the Communist Party between 1946 and 1950 prevented it from developing Anthony's program for women's rights, in fact, those ties actually provided the constituency that embraced Anthony's ideas and put them into action.[69] The CAW's program for women's rights, embodied in Susan Anthony's "Report of the Commission on the Status of Women" and Betty Millard's "Woman against Myth," served as the basis for the American Communist Party's analysis of women's oppression and its work for women's liberation during the decade 1946-56. By exposing Communist women and men to its radical analysis of women's oppression and motivating them to work for women's liberation, Anthony and the CAW effectively revived many of Mary Inman's ideas and ushered in a new era of Communist organizing on the woman question. It was that work, sometimes very sophisticated and sometimes quite flawed, that sustained a radical women's movement into the 1960s.

# II
# TRANSFORMATIONS

# 4 Women's Work Is Never Done: Communists' Evolving Approach to the Woman Question, 1945–1956

IN JUNE 1946, a group of four women from San Francisco wrote to the editor of the newly established women's page of the Communist Party's Sunday newspaper, the *Worker*. In response to an earlier letter from a woman who asked for advice about how she and her husband could combine marriage and parenthood with political activity, Hodee Richards, Helen Linia, Jane Renaker, and Anne Taylor criticized the Party for denying that "the rights and duties of women members are complicated by the fact that women are oppressed as a sex under class societies."[1] After charging the Party with "losing" women in the revisionism of the Browder years, these women reported that the California CP had "set up a Commission on Work among Women in San Francisco County." The group closed their letter with the following demands: "So here's for the solution of our problem: an end to the separation of 'personal' and 'party' life. Special help to women because of their double oppression under capitalism!"

This letter, along with a handful of others published in the Party press in 1946, was among the first signs that at least some rank-and-file Communist women (and a few men) would no longer sit back and allow the Communist Party to maintain its long-held inadequate position on the woman question. Over the next two years many progressive women began to take up the call promoted first by Mary Inman, and later by Susan B. Anthony II and Betty Millard, and to protest against all forms of sex discrimination. What began in 1946 as a trickle of dissatisfaction quickly became a torrent and the CP, ordinarily a fairly rigid, top-down organization that suppressed dissent, was forced to respond. Communist leaders, anxious to maintain and even build the CP's female constituency, began to adapt its position on the woman question to fit the changing circumstances women faced in the postwar United States. By 1948 the Communist Party had abandoned its strictly economic theory of women's oppression in favor of the more complex analysis offered by the Congress of American Women's Commission on the Status of Women.

In order to satisfy the demands made by rank-and-file Communists like those from San Francisco, the Party also explored political solutions for women's so-called personal problems and, through the creation of women's commissions at the national, state, and local levels, worked harder than ever before to insure that Party practice at all levels followed Party theory. Communists ultimately recognized that women's oppression was social and cultural as well as economic and emphasized the need to fight women's oppression *and* male supremacist ideology and behavior. These new policies put the Communist Party far ahead of other leftist groups that endorsed women's rights before the 1960s; they also made the gender politics of the Communist Party more radical and, by present-day standards, more feminist than those of other feminist organizations of the time, including the National Woman's Party.

## Postwar Promises and Problems

At the end of World War II, the American Communist Party's official analysis of women's oppression was little different from the one it had endorsed more than a decade earlier.[2] Between 1922, when the CP established its first Women's Bureau, and 1945, when it reestablished its National Women's Commission after a wartime hiatus, the Communist Party continued to take most of its guidance on the question of women's oppression from the Marxist classics: Marx's *Capital* and *The Communist Manifesto*, Engels's *Origin of the Family, Private Property and the State*, Bebel's *Women and Socialism*, and Lenin's *Women and Society*. Although some women began to insist that discrimination existed inside the Party as well as outside it during the years between the two world wars, Communist leaders had never formally expanded the classical Marxist analysis of women's oppression to explain or deal with the variety of problems women faced daily. In 1945 many Communists still dismissed male supremacy as a divisive concept imported to the working-class by bourgeois feminists and as a serious symptom of the false consciousness exhibited by a few misguided progressive women who did not understand that class, not sex, was the fundamental contradiction in capitalist society.

In 1944 and 1945, once it had become clear that the Allied Powers would defeat the Fascist armies of Europe and Asia, American Communists began making plans for the Party's work in the postwar world. After the dismissal of the national chairman, Earl Browder, the leaders of the newly reconstituted American Communist Party expected that they would be able to resume the struggles from which they had retreated in 1940, including the fight to improve women's status in the United States. In order to recruit women more effectively and fulfill their longtime pledge of support for women's rights, Communist leaders renewed their commitment to family and community issues, demanded an end to the idea that women's place was in the home, and promised to lead the fight to protect women's jobs and wartime child-care centers.[3]

Although Communists resumed their hard work to protect women's rights in labor unions and in the workforce, they also devoted considerable attention to the idea that women had made tremendous progress since 1940 and suggested that, because of their contributions to the war effort, American women were "on the threshold of [their] political maturity." Leaders like Elizabeth Gurley Flynn argued that whereas most women had been somewhat "backward" before World War II, they were finally ready to play an equal role with men in progressive politics in the postwar period.[4] Communist strategists hoped that their efforts, combined with those of the Congress of American Women, would inspire traditional housewives and mothers, angry working women, and experienced peace and women's rights activists to join with men in the struggle to build a peaceful, just, and democratic America.

Communist Party leaders in the United States made several major miscalculations in the immediate postwar period. Their decision to comply with Soviet leaders' demand that they dissolve the Communist Political Association and reconstitute the American Party came in part from their naïve glorification of the Soviet Union and in part from the mistaken belief that the political atmosphere of postwar America would be even more conducive to radical political change than that of the 1930s. Similarly, Communist leaders' assumption that wartime opportunities prepared the way for women's equality inside and outside the Party came from their belief that women's oppression was primarily economic and their failure to recognize that male supremacist ideology also limited women in a multitude of ways. But although it took them more than ten years to acknowledge that Stalin and the Soviet Union had major shortcomings, and four years to concede that conservatives and not radicals would dominate the postwar political agenda, Communists figured out relatively quickly that the opportunities women won during wartime had not solved their problems.

As early as 1946 and 1947 the Communist Party began to explore the notion that women's oppression included cultural and ideological components as well as economic ones and to alter its day-to-day operations so that more women could take part. By 1948 the CP officially recognized that, although male supremacist ideology had economic origins, it operated independent of class exploitation and therefore warranted its own struggle, separate from the fight for women's equality in the workforce and politics. The Party's relatively quick realignment on this issue occurred not because Communists were somehow smarter about women than about other matters, but because Communist women, who had been promised equality in progres-

sive settings for many years, finally insisted on it. In the absence of a comprehensive Soviet policy on the woman question in this period the American Party was able to deal with the issue in its own way and, in doing so, to
embrace women's demands rather than repressing them.

After the inequities of the 1930s and the war years, Communist women
must have been pleased to hear that the CP's leaders intended to take them
more seriously in 1945. But if they had ever really believed that Party leaders' declaration of women's equality in Communist circles was enough to
make them equal (and whether women believed this is certainly question-
able), they were soon disappointed. The demanding realities of family life
during the postwar baby boom quickly brought many young Communist
women to the realization that as wives—and especially as mothers—their
ability to participate in the political and social life of their Party was actually more restricted than before. In her letter to the editor of the women's
page of the *Worker* in April 1946, Joan Garson reported that, as a local Party
leader who was also a housewife and the mother of a new baby, she was
much less active in CP activities than she wanted to be.[5] Garson's letter articulated the ways that even leading Communist women's "personal" circumstances interfered with their political equality and sparked a wave of
rank-and-file protest among Communists that, unlike the dissension of the
1930s, did not go unheard.

The publication of Garson's letter in the pages of the *Worker* coincided
with an increase in the quantity and quality of coverage of women's issues
in the Party press. Garson's letter appeared on April 21, just four days before
Flynn called women "the most decisive group politically in all advanced
countries" and invited "every woman, in the trade unions, in the ranks of
the Negro people, as well as the wives and mothers on the farms and in the
homes and cities" to join the CP. Only a few weeks later the *Daily Worker*
published a series of articles that generously praised the newly organized
Congress of American Women for its pledge to fight "discrimination against
women because of sex or marital status, economically, legally, politically
or socially."[6]

The hypocrisy evident in the Party's simultaneous defense of women's
equality and disregard for the problems of women in Garson's position did
not escape other readers' notice. In the wake of Garson's letter several readers wrote to the *Worker* to affirm that they experienced similar difficulties
and to admonish the Party for its inadequate understanding of women's
predicaments. Nora Brent wrote to say, "It seems to me that our whole approach to housewives is slightly antiquated and a little sectarian." S.T., from
New York City, articulated the serious consequences that lack of support for
women could have on Party membership. "Joan Garson's letter," she wrote,

"touched on the very real problem of the housekeeper-mother who still wants to be politically active and yet not deny her family any of her time." Like Garson, S.T. confirmed that "it takes an almost superhuman effort on the part of the wife to overcome the scorn and ridicule of the type of husband who feels his wife's place is in the home." Not only did this problem have personal implications, it had political ones. As S.T. suggested, "This leads to real strife and discord, and if not solved in some manner, sometimes leads to a really sincere comrade having to drop out of party work entirely."[7]

Hodee Richards, Helen Linia, Jane Renaker, and Anne Taylor also confirmed that they were "in the same boat with Mrs. Garson" and that Garson's problem was "so general, so agitating, and so in need of a solution." But this group was particularly interested in making CP leaders and members aware that "if a branch elects a woman to a position, it is petty-bourgeois to allow her to sink or swim with that responsibility." Leaving women no option but to hire babysitters so that they could continue with their activity, the group submitted, was "nothing more nor less than a tax by the Party on its women members as the price for being of use to the Party." "This is intolerable," they declared. "We believe that the problem is the party's problem. The Party is responsible to help work out a feasible solution."

In the remaining months of 1946 the exchange of ideas in response to Garson's letter proliferated in the pages of the *Worker*. In July, just two weeks after the paper published excerpts from Anthony's discussion of women's inferior political status, yet another local Party leader, A. E. Hudson, wrote to the editor of the women's page to report the problems he saw in his district and to add his suggestions to the small but growing rank-and-file campaign to improve the CP's approach to women.[8] Although he acknowledged that "our problem is an outcrop of the general condition of women in the advanced capitalism of the USA," Hudson proposed that Communists could address "the special aspects that confront us within the party, and in the day-to-day work of the district membership department." He reported that he had visited "scores of comrades" in his own district and discovered that "3/4 of our women comrades were among the inactive." When he asked women why they were not participating in Party activities, they responded with a long list of answers. "They could not leave babies alone and had no one to babysit," he reported. "Women with jobs have to do housework in the evenings and are too tired to go to meetings. Husbands didn't really want them to come. Talk in clubs is over their heads." And finally, he concluded, "No other women at the meetings; if there are other women they are often very young. No friendly spirit in the clubs."

Hudson realized that rank-and-file women were not the only members of the CP held back by sexism; he pointed out that even politically savvy women who had been groomed for leadership positions ultimately suffered similar problems. "What happens to them as time goes on?" he asked rhetorically. "Some of them marry, and not later than the first baby their 'fate' catches up with them. They submerge in the 'reserve' and become the forgotten generation." But Hudson also clarified that "this is not their fault. They try hard, sometimes desperately to keep up without help from the rest of us. They occasionally manage to come to a meeting, but they aren't called upon to do work because they cannot devote as much time as they previously did." Even those without children, he suggested, had similar problems: "Some do not marry, or marry a party functionary, do not raise families, and become the handy-maids in the party offices who carry so much of the dirty work and get so little of the glory. They become isolated, their lives do not resemble those of other women in the community." Lest Communist leaders conclude that women were to blame for their problems Hudson concluded, "Their weakness is not their own—it is ours. We made them."

Hudson was too conscientious just to complain about the CP's errors in dealing with women; like any good organizer he wanted to propose solutions. He conceded that he did not "know the answers to these problems" and stated that "many of us will have to think, observe, analyze and discuss before we can even hope for a partial solution." Despite his modesty, however, Hudson was willing to suggest some possible steps toward improving Communist women's lot. If women were to achieve equality with men in the Party, he argued, membership personnel needed to "know the membership, their potentialities and personal problems, and should help . . . in the correct utilization of every member within his or her limitations. In order to make such a change possible he suggested that the CP needed to create a system that allowed housewives and mothers to participate in political activity, and to combat sexist assumptions and practices that were so prevalent within the Party itself. "Clubs should use their ingenuity to enable mothers to attend at least one meeting a month," he suggested, and "babysitting should be considered political work on the part of youth." Like the California women before him, Hudson argued that the CP "must learn to use the limited time of women comrades. . . . We must stop the mechanical division between political and organizational work, between political and organizational comrades generally as well as along sex lines. . . . We should develop a real cadre policy in regard to women." Hudson concluded his letter by reemphasizing that "thorough thought should be given to the special education of women for party leadership, with full recognition of their particular problems."

If Communist leaders had been unwilling to acknowledge the personal and cultural aspects of women's oppression in 1945, the CAW's work combined with letters such as those from Garson, the San Francisco women, Hudson, and others called attention to their mistake and obliged them to recognize that women's problems were more complicated than they had previously thought. Throughout the second half of 1946 the Communist press published increasing numbers of articles that focused on women's problems. From Katrina Mauley's insistence that "women shouldn't be forced back into their homes to do the tedious and unstimulating work of the household" and David Platt's censure of the film *Without Reservations* for its attacks on women's "right to participate in public affairs [and] their right to do anything but eat, sleep, love and laugh," to Lenore Garrett's complaints about the restrictions placed on her as a woman sportswriter and Martha Bridger's critique of women's magazines for "poisoning women's minds," Communist authors exposed the ways that cultural assumptions and institutions propagated the myth that women were fit only to marry, keep house, and bear children.[9]

The *Worker* and *Daily Worker* carried many more articles explaining the reasons for women's difficulties, such as excerpts from Anthony's "Report of the Commission on the Status of Women" about their inferior economic, legal, and social status. At the same time it also published articles full of advice about ways that Communist women and men could help to reverse such inequalities by participating in women's rights struggles and supporting the Congress of American Women.[10] Flynn's 1947 pamphlet *Woman's Place in the Fight for a Better World* sought to convince American women that, although they had made great progress through the suffrage and labor movements, they still had much to achieve. The solutions to their problems, she proposed, could be found in the Communist Party, which, by that time, supported the very same list of demands promoted by Anthony and the Congress of American Women. These were:

(1) Equality of women in the political, economic, legal, professional, cultural and social life of our country;

(2) Adequate legislation for maternity and child care to safeguard the health of mother and child;

(3) The right of all women to work; equal pay for equal work; equal training; upgrading and seniority with men in all occupations; legal safeguards for health; minimum wage laws including for domestic workers; old age benefits for working women and workers' wives at age 60; defeat of the misnamed "equal rights amendment" which would destroy indispensable labor legislation;

(4) Removal of legal disabilities on women citizens;

(5) Full equality for Negro women from segregation, discrimination, poll tax, downgrading in employment;

(6) Adequate childcare facilities with federal and state support for nurseries, recreation centers and schools with hot lunches;

(7) Basic 5 day week of 40 hours especially because women workers have double duty of job and care of home;

(8) No discrimination or quota system against women in [education] or the professions;

(9) Equal appointment of capable women to posts in federal, state and city governments and in diplomatic service;

(10) Election to office in legislative bodies, labor unions and all public organizations of capable women, Negro and white; and

(11) Adequate funds for the Women's Bureau, Children's Bureau, and other governmental agencies concerned especially with the needs of women and children.[11]

In 1947, in addition to improved coverage of women's issues, considerable evidence also appeared in CP publications that showed the national leadership was starting to take women more seriously. At least some local Party clubs began in that year to plan special events and programs to make it easier for more housewives and mothers to participate in a range of Communist activities. In February the Party put the National Women's Commission to work for the first time since its revival in 1945. Furthermore, over the course of the year the Party also established twelve lower-level women's commissions in Ohio, Michigan, New York, Illinois, Pennsylvania, California, Washington, New Jersey, and Texas to "assess [women's] needs, concrete problems and ties in the community," and "raise party sensitivity as a whole to the needs of women in general." Echoing Hudson's suggestions, Flynn declared that "In our Party it is our duty to fully utilize the capabilities of our women members in every capacity and to assist them in solving problems which develop during pregnancy and after childbirth so that they will not become isolated and embittered by enforced political activity."[12]

In January the Bronxville section of the CP organized a special women's dinner meeting at which men cooked and served food, minded children, and washed dishes while their wives heard Margaret Cowl speak about "the role of women today," discussed "other problems affecting women," and pledged to sell 100 subscriptions to the *Worker*. In April the New York State Board of the Party announced that it had approved countywide women-only meetings "to spur recruiting of feminine forces for the Party" and to counteract the fact that men were three times more likely to join the CP than women.[13]

By the end of 1947 many local Party clubs, such as the Kings Highway section in New York City, introduced special women's classes to train women for leadership positions. These cadre training schools provided childcare so that mothers as well as women without children could participate and transportation so that women and their children could get to the meetings with minimal hassle. Because some Party leaders finally began to recognize that women could be essentially equal to men and still confront special problems because of their oppression, rank-and-file women who benefited from new programs such as the training schools could report that "they have learned concentration in study, have achieved a greater degree of self-confidence, and have become more articulate in their club meetings," and the CP could boast that the number of women in local leadership positions was approaching 50 percent. One woman, a CP member for ten years, summed up the success of the program when she said, "This is the most wonderful experience I have had in the Party."[14]

The years 1946 and 1947 were important for women in Communist circles because gender-conscious activists successfully used the CP's own rhetoric about women's equality to convince at least some of the state and national leaders that their "personal" problems were actually political problems that deserved recognition and attention. The Party's efforts to make it easier for housewives and mothers to take part in political activities by planning women's classes and providing childcare were commendable and in some ways forward-looking, but such efforts also accepted women's roles in the nuclear family and reinforced the traditional sexual division of labor. Documents from the CP National Women's Commission from 1947 make it clear that Communist leaders still hoped to recruit more women primarily so that the Party could counteract the right's influence on them and organize and lead "women's work" around the traditionally female issues of housing, high prices, child welfare and peace instead.[15] Furthermore, despite the Party's endorsement of Anthony's "Report of the Commission on the Status of Women" and its accommodation to housewives' insistence that it recognize their "personal" problems, official CP theory continued to emphasize the notion that women's oppression was economic, that working-class men did not oppress women, and that class struggle, not the "battle of the sexes" approach of feminism, was the only path to women's liberation.

## Woman against Myth

Nineteen forty-eight was a major turning point for Communists' analysis of women's oppression and their commitment to freeing women from it. In January of that year Betty Millard, an editor at the progressive journal *New Masses* and the CAW member who would soon replace Anthony as the head of the group's Commission on the Status of Women, published "Woman against Myth," a two-part article (later reissued in pamphlet form by International Publishers) that ultimately became the basis for Communists' new and more complex understanding of women's subordination under capitalism.[16] Published to mark the centennial of the American women's rights movement and probably also to appease Communist women's demands for more work on the woman question, "Woman against Myth" reiterated much of what Communists in the United States and Europe had been saying about women's oppression for decades. Borrowing from Engels, Millard argued that women's inferiority was not biological, but rather a historical phenomenon that originated with the evolution of private property and the resultant developments of monogamy and prostitution, which made women "vassals of vassals . . . confined to household drudgery . . . excluded from public life." Taking her cue from Marx, Millard also suggested that the Industrial Revolution "cracked the old prison walls around women" by "undermining the rigid traditions of feudalism . . . substituting the concept of free contract for that of inherited right," and laying "the groundwork for their freedom." Although she recognized that large-scale industry had the potential to free women, Millard was clear that "emancipation by no means took place automatically." She deftly illustrated the ways that women acted as agents in their own emancipation by describing Elizabeth Cady Stanton and Susan B. Anthony's struggles for women's rights and women's suffrage, and the Lowell mill girls' fight for higher wages and shorter hours. She also made it very clear that although women in 1948 had rights they lacked a century earlier, their fight for equality was still extremely necessary.

It was Millard's discussion of the problems that women faced in the contemporary United States that would ultimately help to revise the Communist Party's official theoretical position on the woman question. Millard was not the first person to question the CP's standard assumptions about the extent of women's subordination under capitalism—Mary Inman is her most notable predecessor—but she was the first to succeed in inducing the Communist Party to take her blended analysis of Marxism and feminism seriously. Although her arguments bear remarkable similarity to those in Inman's *In Woman's Defense,* the fact that she has no recollection of encountering Inman's work directly indicates that her analysis probably reflects her involvement with the Congress of American Women's Commission on the Status of Women and her familiarity with the writings of Susan B. Anthony II.[17]

Millard successfully challenged the Party line on women in several important ways. First, she expanded on Anthony's analysis and countered the notion that class exploitation was the sole cause of women's oppression by detailing the ways that religious doctrine, Freudian psychology, laws, customs, and language as well as "day-to-day attacks in books, films, radio shows, and magazine articles" together comprised a hegemonic ruling-class ideology that subordinated all women by belittling their achievements, sapping their confidence, and convincing them that they were really inferior to men. Furthermore, she ventured to suggest that women's oppression affected every woman, regardless of class, when she daringly proposed that although "Women are not lynched . . . or killed by the millions in death camps—as women . . . it might be interesting . . . to consider the question of rape as a form of violence practiced against women. . . . Rape is a violent expression of a pattern of male supremacy, an outgrowth of age-old economic, political and cultural exploitation of women by men."

Millard also anticipated the potential reactions of orthodox Marxists and countered them in advance by linking male supremacy and class exploitation symbiotically: the cultural and ideological bases for women's oppression, she argued, convinced both sexes that women were truly inferior to men; helped to justify and perpetuate discrimination against women in the workforce, politics, and social life; and, by dividing working people amongst themselves, furthered the exploitation of the working-class as a whole.

Millard's second goal in "Woman against Myth" was to reverse Communists' idea that women's equality was the natural and inevitable outgrowth of progressive struggle and to demonstrate that women's oppression was not precisely comparable to racial, religious, or economic oppressions. "Women's attempt to achieve equality with men," she explained, "involves an especially difficult, concealed and subtle struggle because women are not isolated in ghettos, but live in intimate daily relationships with the 'superior' sex, a relationship infinitely complex and entangled with biological, economic and social factors." The result? Millard suggested that even in radical circles, "Many otherwise progressive men cling to their vested interest in male superiority and many women are so committed to the seeming security of their inferior yet 'protected' position that they echo the voteless, propertyless, completely dependent women of a century ago who declared to Elizabeth Cady Stanton and Susan B. Anthony that they already had 'all the rights they wanted.'" In other words, "Woman against Myth" implied, contrary to many Communists' opinion, that even the best of working-class and progressive men could be guilty of contributing to the oppression of the women in their lives.

In order to combat all these elements of women's oppression and to make women truly equal inside and outside of progressive organizations, Betty Millard emphasized that Communists needed not only to struggle against class exploitation and for women's rights but to wage a "serious attack on male chauvinism" in America's social and economic structures, in political organizations like the CP, and in individual relationships between men and women. This was an extremely radical suggestion, both for the time and for the context. But although one reviewer criticized "Woman against Myth" for being "too feminist," another argued that it gave "the correct Marxian approach" to the woman question. Many others thought that Millard had "done a terrific job."[18] That the CP's official publishing house International Publishers issued the pamphlet proves that the CP leadership was not too critical of its content. In the end, Millard's careful arguments about the insidious prevalence of male supremacist ideology, her discussion of its damaging impact on women and men, and her insistence on its potential to hinder the success of the progressive movement convinced many Communists that fighting male chauvinism should be an important component of the struggle for women's liberation inside *and* outside the Communist movement. Once "Woman against Myth" successfully convinced a critical mass of progressive women and men that male supremacy was a serious problem it was only a matter of time before Millard's ideas became a key part of the Party's larger strategy for ending oppression in all its forms.

## Turning Tides

At the beginning of 1948, even though they were aware of Millard's work, Communist Party leaders apparently had no plan to change the Party's orientation toward women significantly. The CP as a whole was still paying much more attention to women's issues than it had before the war and, because they had come a long way toward recognizing women's "special" problems combining motherhood and politics and compensating for them, Communist leaders probably thought they were already doing enough. In the first months of 1948 most CP women's work continued in the direction it had taken in 1947. Party publications printed regular articles to counter right-wing propaganda, such as Elizabeth Gurley Flynn's review that dismissed Ferdinand Lundberg's and Marynia Farnham's popular book *The Modern Woman: The Lost Sex* as a "rehash" of Hitler's *kinder, kueche, kirche* arguments.[19] At the same time CP recruitment campaigns continued to appeal to women in traditional female terms by urging them to "protect their families" and to "fight against monopoly prices and the rising cost of living, in defense of democratic liberties, for peoples' health and education programs, and for peace."[20] Women's branches and cadre training schools proliferated, but they continued to focus on adapting to the problems caused by the traditional sexual division of labor instead of arguing for its elimination.

   Elizabeth Gurley Flynn and Claudia Jones, the joint heads of the Party's

National Women's Commission and CAW leaders, were both known by some in the Communist movement as women who were committed to fighting women's oppression. Flynn was a lifelong socialist activist who had strong ties to the feminist movement of the 1910s. Eleanor Flexner said in a 1982 interview that both Flynn and Jones "raged at the Party's relative lack of concern with the woman question" in this period, and she credits them with being two of the major influences on the evolution of her "ideas about the historical development of the struggle for women's rights."[21] Nevertheless, because they were major representatives of the Party, they tempered their opinions in official statements and publications and, as a result, appeared only somewhat more advanced on women's issues than the CP's more powerful male leaders. They saw 1948 as an inspiring year for women and they hoped to commemorate the hundredth anniversary of the Seneca Falls women's rights convention by intensifying the CP's existing efforts to recruit, educate, and promote women into leadership positions. Flynn's and Jones's January 28 memo to all CP districts suggested that the month of March should be used by all branches to discuss the woman question, to "train women for their role in rent, housing and other struggles," and to educate "men comrades . . . as to the special oppressed position of women, and comradely assistance in the solution of practical problems of the home so that the women comrades can play a full role in Party and mass work."[22] In an article written to celebrate International Women's Day, Flynn declared, "This is a year of destiny. . . . We must be bold to reach the women—in the shops and factories, on the farms, in the homes—to make them part of a peoples' movement for peace, democracy, security, here and the world over."[23]

By the time International Women's Day actually arrived, however, the Communist Party's appeals to women suddenly became considerably more urgent. As CP leaders began to realize that its primary constituency—the labor movement—was becoming increasingly hostile to Communism, they gradually began to pin the Party's hopes on other groups, including women and African Americans.[24] In February 1948, after Claudia Jones, CP General Secretary Eugene Dennis, and other leading Communists were arrested for violating the Smith Act, the Party decided that fascism was threatening American democracy and determined that women, because of their natural interests in peace, would be some of the best fighters against it. Both Jones, who was out on bail, and Flynn took advantage of International Women's Day to act on their beliefs about the importance of women's liberation and to push the existing campaign to politicize and recruit women even further. Jones proposed that women could "decide the outcome in '48" and resist the rising tide of fascism by joining the Communist Party and

voting for Progressive Party candidates in the upcoming elections.[25] Flynn,
arguing that "fascists everywhere struck cruelly at women," urged them to
participate in a "women's campaign for the prompt release of Claudia
Jones, to really stir and arouse the women of our city and nation for her
liberation."[26]

Once CP leaders began to view women's participation in Communist
activities as especially crucial for the Party's survival, their recognition of
the real need to fight against male chauvinism in CP policies and settings
also grew. By spring 1948, Elizabeth Gurley Flynn's widely read "Life of the
Party" column announced that changes were in the works:

> Many of our new members are not aware, and many old members have forgot-
> ten, that there is a Communist position on the woman question and that histori-
> cally Communists are in the vanguard to fight against everything that exploits
> and oppresses women. . . . A general misconception is that work among women
> is "woman's work." We do not take that attitude any longer towards either work
> among Negro people or youth. But our Women's Commission is expected to be
> the conscience of the party, absolving all others from this important field of work.
> A few women comrades can't swing this assignment alone unaided by the entire
> party. There are prejudices to overcome, family problems, the double burden of
> our trade union women of a home and a job—all of which need collective efforts
> to resolve. There are "blind spots" on many of these subjects, even among other-
> wise good trade unionists and Communists. . . . Women are going places in 1948.
> Let's help make it towards us, not into the death grip of reaction. Let's recheck
> our plans in every club. To paraphrase Lenin's famous remark: Scratch every dis-
> trict in this "sensitive spot"—their mentality as regards women.[27]

There was probably never unanimous agreement among CP leaders in
early 1948 that supporting a fight against male chauvinist ideology and behavior should be a high priority for the CP. In the end, top Party leaders
began to concede that such a struggle might be necessary only because
women leaders such as Jones and Flynn argued that addressing the problem of male supremacy might bring more women into the organization and
into the fight against the domestic policies of the Cold War. Almost as soon
as the term *male chauvinism* began to appear in the Party press, however,
progressive women embraced it. For them the issue was important in and
of itself; they regarded the Party's identification of the problem as an invi-
tation to point out manifestations of male chauvinism in a wide variety of
settings. By mid-1948 the Communist Party had an internal rebellion on its
hands. The organization had a well-deserved reputation for quashing internal dissent, but because of its much promoted postwar commitment to

"Women: It's Your Turn Now," Communist Party Election Campaign Committee flyer, circa 1948. Courtesy of the Sophia Smith Collection, Smith College.

women's equality and its vulnerability to accusations of authoritarianism in the wake of anti-Communist arrests and attacks, top CP leaders must have felt that they not only had to allow rank-and-file criticism of CP practices but had to respond to it. By the end of the year the Party had revolutionized its theoretical position on women's oppression and its practical commitment to women's liberation: Communists no longer regarded male supremacy as a dangerous bourgeois concept, but as a legitimate problem that hindered every segment of the Communist movement and demanded opposition.

## Fighting Male Supremacy

Before 1948, complaints about women's experiences with male supremacy appeared only occasionally in the *Worker* and the *Daily Worker*. Typical of these sporadic complaints is a 1946 letter printed in the *Worker* that stated that although one woman's "husband could given an excellent lecture on the necessity to emancipate women," he refused to think about how he colluded in women's oppression by mistreating her.[28] But although letter-writers like this one discussed a problem that most Communist women probably shared, their concerns received little attention. Communist newspapers sometimes printed their letters in the paper, but they received little or no response.

It was only after the publication of "Woman against Myth" in early January 1948 that significant numbers of Communist women began to rally around the issue of male supremacy and to insist that their Party begin to address the problems of male supremacist ideology and behavior. As early as January 28, 1948, one angry woman acted on Millard's directive to fight male chauvinism as well as class exploitation and exhorted that

> We women would like to see some study of male chauvinism in the United States. And we would like a weekly or bi-weekly column in the Sunday *Worker* which would discuss concrete examples of male chauvinism and the Marxist solutions to them—a column which would point out how this attitude of superiority exists even among men in the Communist Party, and how it affects their personal relations and what can be done about it.

In case Party leaders missed her point about the need for all Communists to read this column she ended her request by demanding that they "don't put it on the 'Woman's Page.' Print it where men will read it too."[29]

In the months that followed, as leaders such as Flynn began to reinforce the idea that male supremacy was a legitimate concern, many other women and men took up Millard's call and began to point out manifestations of male supremacist attitudes and behavior in various aspects of Communist Party life. A Brooklyn woman named Diane Naroff wrote to the editor to say that she was "shocked at male superiority talk" in Communist settings. Aware that the Communist Party had recently begun to present itself as the place where women could "get to the core of their oppression and destroy its seeds," she wrote that she was appalled to hear a Communist man declare that "men are superior to women in every respect." This concrete example of the ways in which male supremacy was men's problem as well as women's provoked a spate of responses that called attention to other incidents of male chauvinist behavior among supposedly progressive Communist men. When Margaret Brill wrote to the *Worker* in June to ask what she should do about a husband who believed that it was Communist women's "duty to stay home with the children at night" and to "take care of her husband so he can go to meetings while she protects the family," and who accused her of "nagging" when she argued with him about these questions, dozens of irate readers responded. M.L., from the Bronx, argued that "by his attitude [Brill's husband] has created in his home conditions which are similar to conditions in an open shop and placed himself in the position of the union busting boss." E.E., from Long Island City, blamed Mr. Brill's attitude on the CP and blasted the Party for too often neglecting male chauvinism. "If, after the problem has been explained the comrade insists upon his right to consider women inferior," E.E. wrote, "I consider him as guilty as one who is white chauvinist and I feel he must be expelled." William Holzka charitably assumed that Mr. Brill simply lacked education on the matter. He demonstrated the success of Betty Millard's efforts to explain the dangers of male supremacist ideology when he challenged, "I would ask Mr. Brill 'the great' to read Betty Millard's wonderful pamphlet 'Woman against Myth' and, on completion, to look Comrade Flynn in the eye and still maintain his chauvinistic attitude."[30]

If William Holzka's letter showed that some men had been convinced by Millard's arguments, other responses to Brill's dilemma made it very clear to everyone who read the *Worker* that not all men were quite so easy to persuade. A.G., from Elizabeth, New Jersey, wrote in to say that although "a woman has a right to make a [political] contribution . . . kids should come first." Similarly, J. Gerard contended that "a woman married to a progressive worker must realize that her first responsibility is to manage the home and the children and her husband's first responsibility is to provide and struggle for an increase in the level of provision toward socialism." Defensive but still sure of his position Gerard justified his point of view by declaring:

> If this is interpreted as a position supporting the married woman's place in the home, then you're right. A progressive worker has to have a feeling of security about his marriage. . . . he has to know that his wife is fighting alongside him by taking care of the rear just as the front line soldier needs the worker in the factory. . . . The home is the most valuable possession of the family. . . . I charge that the wife who fails to do her job as a good home manager for the progressive worker is being bourgeois in her understanding and is showing contempt for the progressive movement.[31]

Another reader, identified as G.P., also wrote to challenge Margaret Brill's interpretation of her situation by asking, "What about Mr. Brill's side of the question? Could it be that Mrs. Brill was exaggerating her husband's faults? My wife called me a chauvinist because I wanted her to go away for the summer with the kids!" Using a tactic that Communist men often employed when they wanted to dismiss their wives' complaints about male chauvinism, G.P. concluded his challenge by asking his comrades, "Is that or is that not feminism?"[32]

Many readers were angry enough about the opinions expressed by men like Mr. Brill, A.G., J. Gerard, and G.P. that they, in turn, wrote letters to correct them. J. Gingold argued:

> 'Woman's place is in the home.' Where have I heard that before? Didn't the words spout from the mustachioed mouth of the notorious paper hanger of Germany? . . . Let us fight for equality beginning in the home, and remove the excessive filth of ruling over women. Keeping a wife enslaved keeps her husband enslaved much longer.[33]

An anonymous reader from Rochester echoed Gingold's words when he or she wrote:

> Mrs. Brill's problem is an "occupational disease" among the wives of Communist men, unfortunately. . . . It seems to me that the very first prerequisite for being a Communist is an interest in and love of humanity and a willingness to make life work better for mankind. It seems such an easy thing to start in one's home. And while this may be news to some of our male Party members—their wives are human beings.[34]

Lucille Gold reminded women and CP leaders that the male chauvinist tendencies of some Communist men could not be blamed solely on the men themselves and that Communist women and the Party as a whole needed to take more responsibility for solving the problem:

> For too long the problem that faced Margaret and other mothers in our party has been shoved off on the woman's page and then thrown out to the readers for suggestions and help. It is more than a personal affair. Its answer determines the morale and the activity of our party, and mainly the development of women's concentration work. Therefore I cannot understand the problem remaining in the discussion stage. It indicates that the party has not given the leadership and the direction. It is not for the women alone to find the answers but the responsibility of every branch, section and county. Women's Commissions must be set up to politicize and elevate the discussion of women's role in our party. To lead the way in finding new forms to make women's work feasible. . . . Then watch the women solve their personal problems.[35]

Gold's complaints were echoed by a group of Los Angeles women who argued that "in the past . . . women's relationship to the struggle around such

issues [as peace, welfare, children, and high prices] has been oversimpli-
fied and progressive appeals to them have been flavored by the bourgeois
concept of their adjunct role to the men of their family." Furthermore, they
continued:

> Our recognition of the [woman question] has tended to be vague and mechani-
> cal, largely composed of formal nods in general reports and tributes in our press
> on March 8th to women's historical struggles. In theoretical work we have popu-
> larized no more of Engels and Lenin than their classic formulations concerning
> the "socially unnecessary and barbarously unproductive character of housework"
> and the solution to be found under socialism.[36]

In order to improve the Party's work on the woman question in theory and
in practice, they argued, the CP needed to remove women from the margins and to make them central to every aspect of Party life:

> Commissions to deal specifically with the work among women should be estab-
> lished on county and state levels. The sections and clubs should approach this
> question in the light of its concrete manifestation within their areas. In industrial
> clubs, for example, the problems of women workers and their relation to the
> unions provides the basis for the work. In organizing housewives around child-
> care and other aspects mentioned above. In theoretical work the Marxist classics
> on the subject should be restudied and analysis made of the changing status of
> women and the family under imperialism. Educational material should be pre-
> pared and integrated into all aspects of our Party's education. Our press should
> regularly feature news and comment which reflect the realities of the problem
> rather than, as at present, limiting itself to household hints. Through every avail-
> able means we must expose the slanders and distortions about women that issue
> daily from the mass information and cultural mediums. Within the party at-
> tention should be directed constantly toward eliminating the deeply ingrained
> attitudes of male superiority which reflect themselves in the family as well as
> party life.

Like Gold and others they declared: "This is a political problem, a collective
responsibility."

The number of letters like these that appeared in the *Worker* and other
sources in 1948 made it abundantly clear that there was great disagreement
among Communists about the nature of women's oppression and the role
male supremacy played in perpetuating it. In response to this confusion,
to the evidence that male chauvinist attitudes were hindering Communists'
political development, and to demands such as those made by Lucille Gold
and the Los Angeles women, CP leaders acknowledged that the Party still

"tended to look upon woman as just a sort of female man" and that it was "literally starved theoretically" on the issue of women's oppression. In order to establish more agreement on the woman question the CP National Board appointed the Subcommittee on the Theoretical Aspects of Work among Women to evaluate and revise the Party's analysis of women's oppression, to rethink its presentation of the issues, and to oversee the publication of a new book to instruct Communists about the correct approach to women's liberation.[37]

Unfortunately, the Subcommittee on Theoretical Aspects of Work among Women never issued a book of new Communist theory about women. The rising tide of anti-Communism and the arrests of major Communist leaders beginning in the late 1940s must have made it difficult for any national CP committee to carry out its long-term goals and projects; it is possible that given the hostile political environment the subcommittee decided to rely upon "Woman against Myth," which the Party reissued as a pamphlet in spring 1948, instead of issuing something new. Despite the difficulties it faced, however, the subcommittee did manage to define the position that all Communists were expected to take regarding women's oppression. In November 1948 the group published "On Improving the Party's Work among Women" in the Party's chief theoretical journal *Political Affairs* and did so under National Party Chairman William Z. Foster's byline so that even the most skeptical and male chauvinist CP members would be forced to take it seriously. That short article summarized the subcommittee's new thinking by defending women's "age long fight for equality as workers, citizens, home-builders, and in marital relations"; exposing "pseudoscientific" arguments about women's physical, intellectual, social, psychological and sexual inferiority"; declaring that while "women are different from men they are fully their equals"; and officially endorsing Betty Millard's suggestion that a struggle against the hegemonic ideology of male supremacy had to be a vital component of Communists' larger battle against women's oppression. By the end of 1948, in other words, the American Communist Party resolved that women's "economic, political and social . . . demands and struggles, vital as they may be, are in themselves not enough" and that "an ideological attack must be made against the whole system of male superiority ideas which continue to play such an important part in woman's subjugation."[38]

Leading Communists' belated acknowledgment that a struggle against male supremacy was an important and necessary part of their work represented a great step forward for the CP and its record on women. Leaders such as Foster who finally accepted the idea that American Communists needed to expand the classical Marxist analysis of women's oppression ultimately probably did so not only because they wanted to win a "wider mass following" among working women, but because they hoped to quell arguments over the issue of male supremacy and to promote Party unity in the face of hostile attacks from the outside. What CP leaders did not realize is that by officially condemning all manifestations of male chauvinism they were actually making the Party vulnerable to still more criticism from within its own ranks. In the wake of Foster's article, gender-conscious Communist women and men began to use the CP's official rejection of male supremacy to demand that the Party practice what it preached in all aspects of its work. Nineteen forty-eight was a watershed for the CP's work on the woman question, but in 1949 and later Communist leaders were repeatedly forced to respond to internal criticism by extending the Party's fight against all forms of women's oppression and expanding its efforts to educate progressives about the need for women's liberation.

The first and most striking example of rank-and-file Communists' use of new CP theory about women to force further changes in the Party's practices occurred almost immediately after the appearance of Foster's article "On Improving the Party's Work among Women." One of the major contributions of the article was its discussion of the male supremacist assumptions that lay behind accepted notions about sexuality. Foster broke American Communists' silence on the issue of sex for the first time since the publication of *In Woman's Defense* by repeating points similar to the ones Mary Inman had made ten years earlier. Arguing that "the reactionary contention that nature has made man essentially polygamous and woman monogamous . . . is the theory of the double standard of bourgeois morals which seeks to justify the sexual exploitation of woman," he insisted that Communists "must show both from science and experience how such standards [do] incalculable harm to woman's happiness and her position in society."

Although it appeared in the most esoteric of the CP's theoretical journals, Foster's points were not lost on rank-and-file Communists. Many women and men quickly recognized that this official opposition to the sexual exploitation of women conflicted with the Party press's practice of publishing pictures of scantily clad models, beauty contest winners, and "bathing beauties" with captions that exclaimed "Most Beautiful Legs in the World," and "Mrs. New York—and She Can Cook Too."[39] In January 1949, readers began a campaign to protest against such "cheesecake." Phyllis and Morty from Jamaica, New York, wrote to say:

> Our *Daily Worker* is the best newspaper in this country because it is the only paper
> that consistently fights for the interests of the working class and its allies. In way

of criticism, we feel it is very important for the Daily to eliminate the cheesecake pictures. These pictures have no liberating effect for women and the working class, but on the contrary, are used to perpetuate male supremacy through the idea that sex is women's only attribute.[40]

A. Kutzik, from the Bronx, wrote to support Phyllis and Morty's arguments by comparing "cheesecake" to racist stereotypes:

What would we think if 90% of the pictures of Negroes in our paper were to show them in "zoot suits?" The constant exhibition of women in bathing suits, or worse, of show girls and "actresses" is morally and politically just as inadmissible. It is a most flagrant manifestation of the male supremacy theories which have poisoned the minds of nearly every man and woman in America, including progressives and Communists.[41]

Similarly, A.J.M. wrote to the editor of the West coast paper, the *People's World:*

I have a large and growing file of bathing beauties, stage and screen queens, and other bare and buxom lovelies whose likenesses appear frequently in the *PW*. Now I declare that this custom is at odds with our paper's practice. The historical and social significance of woman's physical charm as a commodity is so well known that I need not labor the point. The pictures—to say nothing of the coy bourgeois captions—are evidence that there are those on the *PW*'s staff who do not know about, or worse, who are cynical regarding the woman question. Every *PW* reader and every progressive group would rise in fury if the bourgeois characterization of the Negro "song and dance man" or the "lazy" Mexican were chronic in the paper. Why then is the cheesecake stuff permitted?[42]

Mary, from Oakland, concurred:

The women today who are aware of the necessity for social change are demanding recognition and encouragement of their efforts to take their rightful place in this major undertaking. For these women, "cheesecake" is a slap in the face, expressing as it does an emphasis on the physical gifts of nature and a total lack of appreciation of the mentality and training necessary to institute any change. . . . I have seen many requests from readers for articles and items on the role of women in this social struggle. Surely you cannot continue to present artistic views of the female body as an answer to this demand.[43]

The controversy over cheesecake in CP publications continued to unfold in the newspapers over the next several months. Most people opposed it, and the few who wrote to defend it only succeeded in proving that male supremacy was indeed still a problem within the CP's ranks.[44] By spring 1949, readers' letters began to indicate that "sufficient protest on your policy of displaying women . . . has been registered" and to suggest that the space currently being used for cheesecake in CP newspapers should instead be used "for the purpose of eliminating and exposing the special forms of oppression of women" and for photographs of "women active in labor unions and progressive political work."[45] Because of the Party's new policy of opposing male chauvinist ideology, the editors of the *Worker* and the *Daily Worker* had little choice but to respond to readers' demands. As early as February 1949 the number of pin-ups in the Party's papers decreased markedly; by June cheesecake disappeared entirely from the pages of both newspapers.

Incidents such as the cheesecake controversy made CP leaders aware that the work they had already done to improve the Party's theory and work on women was not sufficient to solve a problem as widespread and deep-rooted as male superiority. As it became clear that simply calling attention to the existence of male supremacy was not enough to eliminate it, CP leaders tried various new strategies for opposing it. The Party's weapon of choice in its war against the ideology of male superiority was education. In 1949 the Women's Commission and the National Committee began to issue educational materials to supplement the existing literature on the woman question and to promote a broader understanding of the complex nature of women's oppression among the Party's rank-and-file members. In March 1950, for example, the CP National Committee issued a Speakers' Guide for International Women's Day instructing local leaders to use the month of March "to raise the theoretical and ideological understanding of the Marxist-Leninist position on the woman question of the entire Party . . . and to boldly develop and promote woman cadres."[46]

In March and April 1950, in response to readers' demands, the Party overhauled the women's section of the *Worker* so that it too could educate male and female readers about the growing importance of women's work.[47] The old women's page, distinguished by a masthead that read "It's on the House" and the silhouette of a high-heeled woman dusting, was replaced by a new page called "Woman Today" and a graphic of two women's smiling faces, one black and one white. Claudia Jones and Peggy Dennis, the editors of "Woman Today," stopped publishing dress patterns and household hints and instead filled the pages with articles about women's history, their role in the peace movement, and their contributions to political struggles around the world. Furthermore, frequent "Woman Today" articles criticized persistent male supremacist practices such as Americans' tendencies to call adult women "girls," to belittle them, and to make them the objects of "false humor." Most readers loved the new women's pages and wrote to the *Worker* to praise the changes. Ethel S., from Philadelphia, wrote, "I am greatly pleased to see the start of a real woman's page. Please no household hints, cooking and what to do when baby pukes." E.L. agreed when she wrote, "I am extremely happy to see this type of page. I had felt before that a so-called women's page devoted only to care of children and home was to some extent an acceptance of 'woman's place is in the home' thinking." And similarly E.R. from Los Angeles rejoined, "It's such a pleasure to read about women . . . and about organizational activities such as the drive for peace. It's such a relief to be no longer affronted by the (unintentional) male chauvinist line that our problems were primarily our inefficiency as housekeepers."[48]

In addition to praise, many readers also wrote to the women's page to offer additional suggestions for improvement, thereby applying continuous pressure on CP leaders to take their concerns ever more seriously.[49] Even in the hardest times of the 1950s when the women's pages appeared only sporadically in the beleaguered paper, readers continued their demand: "Give us more about women. Tear into the male supremacy that is holding back the movement almost as much as white supremacy."[50] The paper complied by publishing increasingly radical material after 1951 including, for example, Eleanor Flexner's critique of women's exclusion from sports in 1952, Sylvia Jarrico's attack on Hollywood films in 1953, Elizabeth Lawson's lengthy and laudatory review of Simone DeBeauvoir's *The Second Sex* in 1954, and Florence S.'s condemnation of sexual harassment in CP settings in 1956.[51]

At the same time that the CP began to expand its written work on the woman question, it also instituted formal classes and seminars to educate large numbers of people about women's oppression and women's liberation. In spring 1949 the CP National Committee organized nine Conferences on Work among Women to bring regional districts up to speed on the woman question and two regional schools to train additional women cadres.[52] In June the Party sponsored an all-day conference called Marxism and the Woman Question at the Jefferson School of Social Science in New York City—the largest of the many CP-supported Marxist education schools around the country—to discuss the theoretical progress the organization made on the woman question in the preceding year and to educate CP members about its importance.[53] Six hundred men and women attended that first conference to hear speakers Claudia Jones, Betty Millard, Eve Merriam, and Elizabeth Gurley Flynn and to discuss "the family, women in industry and the professions, attitudes of male superiority, and the special problems of Negro women."[54]

Because that conference was so successful, the Jefferson School instituted a regular class on the woman question later that year. The first class, taught by novelist and union organizer Myra Page, emphasized topics such as the "origins of women's oppression, the changing character of the family, and the main roots and problems of male superiority," and stressed the new idea that men, as the "carriers" of male supremacy, had a special responsibility to learn about and fight against it.[55] A later class taught by Eleanor Flexner in 1953 focused on similar topics and also included themes such as special roles of Negro women and of Puerto Rican women. And also in 1953 the Jefferson School published *Questions and Answers on the Woman Question,* a 20-page document by Eleanor Flexner (writing under the name Irene Epstein) and Doxey Wilkerson that condensed the theory and substance from the classes into an accessible question and answer format.[56] Despite financial troubles, declining enrollments and anti-Communist harassment, the Jefferson School continued to offer regular courses on the woman question (taught by various people) and evening forums on topics such as women in music and women in literature every term until 1956, when it finally closed permanently.[57]

Communist leaders made education the most important component of their campaign to improve the Party's work on women, but they also realized that education might not always be sufficient. In 1949, along with their expanded plans for instructing the rank and file about the dangers of male chauvinism, Party leaders also began to formulate a policy to deal with those Communists who were not willing to take male supremacy seriously. In September 1949, Claudia Jones outlined the Party's new position on women's oppression and women's liberation by praising and paraphrasing Foster's "On Improving the Party's Work among Women" and announced that Communists' fight against male supremacist ideology was about to become even more intense. Reminding her readers that "the inequality of women stems from exploitation of the working-class by the capitalist class but the exploitation of women cuts across class lines and affects all women," Jones stated unequivocally that "any underestimation of the need for a persistent ideological struggle against all manifestations of masculine superiority [would] be rooted out" in the future. Essentially, Jones explained, those Communists who failed to acknowledge the seriousness of male supremacy would henceforth be subject to Party discipline.[58]

The Communist Party's campaign to root out male supremacy in its ranks never reached the level of intensity that characterized its simultaneous crusade to eliminate white chauvinism among its members. The Party disciplined and sometimes expelled hundreds of members during the height of the white chauvinism campaign of the early 1950s for infractions such as using phrases like "whitewash" or "black sheep" or for more major offenses such as ignoring their African American comrades. Yet there is no indication in the available sources that the CP ever expelled anyone, male or female, for refusing to resist male supremacy.[59] Nevertheless, sources do show that after 1949 the Party made some effort to discipline those who ignored its policy of opposing male supremacist ideology wherever it appeared.

The most widely publicized case in which a well-known Communist was disciplined for neglecting to take male supremacy seriously occurred in 1950, only a few months after the publication of Jones's article. The incident began after Walter Lowenfels, a frequent contributor to the *Worker* wrote a story entitled "Santa Claus or Comrade X?" which appeared in the paper on Christmas day, 1949.[60] Lowenfels's story was supposed to be an amusing one about the trials of a man who lived in a house full of women—his wife and four daughters—who spent much of their time sewing, washing, ironing, and worrying about their clothes. But although several people wrote to the editor to praise the story, not everyone was amused. Beginning in January the *Worker* printed numerous letters from people who were critical of Lowenfels's stance and angry that the editors published the story. C. and G. Lang, of New York, wrote to point out that "the humor in this story is derived entirely from the ever so funny notion that women are exclusively interested in clothes and their own adornment" and, "as must be obvious to everyone, the pitiful female members of the author's family are distinctly inferior creatures." In order to correct the situation, the Langs proposed, "the editors and the author owe the readers an apology and themselves a critical evaluation of their understanding of the woman question."[61] On the day the Langs' letter appeared, Lowenfels tried to make up for his errors: "I am shocked," he wrote, "that there were not more objections," and "I believe our readers have a responsibility and that we should hear from them beginning with (1) our editors; (2) our staff, particularly our women writers; (3) and especially those men and women who praised this piece!"

Turning the blame away from himself, Lowenfels suggested that every progressive needed to be responsible for the problem of sexism. "Is it possible," he wrote, "that we have all become so hardened to male supremacy attitudes that we no longer even object? As for me, you will hear from me shortly with another piece. I am reexamining the question of men and women. It's time somebody did something about it."[62]

Lowenfels meant for his response to be redemptive, but in the eyes of some readers it only led him deeper into trouble. Citing the latest thinking on the fight against male chauvinism, Rhoda Ashe castigated Lowenfels for suggesting that women writers should have pointed out his errors. "In the effort to rid ourselves of white supremacist thinking," she wrote, "white men and women must put up the greatest fight, not Negro people." In the case of male supremacy, she pointed out, "it is not the oppressed who must make the greatest effort, but in this case, the men. I would therefore amend Mr. Lowenfels's point to read 'our staff, particularly the men writers.'"[63]

Lowenfels's new story, "Our Dirty Wash," intended to atone for his previous mistakes, made the situation worse still. An irate woman named Ruth responded:

> First Walter Lowenfels does a stupid article about "his women" and their clothes. That was criticized but the criticism was answered by a flippant, unselfcritical note by Lowenfels. Then Lowenfels "atones" in his article "Our Dirty Wash." His whole attitude boils down to the fact that the wash in his house is "my wife's dirty wash" not "ours." . . . His flippancy toward the woman question is all too typical of the reaction of many progressive and Communist men. The phrases "male supremacist," "male superiority," and "woman question" are all too often laughed about.[64]

Another comrade, Wendell Addington, concurred:

> Lowenfels ha[s] clearly shown that he consider[s] the oppressed position of women under capitalism a big joke. . . . An even bigger joke, in his opinion, [is] the idea of self-criticism on the woman question. And most ludicrous of all to Lowenfels are the women who challenge manifestations of male supremacy. In an article expanding on his previous attacks on the intelligence of women there is no hint of genuine self-criticism. His main regret seems to be that he has "put his foot into it". . . . The *Worker* readers are due a serious explanation from Lowenfels.[65]

A man identified only as "Friend Husband" also wrote to support Ruth's earlier letter: "In appreciation of your crack at Walter Lowenfels on 'his women' and their clothes washing," he commended, "I just wanted to say that I think he had it coming to him."[66]

In the wake of all this strife, local Party leaders in Philadelphia decided that something had to be done. A group of women met with Lowenfels to discuss his errors with him and to insure that he planned to do better in the future. In the interview, Lowenfels admitted his guilt and issued an apology that was printed in the *Worker* on April 16, 1950:

> I am in the process of re-examining those three recent articles of mine in the *Worker*. I agree with you that they smuggled into our pages, wrapped in a pack-

age of false humor, an incorrect, offensive, belittling attitude about women. The total impact of these pieces was essentially an attack on women, a mockery of their problems, and a caricature of Marxism. . . . When readers objected, my flippant and arrogant note in the letter column evaded the central question. My third piece about the purchase of a washing machine was put forth as "self criticism" and "corrective" but it only carried the original error still further.[67]

When his accusers asked him why he wrote the articles and how he planned to improve his attitude, Lowenfels replied: "I am still trying to get to the root of the matter. Some reasons were underestimation of the woman question, a failure to give any serious consideration to the complex questions involved. So what's to be done now? I would say that self-correction from now on is not a question of words."

On his last point Lowenfels was correct. His public apology alone was not, in the eyes of his accusers, enough to repair his standing in the movement. He, like other men who were charged with perpetuating male supremacy, was sentenced to participate in "the struggle for a correct position and understanding of the specific problems of women and the road to their solution" so that he might avoid similar male chauvinist errors down the road.

Communists continued to discipline recalcitrant male supremacists throughout 1950 and beyond. In September 1950, for example, the Minnesota State Women's Commission confronted a group of men who laughed and joked upon the introduction of the woman question in public meetings and chastised an individual male leader who joked with a woman Party member when she tried to discuss with him an assignment given her husband that involved serious changes for their whole family. The Commission criticized all these men publicly and ordered them to complete "control tasks involving study on the woman question" so that they might change their ideas about women.[68] Similarly, in 1954 the Los Angeles Party disciplined men for "designating mailings and phone calls and so forth as 'women's work in mass organizations' . . . hogging discussion at club meetings, bypassing women comrades in leadership [and] making sex jokes degrading to women."[69] In 1955 the CP connected male supremacy to anti-Communism, calling it "a characteristic of every single male 'stool pigeon' who has yet betrayed the Party," and strengthened its commitment to "assist the great majority of women who resent and struggle against male supremacy."[70] Even in the late 1950s, when the CP was only a shadow of its former self, it did not give up the fight to reform male chauvinists in its ranks. When Communists accused the CP of male supremacy during the reevaluation period that followed Kruschev's revelations about Stalin in 1956, they were not, contrary to Rosalyn Baxandall's suggestion, debating the issue for the first time. Rather Communists were continuing discussions that had begun in 1946 and persisted for the entire decade.[71]

THE COMMUNIST PARTY did much to enhance American progressives' understanding of the problem of women's oppression and to equalize the treatment of women in Party publications and activities between 1946 and 1956, but it was never able to make as much headway in the struggle for women's liberation as some Communist women wished. Despite the Party's efforts to promote understanding about women's oppression and to "root out" all manifestations of male supremacy in its ranks, women continued to voice their dissatisfaction with the CP's penchant for glorifying the roles of housewife and mother and its tendency to neglect the obstacles those roles placed in the way of women's political development.[72] Complaints about male supremacist ideology and behavior at all levels of the CP persisted throughout the 1950s. To be fair, Communists' fight against sexism was definitely hampered by McCarthyism, by the imprisonment of Party leaders such as Claudia Jones and Elizabeth Gurley Flynn in 1954, and by Jones's deportation to England in 1955. To its credit, the CP continued to address women's problems even as it fought for its own survival. Nevertheless, women's discontent with the Communist Party was far from groundless: although the group persevered in its efforts to support women's liberation struggles and to undermine male supremacy inside and outside the Party, men continued to dominate Party leadership at the state and national levels, and women's issues remained secondary to "Negro" issues and class struggle. The Communist Party did a lot to explain women's oppression and to promote women's liberation but, in the decade after World War II it also could have done a lot more.

That the Communist Party's theory and practice on the woman question had many weaknesses is indisputable but, despite its flaws, Communists' work also made several important contributions to the U.S. women's movement between 1946 and 1956. First, by defining women's oppression as an extremely complex phenomenon that operated through a mutually reinforcing system of male supremacist theories and assumptions and economic, social, political, and legal discrimination against women, Communists created an important new body of terminology and theory that emphasized women's common interests, linked their so-called personal problems with politics, and provided a foundation from which a struggle for women's liberation could potentially grow. Second, by demanding that the Party take their concerns seriously and combat male chauvinism with the same passion it devoted to white chauvinism, Communist women exposed the role that even otherwise progressive men played in oppressing women and won considerable respect and legitimacy for women's struggles within the progressive movement even as anti-feminism increasingly dominated mainstream politics. Third, by responding to women's demands and lending considerable support and resources to their efforts to win economic, political, social, and cultural equality inside and outside the progressive milieu, the Communist Party helped to raise the consciousnesses of many more women and men who came to see themselves as vanguards in the struggle for women's liberation as well as in the larger struggle for a peaceful, just, and democratic world.

All of this work represented a dramatic advance in the way that the American Communist Party dealt with women, but Communists also pursued two other directions in their work on the woman question in the decade after World War II. First, they explored the ways that women's oppression varied according to race and class and worked tirelessly to understand and address the "special problems of Negro women."[73] Second, like many radicals who preceded them, Communists pushed themselves to build an alternative radical culture and family life that resisted the degenerate elements of capitalism—including male domination—and anticipated the society they hoped to create through class struggle and socialist revolution. These approaches, combined with the Party's newly expanded theory about women's oppression and its other efforts to improve women's status, made critical contributions to the continuity of the U.S. women's movement across the void of the hostile 1950s and shaped the work of the later women's liberation movement in numerous important ways.

# 5    Claudia Jones and the Synthesis of Gender, Race, and Class

> Every period has its heroines, and this period has too. We honor the con-
> tributions Claudia Jones has made to the struggles against racism in this
> country, for civil liberties, for youth, for peace. We honor her contributions
> to the struggles of women. She has given us dignity. It is through her teach-
> ing that we know that only to the extent that we fight all chauvinist ex-
> pressions and actions as regards the Negro people can women as a whole
> advance their struggle for equal rights.
>
> LEONA THOMPSON, "My Close Friend and Teacher," *Daily Worker*,
> February, 1955

HISTORICALLY THE MAINSTREAM of the U.S. women's movement has had a troubled relationship with working-class women and
women of color. Although the first wave of the woman's rights movement
grew out of the interracial abolitionist movement in 1848, its adherents
never concurred on questions of race and class and they ultimately split in
1869 because of conflicts over the Fourteenth Amendment, which specified voters as "male," and the Fifteenth Amendment, which protected black
men's right to vote but did not mention women.[1] The dominant woman's
rights organizations of the late nineteenth and early twentieth centuries
sought reforms that would benefit the white middle-class women who controlled them, often at the expense of their black, immigrant, and working-
class sisters. Before the achievement of suffrage in 1920, for example, the National American Woman Suffrage Association exploited racist and nativist
fears by arguing that white women needed the vote so that they could counteract the political influence of the illiterate and otherwise inferior "lower
races."[2]

During the four decades after the passage of the Nineteenth Amendment, the self-proclaimed feminists of the National Woman's Party continued to privilege gender over race and class. NWP feminists pushed continuously for the passage of the Equal Rights Amendment, despite working
women's fears that it would overturn protective legislation. They also repeatedly dismissed Southern black women's frequent pleas for support on
the basis that such women were disfranchised and mistreated primarily as
"Negroes" and not as women.[3] Furthermore, although feminists understood

the political importance of women's history, they reserved historical recognition only for other white, middle-class women like themselves whom they saw as the rightful forbearers of their movement. When Earl Conrad, a progressive with Communist connections who was writing a biography of Harriet Tubman, corresponded with former suffrage leader Carrie Chapman Catt in 1939 to ask about Tubman's role in the suffrage movement, she made feminists' indifference to African American women's history very apparent. Catt told Conrad that she had never even heard of Tubman, though she had heard of Sojourner Truth. Later, when Conrad sent Catt his manuscript, which described Tubman's involvement with the suffrage movement, Catt insisted that, "Tubman did not assist the suffragists or the suffrage movement at any time. It was they who were attempting to assist her. That much I know from the nature of things. . . . There was no leadership on the part of the colored people at that time and there is very little even now.[4]

Given these limited views, it is not surprising that the women who embraced predominantly white middle-class feminist organizations saw themselves as advocates only for those rights that were denied to women on the basis of their sex. When African American women or even white working-class women asked for feminists' assistance with their own economic or political problems after 1920, feminists nearly always refused. White middle-class women for whom gender was a primary source of oppression led feminist organizations such as the NWP and, for that reason, those groups defined race- and class-based problems as diversions from their larger struggle to improve woman's position in U.S. society.

The CPUSA always maintained a strong commitment to class and race issues and, for that reason, Communists' approach to women's liberation was very different from that of the mainstream women's movement. Between 1946 and 1949 Communists gradually abandoned the position that only working-class women were oppressed and, like the explicitly feminist organizations of the time, embraced the idea that women's oppression affected all women, regardless of their class or color. But unlike other predominantly white groups that were working for women's rights in the postwar period, Communists also recognized that gender oppression was not the sole cause of every woman's problems. In the decades between the 1920s and the 1960s, the Communist Party actively opposed the passage of the Equal Rights Amendment because of the problems it might create for working-class women and supported reforms that would benefit working women directly, such as higher wages, the creation of single seniority lists, and government-sponsored child-care centers. But what made the Communist Party particularly unusual among other multiracial organizations working to improve women's status in this period before the Civil Rights movement burst on the national scene was that it attempted to analyze and respond to the particular problems that burdened black women along with class and gender oppression.[5] This work, inspired by the Party's leading black woman, Claudia Jones, made the Communist movement unique among feminist organizations that existed before the 1960s and shaped the ways that second-wave feminists would conceptualize the intersections between race and gender oppression in the 1970s and later.

## Seeds of Change

By 1945, when progressive women began their major effort to reform the CP's approach to women's liberation, African American women already had a long history of involvement with the organization. Although their numbers were small in the Communist movement of the 1920s, black women from New York to Birmingham made significant inroads in the CP of the 1930s.[6] As their influence grew in Communist circles during the Popular Front era, African American women's experiences and perspective became increasingly visible in the CP's emerging literature on the woman question. By the end of the decade most descriptions of women's oppression in Communist literature emphasized workplace discrimination against African American women and their vulnerability to rape by white men, especially in the South. Communist publications regularly used the terms "triple burden" and "triple oppression" to describe the status of black women who were exploited because of their race, class, and gender.[7] Among most other predominantly white organizations in the United States before the late 1940s, the Communist Party was the foremost defender of African American women's rights and the chief advocate of their equality.

Despite its admirable attention to African American women's uniquely oppressed status, however, the Communist Party's particular stance on race and gender issues in the 1930s put black women in a difficult position. Communists' emphasis on fighting white chauvinism, their efforts to insure race and gender integration at political and social events, and their comparable lack of attention to women's oppression made African American women quite conscious of the distinctive amalgam of racism and sexism that afflicted many otherwise progressive Communists. Beginning early in the 1930s it was common for African American women Communists to complain that routine relationships between black men and white women in CP circles made it difficult for them to find black partners and that white men's tendency to avoid them at social and political events made it impossible for them to form interracial relationships of their own. In Harlem in 1934 black women grew so resentful of this pattern that they finally asked their section's leaders to ban interracial marriages in the Party's ranks.[8]

In keeping with the CP's willingness to fight racism at the personal level as well as structurally in the 1930s, black women framed their grievances about their difficulties within the Party in terms of white chauvinism. The Party could ease their problems, their complaint implied, by instituting a policy that would force black and white men alike to cast off their white chauvinist notions about black women's supposedly second-rate attractiveness. Communist leaders took the women's demands seriously and, in order to follow through on its commitment to fight white chauvinism, the CP assigned black leader Abner Berry (whose own wife was white) to deal with them. Berry insisted that the Communist Party could not outlaw interracial relationships because it would be "counterrevolutionary" to do so, but he and other leaders initiated changes in the Party's atmosphere intended to improve the situation. Party organizers launched educational discussions about black women's triply oppressed status and made an effort to teach dancing to white male Communists so they would be less embarrassed to ask black women to dance at CP affairs. Apparently, some young black male Communists even chose voluntarily to end relationships with white wives and girlfriends and to seek out black women as partners instead.

These reforms did not end the problem of interracial relationships among Communists or settle all of the tension that accompanied them, but they do show that even as early as the 1930s, African American Communist women could articulate their particular grievances to Party leaders with the expectation that the CP would not ignore them. Although black women sometimes took center stage in the Party's Negro work, however, the same was not true of its early work on the woman question. By the time the Communist Party began to embrace a progressive women's agenda for women's liberation in the later 1940s, it looked as if African American women might once again be left in the cold. Communists and other progressives in the CP milieu did not by any means ignore African American women in this period. During World War II, when it took a relatively conservative stance on many other issues, the CP pressed for black women's permanent access to industrial jobs and argued that they particularly needed the benefits provided by labor unions and protection against all forms of discrimination.[9] The Congress of American Women worked from 1946 to 1949 to address black women's concerns about the unique forms of discrimination they faced and counted several black women among its leadership, but it was never able to make significant inroads into the black community.[10] The Party's 1947 platform for women's rights included demands for the "full equality of Negro women from segregation, discrimination, intimidation, poll tax, and downgrading in employment" and "election to office in legislative bodies, labor unions, and all public organizations of capable women,

Negro and white."[11] In 1948 Communists in New York's East Side participated in a successful campaign to win jobs for black women in five-and-
dime stores throughout the city and ultimately worked to spread that campaign throughout the Northeast.[12]

Despite these activities, when Communist publications mentioned
African American women between 1945 and 1949, they usually did so in a
way that implied that those problems were only a small part of the larger
issue of women's oppression. Communists recognized that black women's
problems were different from those suffered by white women because of the
added complication of racial oppression. For the most part, however, the
differences remained and qualifications about "the special problems of
Negro women" were usually tacked on to more general discussions of
American women's status. Even Betty Millard's otherwise insightful and
prescient "Woman against Myth" failed to address African American
women's condition in any meaningful way. Although she compared the oppression of women to the oppression of Negroes several times in her work,
she made only one reference to "doubly oppressed Negro women" in the
penultimate paragraph of the pamphlet, and she neglected completely the
question of how black women's oppression differed qualitatively and quan-
titatively from that of white women.[13]

Betty Millard's pamphlet became the stimulus for expanding the CP's
theoretical work on women because of its contributions to the debate on
women's oppression in the late 1940s. Indirectly, it also became the catalyst
for expanding the group's theoretical work on black women because of the
questions it overlooked. Partly in response to "Woman against Myth," CP
National Women's Commission secretary and best-known black woman
leader Claudia Jones wrote her landmark article "An End to the Neglect of
the Problems of the Negro Woman" published in *Political Affairs* in June
1949. In this article Jones addressed some of the same concerns about white
chauvinism in social and romantic relationships that the Harlem women
had raised in the 1930s. But unlike those women, whose complaints emphasized the ways they were victimized by white chauvinism, Jones capi-
talized on the Party's new commitment to women's liberation by framing
many of the same issues as concerns about white chauvinism *and* male
chauvinism. In this way Jones not only brought African American women's
experiences and perspectives to the center of Communists' writings and activities on the woman question, but she helped to create the recognition that
women could share gender oppression and still be very different from one
another. Ultimately, Jones conceptualized black women *not* primarily as victims who needed special consideration, but as powerful activists that progressives should respect and desire, both politically and personally.[14]

As a result of "An End to the Neglect of the Problems of the Negro Woman," the American Communist movement expanded its work among African American women in the late 1940s and 1950s. At Jones's urging the Party placed black women at the center of its writings and activities around women's issues and took steps toward extending its interpretations of differences among women to consider the experiences of Jewish, Puerto Rican, and Mexican American women as well. Attention to women's differences made Communists aware that although all women experienced subjugation in capitalist society, their oppression took many different forms and that improving women's status was not, as many others believed, simply a matter of equal rights and equal pay. Communists' efforts to document the history of black women's struggles for freedom and their exploration of the connections between racism and sexism made it clear long before the 1960s that black women's concerns were not marginal to the women's movement and that, unless they opposed the systems of class and racial domination as well as male domination in the United States, women's rights advocates in this country could not hope to realize their goals.

## The Leadership of Claudia Jones

Claudia Jones was born in Port of Spain, Trinidad, in February 1915 and immigrated to the United States with her family in 1923.[15] Like many working-class West Indian immigrants living in Harlem during the depression, she was drawn to the Communist Party by its antiracism work and particularly by the International Labor Defense's campaign to free the nine black men who had been sentenced to death for allegedly raping two white women in Scottsboro, Alabama, in 1931. Jones joined the youth section of the Communist Party in 1934, when she was eighteen years old.[16] Within a few years she had become a leading member of the Young Communist League (YCL), and by 1940 she was the editor of the group's newspaper and its national chairman. During World War II Jones officially joined the Communist Party and quickly rose into upper-level leadership positions within it. In 1945 she was named secretary of the newly restored National Woman's Commission and, although she developed a reputation as one of the chief opponents of male chauvinism within the Party, she also continued to be extremely involved in black struggles in New York City and elsewhere.[17] As a leader in the Congress of American Women and in the CP itself, Jones became the Communist movement's chief spokesperson for black women.

In the late 1940s two political developments spurred Claudia Jones to argue more forcefully about the importance of African American women for progressive struggles. First, as the CP's isolation from the labor movement grew more severe as a result of the effects of widespread prosperity and anti-Communism, Communist leaders began to set their sights on other groups, notably women and African Americans, who had been left behind by the changes in the postwar economy.[18] Second, as the increasingly conservative political atmosphere hampered the labor movement in the late 1940s and 1950s, civil rights struggles took center stage as the most radical activities occurring anywhere in the country. Black women, who frequently kindled those struggles, became some of the most visible radical activists in the United States. Jones realized that if the Communist Party hoped to influence and recruit black women activists in this period it needed to recognize and address their specific problems. Neither the Communist Party's existing efforts to confront black women's problems nor those made by the Congress of American Women, Jones thought, were sufficient. At the same time that Party leaders Pettis Perry and Betty Gannett took initial steps to revive the Party's earlier struggles against white chauvinism in 1949, Jones published "An End to the Neglect of the Problems of the Negro Woman." Jones intended the article to show writers on the woman question such as Betty Millard their errors and to outline a new approach to black women's problems that would place them at the center of the Party's work for both women's liberation and black liberation.[19]

Claudia Jones's first goal in "An End to the Neglect of the Problems of the Negro Woman" was to make white Communists aware of black women's unique and contradictory "super-exploited" status. Using data from the Women's Bureau of the U.S. Department of Labor, Jones detailed the ways that black women suffered economically because of their exclusion from all but the most menial and poorly paid occupations such as domestic work, agricultural work, and employment in nonunionized textile and food processing plants. Because the wages of black women were lower than those of men and those of white women and because they were often excluded from benefits such as social security and workers' compensation, Jones pointed out, African American families were often condemned to "ghetto living conditions" as well as higher maternal and infant morality rates than those of poor and working-class whites. Because black women had little choice but to work outside the home to support their families, she indicated, black women hardly needed to fight against the notion that woman's place was in the home. And despite the rhetoric about its reverence for motherhood and the superior status of American women vis-à-vis women in other nations, black women were frequently subject to sexual attacks by white men and to the personal and economic suffering that resulted from the lynchings and other violence that was commonly perpetrated against black men.

The crux of Jones's position was that black women suffered many of the disadvantages of women's oppression with none of the respect and protection that was offered to white women in white supremacist American society. These problems persisted not only in the South, she proposed, but all over the country as black women were pushed out of industrial jobs after World War II and portrayed in film and literature as "mammies" who were "backward," "inferior," and the "natural slaves of others." Jones tied black women's problems to the Party's new program for women's liberation by concluding that "the super-exploitation and oppression of Negro women tends to depress the standards of all women."

Although Jones purposely and carefully emphasized the super-exploited status of black women, she was also very clear about the fact that they were not simply victims of the conditions under which they lived. In fact, she went to great lengths to demonstrate that black women had always been leaders in their families and communities and that they had been prepared by their harsh circumstances to fight difficult individual battles against their exploiters and to lead mass struggles against oppression. Jones relied on black history to argue that in the West African tribes from which many American slaves came, women's status was much higher than in European cultures.[20] Despite the sexual and physical degradation of slavery, she explained, slaves' persistent reliance on matrilineal practices from Africa and their inability to marry legally meant that black women continued to play a dominant role in their families even in the nineteenth and twentieth centuries. That role, according to Jones, "schooled" black women "in self-reliance, in courageous and selfless action." As "the guardian, the protector of the Negro family," responsible for "militantly shielding it from the blows of Jim-Crow insults, for rearing children in an atmosphere of lynch terror, segregation and police brutality, and for fighting for an education for the children," Jones argued that even individual black women who did not participate in explicit political activity were making important contributions to larger struggles against sexism, racism, and capitalism. Finally, Jones used the "lifting as we climb" perspective of black feminists such as Ida Wells-Barnett and Mary McLeod Bethune to argue that black women's participation in "mass organizations" such as the National Association of Negro Women, the National Council of Negro Women, and the National Federation of Women's Clubs was not "mere charity work" but rather their attempt to resist black oppression at the same time that they worked to improve their own status as women. In their families, communities, and women's clubs and in their efforts to organize unions for textile, tobacco, and domestic workers, Jones concluded, black women demonstrated that they knew how to "undertake action" and that they could make a vital contribution to the "emerging anti-fascist, anti-imperialist coalition."

Israel Amter, with leading Communist women Claudia Jones, Ella Reeve Bloor, and Elizabeth Gurley Flynn at an event celebrating the publication of Bloor's autobiography, 1941. Courtesy of the Sophia Smith Collection, Smith College.

Because of her belief that no struggle for liberation could be effective without the efforts of black women, Claudia Jones devoted the remainder of "An End to the Neglect of the Problems of the Negro Woman" to explaining how white progressives' attitudes toward black women kept them from joining groups such as the Communist Party and proposing ways that Communists could bring more black women into the movement. Most important, she suggested, white Communists needed to guard against white chauvinism in all their personal and political interactions with black women. White women, she said, should befriend black women at social gatherings. And instead of arguing for the prohibition of marriages between black men and white women, Jones suggested that white men should dismiss "white ruling-class standards of desirability for women (such as light skin)" and consider not only "social intercourse" but the possibility of "intermarriage." Furthermore, she suggested, white people should not betray "paternalistic surprise when they learn that Negroes are professional people" or ask black women professionals whether "'someone in the family' would like to take a job as a domestic worker," and white Communists should never tell potential black members of the Party that they are "too backward" and "not ready to join." Jones even suggested that if white Communists needed to hire domestic workers they could acceptably hire black women only if they guarded against the "'madam-maid' relationship of white women to Negro women," treated their domestic workers as equals, and insisted on paying their new employees union wages for their labor.

Treating black women as equals was important, but Claudia Jones believed that white Communists also had a special responsibility to support and join black women's autonomous struggles because they inevitably resisted race, class, and gender exploitation and thereby took aim against the whole capitalist system. She instructed Party clubs to "conduct intensive discussions" about the role of black women and to commence participation in their "key issues of struggle." Her primary concern was the case of Rosa Ingram—the widowed mother of fourteen imprisoned for life in Georgia for the "crime" of defending herself against the indecent advances of a "white supremacist"—because of its symbolic meaning for African Americans and women everywhere. "The case illustrates the landless, Jim Crow, oppressed status of the Negro family in America," Jones argued:

> It illumines particularly the degradation of Negro women today under American bourgeois democracy moving to fascism and war. It reflects the daily insults to which Negro women are subjected in public places, no matter what their class, status, or position. It exposes the hypocritical alibi of the lynchers of Negro manhood who have historically hidden behind the skirts of white women when they try to cover up their foul crimes with the "chivalry" of "protecting white womanhood." [It shows that] white womanhood today, no less than their sisters in the abolitionist and suffrage movements, must rise to challenge this lie and the whole system of Negro oppression.

In order to support black struggles against all these evils she urged all Communists to participate in the campaign to gather a million signatures on a petition to be sent to President Truman on behalf of Rosa Ingram and to push for U.N. action on the case. Jones also advised Communists to fight for better jobs for black women in industry, in government agencies, and in other white-collar occupations, and to mobilize black women into the fight for peace.

Jones closed "An End to the Neglect of the Problems of the Negro Woman" by emphasizing that when black women did begin to join the Party in larger numbers, older white members needed to avoid the tendency to view them "not as leaders but as people who have to 'get their feet wet organizationally,'" to refrain from "confronting them with the silent treatment," and "'blueprint[ing]' them into a pattern" of subordination. Instead, she argued, Communists needed to acknowledge their "organizational talents" and "promote them into leadership." Only after Communists recognized that "the Negro woman . . . combines in her status the worker, the

Negro, and the woman," Jones argued, could they reach the "heightened political consciousness" that would enable black women to assume their "rightful place in the historical mission for the achievement of a Socialist America." Only with black women's input, she concluded, could the Communist Party achieve "the final and full guarantee of women's emancipation": a Communist society "in which contributions are measured not by national origin or color" but in which men and women contribute according to ability and ultimately . . . receive according to their needs."

Claudia Jones overstated her case when she implied that the Communist Party had been guilty of neglecting black women completely. She failed to acknowledge that during and after World War II, and particularly after 1948 when their coverage of women's issues in general improved so much, Communists paid considerable attention to minority women's "triple exploitation," to their contributions to the war effort, and to organizations such as the Congress of American Women and the Progressive Party.[21] As a result, not everyone appreciated her point of view. Harriet Magil, for example, called her "really weird" and guilty of "the most awful reverse chauvinism" and Betty Millard felt as if Jones had misinterpreted "Woman against Myth."[22] Despite such discord, in the extremely race-conscious atmosphere of the Communist Party in 1949, many people found Jones's arguments compelling. Eleanor Flexner remembered that "the few evenings that I spent at long intervals with Claudia made an enormous impression on me. I realized . . . that there was absolutely no mention anywhere of black women's problems or of the women themselves."[23] Flexner and others who realized that civil rights would be the major mass struggle of the postwar era understood immediately that the black women who were a part of such struggles could be a major asset to the CP. After the publication of "An End to the Neglect of the Problems of the Negro Woman," leading Communist writers and policymakers inaugurated a campaign to spread Jones's ideas about the centrality of black women to the progressive movement and launched a simultaneous effort to attract more of them into the Party. Despite these efforts Communists never succeeded in winning over masses of black women but, in the racist and sexist environment of the United States in the 1950s, the Communist Party became a center of writing and thought about the experiences of African American women and a source of support for some of their efforts to "lift" as they "climbed."

Almost as soon as Claudia Jones's article hit the presses in June 1949, the Communist Party began to increase its emphasis on black women's problems and their importance for the process of democratic social change. The Party's strategy was twofold. First, leading Communists hoped to make white progressives more aware of the nature of black women's status and their potential to make important contributions to the movement. Second, they hoped to show black women that Communists admired them and their attempts to resist oppression and to demonstrate that the Communist Party was prepared to support them in their struggles against racism and male supremacy. One good indication of the intensity of the CP's new commitment to discussing black women wherever possible was the testimony of national CP leader Gil Green in the Foley Square anti-Communism trial in New York City in June 1949. Green, who was testifying about the Party's work for women's rights, tried repeatedly to address the problems of black women until the presiding judge, who thought he was repeating previous testimony about black liberation struggles, scolded him angrily. When an insistent Green tried to clarify that the problems of Negro women did not replicate testimony on the "Negro question" the judge cut him off saying, "when we get to that part about the Negro we'll skip that. I think we have had enough of that."[24] Green's effort to publicize black women's problems in the trial was an interesting strategy, but the Communist Party carried out the bulk of its campaign to promote black women in the Party press and in educational forums that it sponsored at Marxist schools such as the Jefferson School of Social Science in New York City.

## Ending the Neglect of African American Women

It was rare, after 1949, for an issue of the *Worker* or the *Daily Worker* not to include at least one article about black women's special "triply exploited" position in American society. Such articles usually recapitulated Claudia Jones's points rather than making new contributions to the Party's understanding of black women's status, yet they successfully demonstrated to everyone who read the newspapers that Communists took black women's problems seriously and that they regarded efforts on their behalf as a fundamental part of their women's work. *Worker* and *Daily Worker* writers such as Eugene Feldman, Jo Willard, Elizabeth Gurley Flynn, and Dora Johnson, apparently achieved some success in making Jones's somewhat esoteric arguments accessible to the general reader who did not regularly peruse *Political Affairs*, the Party's most theoretical publication.[25] By 1951 the editors of the women's pages of the *Worker* congratulated writers for educating readers with their "coverage of the problems of triply oppressed Negro women" and readers wrote in to confirm that they "learned much" from such coverage and to request more of it.[26] In 1953, Eleanor Flexner (again using the pseudonym Irene Epstein) and Doxey Wilkerson included a special section on "Negro Women" in their comprehensive educational booklet *Questions and Answers on the Woman Question*. Over the course of the same period Communists also began to expand their analysis of black women's triple oppression to other women of color. Between 1949 and the mid-1950s, numerous writers discussed the superexploitation and super-militancy of Jewish women, Puerto Rican women, Asian women, and Mexican American women.[27]

In addition to their propagation of Jones's arguments about the "triple exploitation" of Negro women, one of the most important elements of the Communist Party's campaign to make black women more central to its program was a strong emphasis on black women's history. In order to show whites that black women could be leaders and to provide historical role models to guide black women in their current battles against white chauvinism and male chauvinism, Communists explored black women's problems and achievements from the time of slavery to the post–World War II era and presented them in Party literature and in CP-sponsored educational forums. Like Communists' concern with African American women's triply oppressed status, their interest in women's history was not entirely new in 1949 but went back at least several years. In 1943, for example, Earl Conrad's biography of Harriet Tubman discussed her role in the suffrage movement. In January 1949—six months before the appearance of Claudia Jones's article—historian and Communist Herbert Aptheker published his essay, "The Negro Woman," in an attempt to begin to redress the "super-neglected" history of that group.[28] But, once again, it was only after the appearance of Jones's "An End to the Neglect of the Problems of the Negro Woman" that Communists devoted themselves fully to documenting the history of African American women. Much of this new work appeared in the CP press. After June 1949, CP newspapers and journals such as the *Worker,* the *Daily Worker,* and *Masses and Mainstream* regularly published essays and articles about the achievements of heroic women such as Harriet Tubman, Sojourner Truth, Ida Wells-Barnett, Moranda Smith, Mary Church Terrell, and Mary McLeod Bethune.[29]

In 1951, the progressive production company People's Artists performed a musical revue by Eve Merriam and Gerda Lerner entitled "Singing of Women" that included a song called "Ballad for Sojourner Truth."[30] The song, a ballad about an unnamed women's rights convention, began with the words, "Now all the women longed to speak, but none knew how to start 'til Sojourner stood on the pulpit steps and spoke out from her heart" and ended with the Sojourner Truth character responding with the well-known "Ain't I a Woman" speech, set to music. *Questions and Answers on the Woman Question* honored African American "women leaders" such as Tubman, Truth, Wells-Barnett, Terrell, Jones, as well as Shirley Graham, Moranda Smith and others. Similarly, in 1955, *Masses and Mainstream* editor Samuel Sillen's book *Women against Slavery* also included chapters about black women abolitionists Sojourner Truth, Harriet Tubman, and Sarah P. Redmond.[31]

In addition to publicizing the achievements of famous black women such as Truth and Tubman, Communists also made an effort to document both the political sophistication of the masses of black women and their contributions to a variety of social justice movements. In 1951, for example, one unidentified author compiled a group of primary sources that included, among other things, an 1827 letter from a woman named Matilda to *Freedom's Journal* protesting their neglect of black women, an 1859 letter from "a mass meeting of Negro women" to John Brown thanking him for his efforts at Harper's Ferry, and an 1872 letter from Mary Olney Brown to Frederick Douglass demanding that he work to include black women in the Fourteenth and Fifteenth amendments.[32] In 1954, Peggy Dennis discussed the contributions of the "Negro women workers in the laundry, domestic and food industries" who were among the "90,000 Negro members" in the Knights of Labor and the "300,000 Negro women" in the Colored Farmers Alliance of the 1880s.[33] Articles such as these made it clear to white and black readers alike that far from being just passive victims of their triple oppression, black women had a long history of standing up for themselves and, in the process, actively resisting race, class, and gender exploitation.

Communists' strategy of teaching progressives about African American women's past and present conditions and activities through the Party press was a good way to reach many people simultaneously. But despite its efficiency, the Communist Party did not rely solely on such written material to educate its members and supporters about the crucial importance of black women to the movement. In addition to CP literature, Communists also organized numerous public classes and programs that sought to make people aware of black women's problems and achievements, and their potential to contribute to Communist struggles. It is not clear from the evidence exactly when the Party's Marxist schools began to include such courses in their curricula but by the early 1950s teachers such as Lorraine Hansberry, Claudia Jones, Charlotta Bass, Eleanor Flexner, Yvonne Gregory, and Doxey Wilkerson offered lectures and courses that explored topics such as "Negro Women in the Struggle for Peace and Democracy," and "Negro Women in Political Life."[34]

In 1951, Flexner (using the name Irene Epstein) compiled a comprehensive "Bibliography on the Negro Woman in the United States" that included more than fifty books and articles to support the classes.[35] The bibliography could still stand as an excellent reference to sources on African American women published before 1950. Under the categories Marxist writings, women under slavery, women since the Civil War, women workers, women's organizations, women leaders, and general reference, Flexner included many diverse writers, such as Herbert Aptheker, Carter Woodson, Alexander Crummell, and Elizabeth Davis.[36] Her inclusion of books such as *Incidents in the Life of a Slave Girl,* by escaped slave Harriet Jacobs, and articles on women such as Maggie Lena Walker demonstrates that Communists were familiar with these current black feminist heroines long before second-wave feminists rediscovered them in the 1970s and 1980s.[37]

All of these efforts the Communist Party conducted to empower black women and to make them more central to Communist politics were important. In the racist and sexist atmosphere of the 1950s Communists were probably the only white political activists who were thinking and writing so much about black women's particular social, economic, and political circumstances. Their analysis of the intersections of race, class, and gender integrated Marxism with black women activists' theories about their own position in society and was, in many ways, very forward-looking. But it is also important to note that Communists' commitment to black women did not just exist on paper, in classrooms, and in lecture and performance halls. In the 1940s and especially in the 1950s, Communist leaders pushed rank-and-file members to act on their belief that all progressive people had a personal responsibility to support black women's struggles and to welcome black women into the movement with open arms. Between 1949 and the mid-1950s, Communists worked for black women's rights through existing women's organizations, such as the Congress of American Women and American Women for Peace, and through labor unions and organizations such as the United Electrical Workers' Union, the Hotel and Restaurant Workers Union, and the National Trade Union Conference of Negro Rights.[38] At the same time they also worked to organize and support a Domestic Workers' Union with the hope that it could improve wages and working conditions for African American domestic workers around the country.[39]

In 1951 and 1952, Communists lent a great deal of leadership and support to Sojourners for Truth and Justice, a new organization of black women established to heed "the historic calls of Harriet Tubman and Sojourner Truth," to "stimulate united front activity among all Negro women's organizations . . . in every community of the nation," and to fight for "Negro liberation." Throughout the 1950s the Communist Party also continued to work tirelessly for the release of Rosa Ingram and, by the later 1950s, the CP held up non-Communist activists such as Rosa Parks, Autherine Lucy as well as Rosa Ingram as some of the finest examples of resistance to the interlocking systems of male supremacy and white supremacy.[40]

In order to make black women feel more welcome in the Party Communists not only tried to combat their own white supremacist attitudes but named local clubs in many cities after famous black women leaders such as Harriet Tubman, Sojourner Truth, and Moranda Smith. They also made an earnest attempt to promote black women and other women of color into leadership at all levels of the Party. In addition to Claudia Jones, who was secretary of the National Women's Commission, women of color such as Johnnie Lumpkin, Mary Adams, Geraldyne Lightfoot, and Mercedes Arroyo held state and local leadership positions.[41] These efforts never inspired African American women to join the Communist Party en masse, as Communist leaders hoped they would, but they did convince at least a small number of black women that the CP had their best interests at heart. By 1956, the Communist Party had made much progress toward ending the neglect of the problems of Negro women in its own ranks and contributed more than any other interracial radical organization in the U.S. to black women's own attempts to raise the status of their race as they improved the conditions of their own lives.

THE CP'S ATTENTION TO RACE and class issues as they intersected with women's oppression also made it unique among racially integrated organizations working for women's rights between 1945 and the 1960s. Unlike NWP feminists, many of whom saw race issues as divisive, and women's rights advocates in the labor movement, who debated the wisdom of challenging race and sex discrimination simultaneously, Communists understood that race and gender issues were inseparable—that there could be no women's rights unless black women and other women of color were freed from racial discrimination. It is no coincidence that while the NWP clung to such nineteenth-century terminology as *woman movement* and *woman's rights,* the Communist Party shifted in the 1940s to the plural *women's* movement and *women's* liberation. For Communists this distinction had more than rhetorical significance: to them it meant race and class were not differences that drove women apart, diverting them from a universal "woman's" cause, but attributes that could bring women together to fight against gender, race, and class oppression and, in that way, to achieve real liberation for women and men alike.

By the early 1950s, Claudia Jones had successfully convinced many American Communists that "ending the neglect of the problems of Negro women" was an important and complex task, one that they needed to embrace. In doing so, Communists broadened their theoretical approach to the woman question by adopting a black feminist perspective and extended their women's work to include writing and popularizing black women's history, appointing Communist women of color to local leadership positions, and lending support to black women's efforts to improve conditions for themselves and their families. In addition to bringing African American women to the center of the Communist movement's gender politics, however, Claudia Jones also articulated the ways that the combination of racism and sexism hampered black women's struggles and challenged every white progressive to reexamine their assumptions about and interactions with black women. Jones's firm stand on this point not only reinforced progressive women's emphasis on the connections between personal and political issues but, because she was the CP's leading black woman, increased support for their demand that the CP take male supremacy more seriously. By the early 1950s, Communist leaders insisted more than ever before that the Communist movement should be a model of racial integration and harmony. Probably not coincidentally many of them also encouraged progressives to guard against male supremacist behaviors, to adopt egalitarian gender roles, and to live out their politics in their day-to-day lives at work, in their interpersonal relationships and at home.

# 6 Communist Culture and the Politicization of Personal Life

In April 1951, after the debut of Gerda Lerner and Eve Merriam's musical *Singing of Women* at the Cherry Lane Theatre in New York City, *Daily Worker* reviewer Eleanor Flexner billed it as "another important event in this year's renascence of the progressive theatre."[1] The two-act musical dramatized "the history of American women dating back to the time when women were sold for 20 pounds of tobacco 'because they would make good workers and had a fine set of strong teeth.'"[2] Although Flexner thought the revue was too large in scope to be fully effective, in her review she praised its emphasis on "the fight for women's rights and its integration with other progressive struggles such as Abolitionism and trade unionism," on "specifics" including "the question of male supremacy, the dual exploitation of woman as housewife and worker, unequal pay, her international role in the fight against fascism and the emerging peace movement," and on "the oppression of Negro women." Flexner concluded by calling the revue a "pioneering achievement" and suggesting that *Singing of Women* should stimulate further attempts to use the rich experiences of the women's rights movement as a vehicle for the education of both men and women to the need for building a strong women's movement in the fight for peace and socialism.

A musical production like *Singing of Women* is not the first thing that comes to mind as an example of Old Left political activism. In the 1940s and 1950s, as in the two preceding decades, Communists and progressives directed most of their political energy toward aiding the class struggle by organizing the unorganized, supporting strikes and meat boycotts, opposing unemployment, and defending the rights of African Americans. Although they devoted a great deal of effort to workers' struggles against the material aspects of their exploitation, Communists were also very much aware that capitalist domination extended beyond the formal economic, social, and political systems. Long before Antonio Gramsci's writings about cultural hegemony or critical theorists' critiques of mass culture permeated the U.S. Left, American Communists and progressives argued that because "bourgeois culture" and "bourgeois morality" were instrumental in perpetuating the oppressive class system, the creation of an alternative "peoples" culture and value system was necessary to achieve a classless society.[3]

In the late 1940s and 1950s, when the political context of the United States was decidedly unrevolutionary and both CIO unions and reformist organizations such as the NAACP and the ACLU barred Communists from their ranks, cultural and personal politics became more important within the Old Left than ever before. Although Communists and progressives continued their activism in the labor movement, the early Civil Rights movement, and other struggles whenever possible, many turned their revolutionary impulses inward. As it became increasingly difficult for them to influence social and cultural institutions within mainstream society, Communists concentrated on creating an alternative culture and lifestyle that reflected their deeply held political principles and beliefs. By the 1950s many Communists and their allies were devoting considerable energy to developing for themselves the cultural institutions and artifacts they wanted to see in the future and modeling the egalitarian interpersonal relationships they hoped every American would be able to adopt when socialism finally triumphed in the United States.[4]

American Communists' commitment to the creation of a prefigurative political culture was not new in the McCarthy period, but their attention to culture and individual relationships was substantially different from before.[5] Because of the new emphasis that Communists placed on fighting male supremacist ideology and the cultural, interpersonal, and psychological elements of women's oppression, their efforts to create an oppositional subculture in those years naturally included attempts to counterbalance the sexism that was prevalent in mainstream culture and society. After progressive women began to criticize images of women in books, magazines, newspapers, and movies, Communists made a conscious effort to create new cultural artifacts that portrayed women as strong and intelligent. *Singing of Women* is an excellent illustration of this change. At the same time, after Communist women began to argue that male supremacist ideology influenced individuals and the family as well as society at large, the Party began to insist that progressive men guard against male chauvinist attitudes and behavior in their roles as husbands and fathers as well as in political settings. Female-male and even parent-child relationships, Party leaders suggested, should be respectful, egalitarian, and mutually satisfying.

Some might argue that Communists' emphasis on the creation of an alternative culture and community in this period was actually their way of withdrawing from politics and creating an isolated refuge away from the reaction and repression that dominated the United States in the 1950s. But progressives had long stressed the critical relationship between culture and politics, and Communists, in particular, underscored their responsibility to practice what they preached. Even before the full onslaught of McCarthyism, when Communists were still optimistic about the possibilities for the Left in the United States, *Daily Worker* articles reminded readers about the value of "personal revolution" and the importance of integrating the "decisions and programs of the Party" into "our personal and emotional lives."[6] In the 1950s, when McCarthyism severely limited progressives' opportunities for public political activism, working toward this kind of "personal revolution" might have been the only way for most of them to maintain some kind of visible commitment to their political ideals.[7]

Communists were not the original proponents of cultural or personal politics in the United States, but, like many activists before and after them, they strove to model the egalitarian and classless society they ultimately hoped to create. Even as their influence in U.S. society was declining rapidly in an era dominated by the Cold War, McCarthyism, suburbanization, and television, Communists' efforts to create an alternative way of life for themselves made them quiet but persistent vanguards of a new era of American political activism in which conduct and appearance mattered as much as ideology. Certainly there were major differences between the Old Left and the New. The two generations of activists had diametrically opposed positions on the nature of the Soviet Union, on hierarchy and structure, and on the relevance of Freudian psychoanalytic theory for understanding the modern world. Despite these differences, it is clear that Communists' brand of "personal politics" helped to shape those that the participants in the new movements of the 1960s thought they invented.

## Communist Culture and Communities

At the end of World War II Communists already had a long history of efforts to develop an alternative culture and lifestyle that included art, literature, music, and theater that represented "the people" and had the potential to empower them. In the 1920s, for example, a group of Communists who were primarily Jewish garment workers formed the United Workers Co-operative Association and built two apartment buildings—the Allerton Avenue Co-operative Houses, also known as "the Coops"—in the Bronx, that housed three thousand people at any one time. From the 1920s to the 1950s, the Coops supported a self-contained radical community that included clubrooms, meeting halls, a library, a nursery school, a community center, and an auditorium and allowed Communist residents to live out their politics on a daily basis.[8]

Progressive summer camps and children's programs at Marxist schools served a similar purpose for those who lived outside of such communities. Communist parents sent their children to summer camps at Camp Woodland, Camp Kinderland, Camp Wo-Chi-Ca (Workers' Children's Camp), and Camp Calumet so they could spend time with other "red-diaper babies" and absorb progressive politics and values through sing-alongs, art projects, and storytelling.[9] In the 1930s and early 1940s, as the Party grew in size and influence, it attracted numerous writers and musicians whose artistic labors reflected their political commitments and helped to build Communist culture.[10]

Throughout this period Communist authors wrote novels, plays, and children's books with revolutionary themes and strong working-class heroes and heroines. Singers Pete Seeger and Woody Guthrie held "hootenannies" at which Communists and their supporters gathered to sing politicized folk songs. The CP leadership demanded that whites interact with blacks as equals.[11] At the same time Communist scholars also began to research and write about labor history in order to provide activist role models for the working class and create a usable past for themselves. Despite their Party's longstanding emphasis on the importance of economic and political workplace and neighborhood issues, American Communists always recognized that cultural activities were important components of the fight to build a better world.

The Communist movement's efforts to develop a counterhegemonic "peoples" culture between 1919 and 1945 were, by and large, extremely progressive. In contrast to the increasingly pervasive mass culture of the United States, which accepted and promoted imperialism, racism, nationalism, competition, and consumption, Communist-influenced art, music, literature, theater, and daily life emphasized cooperation, racial equality, and international peace. The movement also celebrated the proud heritage of the working class and praised progressives' efforts to resist the decadent, bourgeois values that increasingly dominated the nation. Advanced though it was on race and class issues, its record on gender was considerably less impressive. As was clear from the cheesecake in the *Daily Worker* and the expectation that women cater to men, before 1945 Communists actually adopted sexist ideas and practices from mainstream culture more often than they opposed them.

Not surprisingly, as Communists began to expand their theory on the woman question at the end of World War II and to acknowledge that male supremacist ideology *and* class oppression subordinated women, all of this began to change. In fall 1946, after a published excerpt from Susan Anthony's "Report of the Commission on the Status of Women" criticized "the press, periodicals, films, radio and theater" for perpetuating male supremacy by presenting women exclusively in terms of negative female stereotypes, many Communists began to consider the effects of cultural messages on women more seriously.[12] In 1948, after Betty Millard published her observation that even progressive men often displayed sexist attitudes and behaviors, Communists also began to think about how male supremacy operated at the individual as well as the group level. It seems likely that once Party leaders realized that individual men's capitulation to sexist stereotypes and behaviors compromised the organization's ability to recruit women, they adopted a new stance for the CP. In the late 1940s, when the Party's ability to influence the public had sharply diminished, leading Communists broadened their efforts to replace the sexist images in their publications with empowering ones and strove to eliminate the male chauvinist attitudes and behavior that restricted the activities of girls and women in so many rank-and-file Communist families and relationships. By the 1950s, although sexism certainly persisted at all levels of Communist Party life, Communists publicly condemned male supremacist attitudes and behavior in the family and personal life and disdained sexist images almost as loudly as they repudiated white chauvinism, Aunt Jemima, and minstrel shows.

## Progressive Feminism and the Revision of Communist Culture

The Communist Party's attack on male supremacy in bourgeois culture began almost immediately after the *Worker* published "Jimcrow against Women," Susan Anthony's analysis of the cultural oppression of women. Once Anthony articulated the ways that constant misrepresentations of women effectively saddled them with a "sex inferiority complex," other Communist writers followed her lead and initiated what became a lengthy process of exposing and condemning the cultural messages that shaped and limited women's lives. The first critiques of sexism in mainstream culture that appeared in the *Worker* and the *Daily Worker* simply tended to repeat Anthony's points about the damaging effects of stereotypes using specific examples from movies and magazines. David Platt, for example, denounced the movie *It Happened One Night* as "an insult to every woman who ever contributed to social progress" and Martha Bridger called women's romance magazines "one of the most formidable types of propaganda . . . this nation possesses."[13] It was not until after 1948, when Betty Millard explained concretely the variety of ways that language, customs, and stereotypes helped to perpetuate women's inferior status, that other authors began to develop their ideas further.

After 1948 articles criticizing portrayals of women in popular culture proliferated in Communist Party publications. Instead of limiting themselves to the subjects of movies and magazines, writers branched out and addressed every variety of chauvinistic language. They denounced not only anti-black, Asian, Gypsy, Irish, and Canadian terms but misogynist expressions as well.[14] They also frequently discussed misrepresentations of women in literature and, as soon as television became an important element in American culture, Communists began to argue against the way TV shows depicted women and girls.[15] N.E., of New York City, for example, wrote to the *Daily Worker* to warn fellow progressives against "a most disgusting program," the "Horn and Hardart Children's Hour," on which "male supremacist songs are twittered forth by precocious little girls," and Vic Miller's article "Looking at TV Shows Featuring Women" argued that most series portrayed women as "zany scatterbrains with long-suffering menfolk."[16] Sexist advertising became a target of Communists' attacks, as Ted Tinsley and W. Greer of Brooklyn each condemned the use of scantily clad women for purposes such as selling cars and justifying phone rate increases. Communists also began to write in this period about the evils of women's fashion, comparing the expectation that American women wear high heels to the practice of binding women's feet in China.[17] Elizabeth Gurley Flynn criticized conventional standards for women's attractiveness in her regular column "Life of the Party," arguing that "the idea that women must be beautiful at all costs is a slave idea, as is the whole concept that they must be gentle, sweet, low-voiced and pliable."[18]

By the early 1950s Communists simply accepted the notion that one of the explicit purposes of bourgeois culture was to keep women down. Progressive writer Margrit Reiner's *Masses and Mainstream* article "The Fictional American Woman" stated decisively that the typical fiction writer "not only reflects in his writing the male supremacist attitudes he observes in the world around him," but that "his treatment of women in fiction is designed to justify and perpetuate these attitudes." David Carpenter effectively summarized the Party's new position on the role of culture in women's oppression in 1951 when he wrote:

> One of the worst crimes of American monopoly capitalism against humanity in this period when it dominates the whole capitalist world is its debasement and degradation of women. At the very time when the productive forces and creativeness of humanity make possible the liberation of women after long centuries of super-exploitation, the capitalist overlords of U.S. imperialism increasingly defile women. The entire cultural power of the capitalist class—movies, books, magazines, radio, schools, churches, etc.—attacks women, particularly of the working class, almost from birth, to destroy their minds and creative social abilities. Every word, every picture, is aimed at making women accept sexual and kitchen slavery as their destiny.[19]

The number of articles like these published in the Party press demonstrates that by the late 1940s and 1950s American Communists recognized and exposed the ways that mainstream culture damaged women's status and self-esteem. But, because they were activists as well as social critics, Communists and their allies also agreed that it was necessary to attack oppressive representations of women whenever they could. Anthony suggested in 1946 that the best way to oppose sexism in culture was to mobilize the masses of American women to protest against degrading images in the press, fiction, films, and the like. But in the increasingly reactionary environment of the postwar period organizing such mass-based resistance was virtually impossible. Because they had no hope of reforming those who produced mainstream women's magazines, textbooks, movies, and radio shows, progressives must have decided that their only hope for winning the battle against bourgeois culture was to create their own. If images of women as sex symbols, doting mothers, and scatterbrained housewives in popular culture were supposed to make them accept their subjection, Communists believed, then an alternative peoples' culture needed to provide new images of smart, strong, powerful women that could inspire them to fight the forces of reaction and resist their own oppression.

One way that Communists tried to create such images was by rethinking the CP press's portrayal of women. The editors of the *Worker* and the *Daily Worker* promoted positive images of women in 1949, when they declared a moratorium on cheesecake, and in 1950, when they removed the picture of the high-heeled woman dusting at the top of the woman's page. In keeping with Margrit Reiner's guidelines for moving beyond "the male supremacist patterns of omission, stereotype, distortion, violence, and isolation" in their fictional portrayals of women, progressive authors also worked during this period to add to an existing body of progressive poetry and fiction that contained realistic female role models. Authors such as Meridel LeSueur, Eve Merriam, and others all published poetry and fiction that reflected real women's problems and experiences, such as forced sterilization, prostitution, pregnancy, rape, and unemployment, and sought to empower women by highlighting their past and present militancy.[20]

Art (and other visual representations of women) and literature were both important parts of Communists' crusade to improve upon the sexist and misogynist images presented in mainstream culture. But between 1946 and 1956 Communist writers spent less time inventing positive fictional images of women and concentrated instead on uncovering the creative and political achievements and contributions of real heroines from the American past. The first discussions of U.S. women's history appeared in the *Worker* and *Daily Worker* in fall 1946 as part of the Party's larger efforts to draw more women into the CP's milieu. These articles sought to show progressives that women had long been contributing to social justice movements. They also strove to demonstrate that women could participate in campaigns for social and political reform even though they were excluded from the formal political system. Only one of these early stories—Virginia Warner's "Battle for Women's Rights Began in 1848"—focused specifically on the nineteenth-century woman's rights movement. The others conceived of women's movements more broadly and emphasized women's contributions to other nineteenth-century social movements as well.[21] Samuel Sillen, for example, wrote about the Boston Female Anti-Slavery Society and Virginia Warner about the contributions of women such as the Grimke sisters and Lydia Maria Child to the abolitionist movement.[22] Similarly, Philip Foner presented Sarah Bagley and the Lowell Mill girls as pioneers in the American labor movement. In order to oppose the notion that suffragists were selfish middle-class women concerned exclusively with winning rights for themselves, Virginia Gardner discussed the coalitions that some suffrage advocates formed with groups such as the Knights of Labor and the American Socialist Party.[23]

*Worker* and *Daily Worker* readers responded very favorably to the women's history articles that appeared in the newspapers in late 1946. E.R., from Woodside, New York, wrote to the editor of the *Daily Worker* in October to say that he or she "liked the article on women in the abolitionist movement" and to express the opinion that "we need more information on the historical role of women in America." In January 1947 another reader wrote to the *Worker* to say "the articles . . . on the history of the women's equal rights movement have been a wonderful relief from the conspicuous lack of material on the subject" and to request "more data on the American women's movement—specifically on the struggle for equality in the shops, in unions, in politics." In response the editor promised, "We'll see what we can do about getting more of it."[24]

From then on, women's history features appeared frequently in the *Worker* and the *Daily Worker* and occasionally in other publications such as *Political Affairs* and *Masses and Mainstream*. Beginning in 1947, both CP newspapers published regular articles presenting female activist role models such as Anne Hutchinson, Carrie Chapman Catt, Mother Jones, Kaethe Kollwitz, Sarah and Angelina Grimke, Lucretia Mott, Elizabeth Cady Stanton, Susan B. Anthony, Lucy Parsons, Harriet Tubman, Prudence Crandall, Sojourner Truth, Florence Kelly, and many others, all of whom demonstrated that women could overcome the limitations set for them and achieve significant influence in politics and social life.[25] At the same time CP publications also began to print regular columns on the history of the U.S. women's movement that included the contributions of African American and working-class women as well as those made by well-known nineteenth-

"Needed: Still Newer Look at Women's Problems," Communist Party USA *Discussion Bulletin* no 2, 1956.

century feminists such as Stanton and Anthony. Articles such as Elizabeth Gurley Flynn's "1948—A Year of Inspiring Anniversaries for Women" and "'Petticoat Revolt' They Sneered," and Peggy Dennis's "World Labor's Debt to American Women" argued that women's struggles to improve their own status were irrevocably linked to the abolitionist movement and the labor movement and that women had been central to the successes of all three.[26]

In 1953, Communist historian Herbert Aptheker published a series of three articles on the woman suffrage movement in the *Daily Worker* to refute American Historical Association president J. G. Randall's "appalling" and "male supremacist" statement that "Woman suffrage in the United States was obtained not by a revolution or a kind of Amazon's Bastille Day, but by orderly processes under mere male control."[27] In these works Aptheker analyzed the history of the suffrage struggle from its origins in Seneca Falls in 1848, to the mass arrests and gross mistreatment of suffragists picketing in front of the White House in 1917, to the ratification of the Woman Suffrage Amendment in 1920. The examples set by the suffragists and other women activists from the nineteenth and early twentieth centuries, Aptheker and other Communists believed, were particularly important for progressive women of the 1950s who were fighting "so courageously . . . against McCarthyite, Smith and McCarran Acts persecutions."[28] Stories about real women activists who triumphed despite persecution in the past, they thought, could inspire radical women to persevere in spite of the subpoenas, blacklisting, and arrests that threatened them throughout the late 1940s and 1950s.

Other progressive writers also developed an interest in women's history after 1946. Lerner and Merriam's pursuit of the subject led to the production of *Singing of Women*, which they explicitly intended to "take the starch out of theories and myths which depict women as the 'weaker and feeble-minded sex.'"[29] The first act of the two-act production dramatized women's militancy through historical events including women's efforts to keep prices down during the Revolutionary War, the Women's Rights Convention of 1848, the earliest strike of women textile workers, the fight for women's suffrage, women's struggles for the eight-hour day, and the establishment of International Women's Day. The second explored "the problem of male supremacy, the dual exploitation of woman as housewife and worker, unequal pay, and women's international role in the fight against fascism and the emerging peace movement." In postwar United States, where most cultural representations of women functioned to keep them from challenging the status quo, it was clear that women's history in general and programs such as *Singing of Women* in particular provided positive images that Communists hoped could both inspire women to action and serve as "a vehicle for educating . . . men and women [about] the need [to] build a strong women's movement within the fight for peace and socialism."[30]

The Communist Party's campaign to denounce sexism in popular culture and to present more positive and inspirational images of women in Party publications such as the *Worker* and *Daily Worker* was an important step forward in its campaign to recruit more women and create a way of life that reflected its theoretical commitment to women's equality. More women joined the CP and participated in the events and activities it supported after 1945 than had before the end of the war, but it quickly became apparent to Party leaders that it would not be easy to equalize the participation of women and men in Party life. There was new theory on the woman question, special classes and activities for wives and mothers, and favorable representations of women and women's issues in the Party press, but both the Communist Party's leadership and its day-to-day operations were still, by-and-large, dominated by men. The true equality Communists had hoped to create for themselves while they worked for a revolution was still a long way off.

If Communist leaders were confused in the late 1940s about why their efforts to promote greater equality between women and men in CP life were not succeeding, they did not have to look far for an explanation. They had only to turn to the women's pages of the *Worker* to read women's complaints about the ways that economic discrimination and exclusion from politics exploited them as a group *and* about the ways their husbands' attitudes and behavior oppressed them as individuals. In June 1946, for example, S.T., from New York, wrote to the paper to suggest that although the Party's efforts to compensate for women's oppression in society at large might help to recruit some new women members, others were still limited by their personal circumstances. "It is the unsympathetic husband who throws every obstacle in the path of a political alert wife who is the real problem," S.T. argued. "It takes an almost superhuman effort on the part of the wife to overcome the scorn and ridicule of this type of husband who feels his wife's place is in the home."[31] In November of that year W.O. wrote to confirm that her husband was indeed her problem and to suggest the widespread nature of this phenomenon:

> My husband could give an excellent lecture on the necessity to emancipate women. He spends hours reading and improving his mind. Politically he is really well educated. But what about his wife? I work 16 hours a day, seven days a week. If I have the time to read the editorial in the *Daily Worker* I am lucky. I can jump up from a meal a dozen times, but my husband will pass the knife for me to cut him a slice off the loaf. He would never dream of helping me with the children, or doing the dishes, or putting things away when he uses them, or planning to stay home one evening occasionally so I could get out for a change of atmosphere. He is waited on hand and foot and expects it. . . . He would think any other man described like this was a poor comrade, but if he suspected this meant himself he'd be angry at me. He is not the only one; I've met dozens like him.[32]

NUMEROUS OTHERS ALSO WROTE to the women's pages to validate the notion that committed Marxists could also be male chauvinists and to demand that the Communist Party "pay closer attention to the personal and emotional problems of [its] people through a clearer delineation of Marxist behavior in human relations."[33]

Since the 1920s the Party had always maintained that the exploitative conditions of capitalism, not men, were responsible for male supremacy. In 1946 and 1947, when Communist women first began to air their grievances about the ways their male family members enacted women's oppression, CP leaders tended either to ignore their arguments that their husbands limited their participation in progressive activities or to dismiss their complaints as a "battle of the sexes approach" to women's problems. In the late 1940s, however, despite the CP's insistence that they were not approaching the problem of women's oppression correctly, more and more rank-and-filers insisted that the Party had a responsibility to require progressive men to live out their politics in their personal lives.[34] In summer 1948, for example, Joseph Gingold wrote to the *Worker* to say that "the fight for equality begins in the home" and E.E., from Long Island City, proposed that "it is essential that when people join the party they understand that there is a Communist way of life and they will be expected to live it as well as to preach it."[35] Another reader wrote to the *Worker* to point out that male chauvinist husbands "created in [their] homes conditions which are similar to conditions in an open shop and placed [themselves] in the position of the union busting boss."[36] Letters like these apparently forced the Communist Party leadership to acknowledge that the male supremacist attitudes and behaviors perpetrated by individual men did sometimes keep women tied to home and children. As a result, Party leaders gradually began to take women's complaints more seriously. By the end of the 1940s, as the political climate made it increasingly difficult for Communists to mount a public challenge to the economic, political, and social status quo, CP leaders began to place more emphasis than ever before on the need for Party members and supporters to reform their personal and family lives.

## Raising Communists' Consciousness

It is interesting (and, some would say, ironic) that Communists' campaign against individual manifestations of male supremacist thinking and behavior in the home and family emerged at the same time that CP leaders publicly rejected Freudian psychoanalysis—a method for reforming individuals' consciousness and behavior that they had previously accepted—as a tool of the bourgeoisie. Many have assumed that, by rejecting Freud, Communists also necessarily dismissed the idea that an indvdidual's consciousness has political relevance.[37] In fact, as the white chauvinism campaigns of the 1930s and 1950s demonstrated, Communists consistently accepted that consciousness and politics were inextricably linked. Their repudiation of Freudianism in the late 1940s did not require them to deny the political importance of consciousness raising and, in fact, probably even aided progressive women's struggles to draw attention to male supremacy's central role in the perpetuation of women's oppression.

Like many contemporary feminists, Joseph Wortis, the most influential Communist opponent of Freudianism, actually based his critique of Freudian theory on its essentialist assumptions and middle-class biases. He argued that no human behavior was instinctual or innate and that "social structure . . . determines human behavior together with ideas and ideologies which motivate behavior." He went on to suggest that "Not even the pattern of normal sexual activity can be regarded as instinctive and innate: contemporary normal patterns of sexual maturity owe their development to a social context in which the monogamous heterosexual family is dominant."[38] Furthermore, Wortis suggested, although Freudianism "sometimes disclaims any interest in morals or ethics it has an implicit acceptance of most contemporary middle-class standards" which is "revealed in its attitude toward women, in its notion of what is normal, in its standards of success and failure, in its attitude toward social progress, and in its fundamental pessimism." Most of all, Wortis and other Communists objected to Freud and his school of psychoanalysis because it regarded "comfortable adaptation to a static social order as either a possible or desirable standard of psychotherapeutic goal." When an individual expressed or acted upon pathological racist or sexist assumptions, Communists believed, his or her consciousness needed attention. But for them reforming individuals' beliefs and behavior was not an end in itself. Rather, Communists saw consciousness raising as a means of building a successful political movement that could, in the end, revolutionize the social order.

It is unclear whether or not Wortis's efforts to challenge progressives' acceptance of psychoanalysis at the end of the 1940s actually influenced progressive feminists in any significant way. What is clear is that progressives' understanding of the impact of male supremacist ideology and consciousness on women was founded on the new and deeper understanding of the role of culture in perpetuating women's oppression that progressive writers had forged at the end of World War II. In addition to demonstrating the ways that sexist images in bourgeois culture damaged women's self-esteem and made them hesitant to ask for a better place in the world, a few Communist writers also recognized that male chauvinism in culture "corrupt[ed] men into becoming its agents for keeping women sexual and kitchen slaves."[39] This argument was key to convincing Communist leaders that the Party could address the problems of male supremacy in the family without deviating from its longstanding position that capitalist class relations (and not individual men) were responsible for women's oppression. Once they recognized that progressive and working-class men's oppressive attitudes and behavior stemmed from structural causes, CP leaders could acknowledge that "women in the modern bourgeois family [function] as 'the proletariat' of the man who assumes the place of 'bourgeoisie'" and that "there are many Communist men . . . who believe that a woman's function is to make love, have children, do the cooking, the housework, and wait on her lord and master."[40] By the end of the decade they began to implement a strategy for reversing this un-Communist but not uncommon point of view.

As early as 1948 CP women's leader Margaret Krumbein insisted that the Party institute a program of education for men on the woman question that included, among other things, instruction on "Communist ethics."[41] In the early years of its campaign to encourage Communist men to live out their politics by treating their wives and other female comrades as equals, the Communist Party followed Krumbein's advice. If Communist men had been corrupted by bourgeois ideology, CP leaders must have reasoned, then the best way to free them from that ideology was to explain where it came from, how it affected them, why it was bad, and how they could do things differently. Initially they relied primarily on the CP press, especially the *Worker* and *Daily Worker*, to do this. From 1948 into the 1950s the newspapers carried regular articles and features that were intended to point out day-to-day examples of male chauvinism and give hints about how Communist men could mend their ways. In April 1948, for example, the caption under a photo of three chimpanzees dressed as people performing household chores read, "Household drudgery: Even in the St. Louis Zoo male superiority rears its ugly head as Ma Chimpanzee wields the mop, the youngster polishes the table, while Papa Chimpanzee sits back and takes it easy."[42] In April 1949 the caption under a photo of a small child eating lunch with her father read, "It does a girl good to have lunch with one of her favorite men occasionally, and it's especially good if the child is very young and the man is the child's father. Families are stronger and happier if the father knows how to fix the cereal, tie the bibs, and take care of the youngsters."[43]

Scores of articles and letters also appeared in the CP papers in this period condemning men who refused to treat their wives respectfully and reminding them that Communist living meant that they should help with the dishes and take real responsibility for some aspects of housework and childcare. In 1950, for example, an "irate husband" spoke for many when he wrote, "I think we must be more alert to certain subtle acts of male supremacy that are keeping many women tied down to the home. . . . Communist women today should be relieved of their household drudgery so that they can once and for all do the key political job which has been denied them before. The main responsibility lies with male Communists. They must begin to recognize that cooking, cleaning and looking after kids is not a woman's responsibility, but a joint one."[44]

In 1954 *Worker* writer Jean Josephs took this analysis even further when she criticized the way progressives called men who performed household responsibilities "wonderful" and "remarkable" while they took it for granted that women were supposed to have two jobs, one outside the home and one within it.[45] Until social legislation could achieve better day-care centers, socialized housekeeping and communal cafeterias, she argued, husbands and fathers needed to take on their share of the family responsibilities so that women could pursue political activities. Later that year Elizabeth Lawson published a laudatory review of Simone DeBeauvoir's *The Second Sex,* which she called a "magnificent contribution" and a "trumpet call to women's liberation" that, despite its problems, progressives should read in order to benefit from its freshness, originality, and continuous revelations and delights.[46]

Articles and letters encouraging men to fight male supremacy in their personal lives were one important part of the CP's educational campaign against individual manifestations of male supremacy, but they were only half the story. In its quest for a satisfactory resolution to Communists' version of the "battle of the sexes" in the early 1950s, the Party also sponsored classes on topics such as "Marriage and Family Life" and "Male Supremacy and Family Relations" at the Jefferson School. They hoped that such classes might persuade more men to renounce the privileges they gained from male supremacy and to work for genuine egalitarianism in their relationships with their wives.[47] These classes reminded men that, despite their allegiance to the Communist Party, they were not necessarily ideologically pure. On the contrary, according to the Jefferson School faculty, male supremacist ideology "infected" both the working class and the progressive movement. Even the most progressive men, they argued, commonly exhibited their male chauvinist attitudes by

> neglect[ing] their responsibility in problems of child up-bringing, the family, household chores, etc., leaving these necessary tasks for women to perform; discouraging one's wife from participation in political and other community activities (or not making it possible for her to do so); passing jokes and derogatory comments about women in general; preoccupation with women solely as "sex beings," rather than as equal companions in rounded social relationships; accepting the "double standard" of morality; and refusing to take a serious approach to the woman question, to study and understand it as a special question of prime importance for the triumph of the working class over imperialist reaction.[48]

Furthermore, the courses explained that male supremacist attitudes and behaviors were one of the primary sources of marital friction between progressive men and women. They argued that male supremacy in relations between men and women was especially dangerous because it obstructed the advance of the entire working class.[49] Because men, not women, were the "carriers" of male supremacist ideology, the classes stressed, men had the main responsibility for struggling against it. Teachers such as Joseph Fuerst, Herbert Aptheker, Eleanor Flexner, and Doxey Wilkerson urged men to fight male supremacy by working for the "full equal rights of women on the job, in the union, and in the home." They also taught that men needed to raise their own consciousness on the woman question by engaging in "the regular and constructive use of criticism and self-criticism," a practice that "alerts the individual to the role of anti–working-class ideas in his own life and that of his associates, and directs the collective efforts of the whole group toward the ideological strengthening of each member."[50] In other words, these teachers stressed, not until progressive men began to identify and correct male supremacist tendencies in themselves and others would the Communist Party be able to proceed in its struggle to emancipate women and to move forward on the road to socialism.

Communist leaders undoubtedly realized that classes were beneficial only to those who enrolled in and attended them. They also recognized that the most sexist men were not likely to register for a course called "Male Supremacy and the Family" so they insured that regular Party educational forums and lectures also addressed similar topics. Claudia Jones and Elizabeth Gurley Flynn often delivered lectures and speeches that emphasized issues such as the importance of equality within the home.[51] CP National Education Director Betty Gannett also lectured on topics such as "The Morality Demanded of a Marxist" and "Morality in Marriage."[52] Although she did not bill herself as an expert on the woman question, Gannett regularly incorporated anti–male chauvinist messages in her explanations of how to live as a good Communist and reminded Communist men that Marxist morality required them to "appreciate and respect their wives as human beings and companions." The "moral duty in marriage demands daily cooperation with one's partner," she wrote, and "joint handling of marital problems; and marital fidelity."[53]

Peggy Dennis, the wife of prominent CP leader Eugene Dennis, suggested in her memoirs that their relationship was not an egalitarian one, but the CP's efforts to educate Communists about the importance of gender equality in the home clearly convinced some Communist and progressive men that they needed to practice what they preached on the woman question.[54] In his memoir, for example, Communist Steve Nelson reported that even while he was a busy local Party leader he "managed to come home every day to help with dinner and clean up" before he rushed out to a meeting.[55] Similarly, progressive activist Joan Acker described how after she married one of her comrades from the Wallace for President campaign in 1948, her new husband "really tried to live according to the basic notions of equality." Rose Kryzak reported that she and her husband "always shared" the housework and child-rearing, and Ann Fagan Ginger explained that many Communist and progressive men "were excellent cooks" who also did their share of "taking care of the kids" both at public meetings where child-care was provided and in their own homes.[56]

Despite such examples of egalitarianism, women persisted in complaining about their progressive but sexist husbands in the *Worker*. In response to complaints about incorrigible male chauvinists, local Communist Party officials at least sometimes resorted to disciplinary measures. Dorothy Healey recalled that as the district organizer in Los Angeles in the late 1940s and 1950s she occasionally visited individual Communist men in their homes to confront them about the sexist ways they treated their wives. According to the FBI, in 1954 alone, the Los Angeles district of the CP intervened in at least three cases of male supremacy including: (1) an unmarried male who carried on a series of affairs with a number of women without any intention of marrying; (2) a married male who suggested wife swapping with his closest friend; and (3) a man who struck his wife and later said there was nothing political in his actions.[57]

State and local level women's commissions also confronted individual men's male chauvinist behavior and urged them to mend their ways. In 1950, for example, the Minnesota Women's Commission investigated and intervened in numerous cases including those involving a local Party leader who brushed off his wife's attempts to confront his male chauvinist behavior by joking with her about "feminism" and who later insisted that his daughter learn to wash dishes so she might "make some man a good wife," a second man who was "super-critical of the way his wife did housework," and a third man who "habitually lectured his wife on politics instead of discussing political questions with her as an equal."[58]

Typically, the CP charged such men with male supremacy, subjected them to the criticism of their peers, and sentenced them to "control tasks involving study on the woman question" so that they might unlearn the poisonous ideology of male chauvinism. Relieving individual men of their male supremacist tendencies, CP leaders must have reasoned, would both insure the stability of Communist families and build support for a mass movement for women's liberation.

In the mid-1950s Communists continued to denounce male supremacist ideology, criticize its reflections in mainstream culture, and work to reverse its effects on the lives of progressive women and men. But in addition to counseling progressives about how to avoid male supremacy in their relationships, some Communists also began in this period to expand their vision of a radical subculture to incorporate a variety of new efforts. They hoped to encourage others to move beyond patriarchal assumptions and customs in every area of family life and to set an example of real egalitarianism for the rest of the nation. Between 1952 and 1956, for example, a few Communist women began to argue against the notion that women were fated to suffer severe pain in childbirth. Some of them began to participate in the earliest American movement toward natural childbirth practices in order to empower women, to encourage the participation of husbands, and to publicize the relaxation methods that the French doctor Lamaze learned in the Soviet Union.[59] Others began to argue that the subordination of women and the subordination of children in the family came from the same sources and that it was just as important for progressives to protect children's rights as to protect women's rights. The best way to respect children and raise self-confident, political adults, Communist advice columnists argued, was to allow them to question and challenge the status quo and to involve them in family decision-making as often as possible.[60]

This analysis had a significant impact on the way many Communist parents actually raised their children. Jane Lazarre and other children of Communists from this period report that their parents "always encouraged open discussion and debate," expected their children to participate in adult conversations, and urged them to express their opinions on topics ranging from racism, to imperialism, to the Army-McCarthy hearings. Not surprisingly, daughters of Communists also report that their parents expected them *and* their brothers to grow up to become adults who combined work, family, and political activism.[61]

Communists' most public effort to demonstrate that individual men and women could free themselves from patriarchal assumptions and customs and transcend the sexism and classism so pervasive in bourgeois culture was the making of the film *Salt of the Earth* in 1953. Made by black-listed progressive filmmakers Michael Wilson, Herbert Biberman, and Paul Jarrico, all of whom were deeply influenced by CP thinking about the politics of culture, *Salt of the Earth* immortalized the events that surrounded the International Union of Mine, Mill and Smelter Workers' strike against Empire Zinc in New Mexico in 1950-52 and showed how surpassing traditional gender roles had the potential to liberate an entire community.[62]

Jarrico, a Communist screenwriter who had just formed his own production company and was looking for a good political story to be the subject of its first film, learned about the mine and mill workers' strike against Empire Zinc from Clinton Jencks, a longtime progressive activist and a local United Mine, Mill and Smelter Workers' Union official in New Mexico. After a quick visit to the strikers' picket line, Jarrico knew he had found his story.

He engaged screenwriter Michael Wilson and director Herbert Biberman, one of the Hollywood Ten, to join him in completing the project.[63]

*Salt of the Earth,* which cast Mexican American mine workers and their families to play themselves, opened with the working men of the community deciding to go on strike for higher wages and safer working conditions but refusing to listen to their wives' suggestions that they add sanitation and running water in company housing to their list of strike demands. In mid-film, after an injunction forbade the men to picket, the women fought against their husbands' male chauvinist attitudes and won their permission to take their places on the picket line. By the end of the movie the women had been empowered by their crucial role in maintaining the strike and the men, who had taken care of their homes and children while their wives continued the strike, appreciated the importance of the women's work and their demands for better company housing.

Throughout, *Salt of the Earth* focused on the Quintero family, showing how the husband Ramon initially attempted to limit his wife Esperanza's participation in the strike and maintain his own power as head of the household. Against her husband's wishes Esperanza became a leader in the strike and for the first time forged a life for herself outside of her household. Although this action initially led to discord between them, Esperanza's political successes eventually persuaded Ramon to accept her new role and, by extension, to live according to a new model of family life. To illustrate his realization that male chauvinism could only retard the progress of the union's struggle, Ramon says to Esperanza at the strikers' victory in the closing scene of the film, "Thank you for your dignity. You were right. Together we can push everything up with us as we go."[64]

*Salt of the Earth* maintained the Communist tradition of using oppositional culture to portray women as strong and herioc figures, but it also incorporated Communists' new insights about the importance of transforming personal relationships between individual men and women. Because of the importance of the political messages emphasized in the film, everyone involved in the production process persevered in the face of enormous anti-Communist opposition. The Pathé Laboratory canceled its contract to process the film and local businessmen in New Mexico boycotted the production. HUAC member Donald Jackson denounced *Salt of the Earth* on the floor of the House, promising to "do everything in my power to prevent the showing of this Communist-made film in the theaters of America." Immigration and Naturalization Service officials arrested Mexican actress Rosa Revueltas, who had been cast in the lead role, and held her without bail in El Paso, Texas. On location in Grant County, New Mexico, local anti-Communist vigilantes set up loudspeakers to play patriotic music and threatened an armed attack on the ranch where the filming was taking place.[65]

Despite these and numerous other obstacles encountered during processing and editing, Jarrico, Wilson, and Biberman refused to give up their fight and went deep into debt in order to complete *Salt of the Earth* in 1953. But once the film was ready to exhibit they faced still more obstructions. Newspapers and radio stations refused their advertising, theater owners refused to book it, and International Alliance of Theatrical Stage Employees projectionists refused to run it. Effectively hindered by these efforts to censor their work, Jarrico, Wilson, and Biberman finally arranged showings of the film in only fourteen theaters between January and September 1954, making *Salt of the Earth* a commercial disaster. As historian Ellen Schrecker points out, their tenacity attests to the strength of their political convictions.[66] According to Wilson, the movie played primarily in theaters on the East and West coasts, most frequently in New York and California. It also got bookings at three theaters in New Mexico, in Silver City, Arbada, and La Habra. Several other theaters in New York and California expressed interest in the film and even signed contracts but backed out at the last minute because of pressure from the major motion picture distributors.[67]

Few reviewers liked the movie. Critic Pauline Kael dismissed it as "clear a piece of Communist propaganda as we have had in many years," and groups such as the American Legion warned Americans that they should "guard against one of the most vicious propaganda films ever distributed in the United States." Nevertheless, neither warnings issued by mainstream critics and conservative patriotic organizations nor protests that occurred outside theaters showing the film prevented Communists and progressives from attending in droves. In the two New York theaters where it was shown, it played continuously all day long to accommodate all those who wanted to see it.[68]

CP commentators on the film included David Platt, Betty Millard, and Elizabeth Gurley Flynn, all of whom gave it the highest praise.[69] The film had a significant impact on those rank-and-filers who saw it as well. When David Platt interviewed progressive workers who had seen the movie, they all commented on the power of its anti–male chauvinist message.[70] In May 1954, Saul Gross wrote to the editor of the *Daily Worker* to report that he had taken his fourteen-year-old son to see the film and that even he had been "completely involved in the happenings being recounted on the screen."[71] "After we left," Gross wrote, "he asked questions about the background of the film and we had a discussion about the events portrayed in it, especially the part played by the women." Another woman commented to the paper after viewing the film, "I have been so emotionally stirred I am all washed out and shaking. I have never seen any film deal with women in the way this one did."[72]

*Salt of the Earth* stands today as one of the most explicitly feminist cultural creations to come out of the predominantly antifeminist 1950s. It shows that the Communist Party and its supporters did not ignore the personal and cultural aspects of women's oppression and that they actually took such concerns very seriously. Many second-wave feminists who saw the film for the first time in the early 1970s were mystified about the origins of its feminist message. They "expressed surprise that so 'old' a film should portray with such passionate comprehension the sometimes conflicting claims of feminist, ethnic and class consciousness." But the film was a direct reflection of Communists' efforts to develop their understanding of the relationships among class, gender, and race and to politicize culture and personal life in the decade between 1946 and 1956.[73] It revealed the impressive progress that Communists had made by the mid-1950s in their struggles to create cultural artifacts that empowered women, to educate their supporters about the politics of individual relationships, and to promote an alternative subculture that abandoned patriarchal customs and modeled egalitarian family life for all those who were exposed to it.

Despite all these apparent successes, however, Communists were never able to formulate an answer to the woman question that satisfied everyone. After Kruschev's revelations about Stalin in 1956 led the Communist Party to initiate a systematic reevaluation of the organization's past policies and practices, many women and men wrote to the *Worker* and *Daily Worker* to emphasize the Party's deep need to reexamine its work on women as well as its orientation to the working class and the Soviet Union. In the *Sixteenth National Convention Discussion Bulletin* a letter nearly a full page long by E.R.R., from Minnesota, under the bold headline "Needed: Still Newer Look at Women's Problems," called the CP "guilty of serious weakness on this score."[74]

Throughout that year, CP publications were fuller than ever of discussion and debates about sexual harassment in Party settings; male supremacy in the home and in the Party; the politics of housework; the difficulties women had combining work, family, and politics; progressive men's failure to free themselves of male chauvinist attitudes and work to free their families of hierarchy and authoritarianism; and the true extent to which women in the Soviet Union had been liberated.[75] One writer went as far as to suggest that even the phrase "strengthening the Party's approach to women" was problematic because it is impossible to strengthen a subject about which "there is no discussion at all."[76] Statements like this one were not unique. They made it clear that many progressives believed that the Party still had a long way to go before it could claim that Communists had solved women's problems. But the debates of 1956 also made it clear that many Communists and their supporters believed that the Party's efforts to create a new and more democratic structure after 1956 would provide a long-awaited opportunity to push the struggle for women's liberation further than ever before.

UNFORTUNATELY FOR THOSE COMMUNISTS who were interested in women's liberation, 1956 proved to be the year that the Communist Party finally ceased to be a significant influence in U.S. politics and culture. It was not, as many had hoped, a renaissance for the Communist movement. By the end of that year the dual influences of McCarthyism and top Communist leaders' continued allegiance to the Soviet Union led all but the most dedicated members of the CP to resign from the organization.

In the wake of 1956 many former Communists even renounced their socialist politics altogether. But the progressive women who recognized that their oppression stemmed from cultural norms and attitudes as well as from economic sources, who applied their new knowledge about women's oppression and male supremacy to their home and family lives, and who realized that their personal problems might have political solutions refused to abandon their newly raised gender consciousness. In fact, during the dozen or so years between the demise of the Old Left and the birth of the women's liberation movement many of these women continued to act on their progressive gender politics in numerous ways. Although they often did so quietly and as individuals rather than in groups identified as Communist or feminist, progressive women managed to carry significant elements of the Communist Party's analysis of the woman question across the void of the 1950s. Ultimately, they passed on their ideas, through various means, to the next generation of feminists.

# III
# CONNECTIONS

# 7 Old Left Feminism, the Second Wave, and Beyond

In 1972, ELEANOR FLEXNER spoke with journalist Ann Shanahan in Northampton, Massachusetts, about her contributions and approaches to women's history and feminism. At one point in their conversation Flexner confessed to Shanahan that "one of the things that bothers me is that many women's liberation spokesmen don't give any credit to the people who laid the foundation for them." She also conceded that although "many ideas of the women's liberation movement are not just hatched . . . [they] are given new clout by the movement."[1] As one of the women who participated in the postwar efforts to broaden the Old Left's approach to women, Flexner could clearly see that she, along with women such as Susan Anthony, Claudia Jones, Betty Millard, and others, originated many of the ideas that younger feminists claimed as their own. But she also recognized that although progressive women developed an important new framework for understanding women's oppression and working toward women's liberation, their ties to the Communist movement also limited their efforts to spread their ideas or win others to their point of view.

It is both interesting and ironic that while Flexner expressed bitterness about feminists' failure to recognize Old Left women's contributions to the women's movement, she also continued to conceal both her ties to the CP and the fact that she had gained much of her knowledge about women's oppression and women's history through her years as a writer and teacher in the Communist movement. When Shanahan asked Flexner in the 1972 interview how she came to write *Century of Struggle*, Flexner explained that "in 1954 [she] went looking for a book about the women's rights movement in this country." When she found "that particular shelf was bare," she decided to write the book herself. Even when she spoke with interviewer Jacqueline Van Voris in the late 1970s, Flexner still insisted that she could not really recall when she became interested in the history of the women's movement but said she thought it had been around 1950, when she "started buying books about it." Flexner finally admitted to Van Voris in a 1982 interview that she attributed her "concern and interest in women" to her "connection with the radical movement in the 1930s," to the Congress of American Women, and to her associations with Elizabeth Gurley Flynn and Claudia Jones. She came out as an ex-Communist to Van Voris but, because of the persistent legacy of McCarthyism, felt unable to reveal her political background more publicly. Although various historians speculated about her radical past in the early 1990s, it was not until after her death in 1995 that Flexner's papers confirmed the origins of her race- and class-conscious feminist framework and her path-breaking book.[2]

Flexner's history is not unique. She, along with Eve Merriam, Gerda Lerner, and other participants in the Communist movement, played a part in creating a new framework for understanding women's oppression, a new terminology for expressing it, and a new literature on women's history. Alongside *Century of Struggle* their work ultimately played a major role in shaping both the second wave of the women's movement and the discipline of women's history. But these pioneers did not explicitly discuss the origins of their ideas.[3] Understandably cautious about damaging their reputations as respectable writers and citizens, Flexner, Lerner, Merriam, and many other lesser-known women quietly continued in the 1950s and 1960s to articulate the feminism they had fashioned in the Old Left as writers, parents, and activists. In this way they preserved the tradition of progressive feminism in the United States through the hostile McCarthy era and helped to ignite the new feminist movement that flourished after the 1960s.

When a new radical women's movement began to coalesce within the Civil Rights and student movements, young women activists applied the New Left's analysis of oppression to their own lives and realized that they, like African Americans and other minority groups, occupied an oppressed position in American society.[4] Although it was loosely organized and composed primarily of local collective structures, it was not long before this new movement achieved national influence. By the early 1970s a broad-based women's movement consisting of radicals and liberals attracted thousands of women who worked both inside and outside the formal political arena to challenge legal and political discrimination against women, sexist cultural attitudes and assumptions, and male chauvinism in the family and personal relationships. Calling their movement the "second wave" of American feminism these women believed that they rekindled a struggle that had been dormant since the suffrage victory in 1920. They believed they pioneered the concept that the personal is political.[5] Many second-wave feminists probably would have found the suggestion that they were building upon a foundation laid in part by a Communist women's movement in the 1940s and 1950s quite laughable, even absurd.

Certainly when the political climate shifted and radical activism reemerged in the 1960s after nearly twenty years of reaction and repression, the Communist Party, as an organization, was in no position to influence the new movements directly. Not only had McCarthyism and Stalinism decimated and discredited the CP, but 1960s activists felt vulnerable to red-baiting and carefully distinguished themselves from the progressive movements of the past. When they wrote the Port Huron Statement in 1963, for example, founders of Students for a Democratic Society (SDS) quite consciously called their movement the "New Left" to differentiate themselves from the Communist-dominated Old Left of the 1930s, 1940s, and 1950s.[6] Despite such efforts, 1960s movements could not elude the influence of progressive activism that preceded them. The Communist Party itself was not a significant political force by the 1960s, but important elements of its materialist analyses of race, class, and imperialism survived into that decade. Not surprisingly, the Party's framework for explaining women's oppression and achieving women's liberation also persisted into the 1960s, albeit only in parts and pieces. In a social and political context in which awareness of women's oppression was virtually nonexistent, however, the CP's work on the woman question provided younger feminists with a foundation upon which they could build their own version of a women's liberation movement.

The Old Left's legacy for the women's liberation movement of the 1960s and 1970s included concepts and terminology for explaining women's oppression and women's liberation and ideology about the importance of race and class differences among women. It also contained an analysis that stressed the political nature of women's so-called personal problems and a framework for conceptualizing women's history as a means of inspiring support for their ongoing struggles. Communist feminists transmitted these components of their work on the woman question to the next generation of feminist activists in three ways. They did so indirectly as radical intellectuals who wrote about women's history and women's experiences in the late 1950s and 1960s and generated a small body of literature that helped the women's movement shape its agenda and guide its future struggles. Second, Communist parents worked to model gender equality in family life and political activity, discussed politics at the dinner table, and encouraged their children to question the world around them. In doing so, they nurtured directly the activists who would build the movements of the 1960s. Finally, as seasoned activists some progressive women and men directly influenced the women's movement as informal consultants to feminists who sought information and advice about how the struggles of the past might be relevant to their current concerns and issues and about how to deal with the intersections between gender, race, and class. Occasionally these veteran activists even served as heroines of feminist activism from days gone by.

## Indirect Influences

The Communist Party's work on women's issues in the 1940s and 1950s laid important groundwork for the women's movement of the 1960s and 1970s, but it is no wonder that most young feminists lacked awareness about the origins of the concepts and vocabulary they used to frame their positions. Significant aspects of the Communist Party's influence on the women's movement did not come directly from the organization itself; rather, that influence was transmitted indirectly through individuals who had been politicized in CP circles in the 1930s, 1940s, and 1950s and who continued to act on their commitments to women's liberation even after they left the Party's milieu. Because anti-Communists so thoroughly stigmatized Communism after World War II, however, many of these individuals chose not to disclose their progressive histories, and some—such as Betty Friedan— went to considerable lengths to conceal their connections with the Communist movement.[7] A few of the older women and men who participated in the movement of the 1960s and 1970s openly discussed their ties to the CP, but the majority understandably preferred not to acknowledge their intellectual and political debts to the progressive movement and culture of the 1930s, 1940s, and 1950s.

Women such as Eve Merriam, Eleanor Flexner, Aileen Kraditor, and Gerda Lerner—all of whom had been active in the Communist Party or in affiliated organizations such as the Congress of American Women (and sometimes both)—survived the repressive 1950s and early 1960s by building upon the analyses of women's oppression and women's history they had learned from the Old Left and publishing new works about women's lives and their contributions to the social justice movements of the past. In the mid-1960s, when feminists began to look for writings about women's history and women's experiences that could validate their grievances and protests and suggest ways to solve their problems, these and other authors had already created a small body of literature shaped by the Communist movement's perspectives on women's oppression and the interplay of gender, race, and class in women's lives and historic struggles. These works helped to quench feminists' thirst for knowledge about women's movements of the past. Perhaps more important, they transmitted Communists' analysis about the importance of race and class differences among women to the new movement that was, by and large, still white and middle class. By developing and refining the approach to women's history they had learned from the Old Left and sustaining it into the 1960s, Merriam, Flexner, Kraditor, and Lerner all laid the foundation for the discipline of women's history that grew up alongside the women's movement of the 1960s and

1970s and transformed historical writing and teaching in the 1970s, 1980s, and 1990s.

Poet and writer Eve Merriam was one of the major literary figures writing about women in the decade before the women's liberation movement emerged. The nature of Merriam's connections to the Communist movement are not entirely clear. She did not discuss them openly during her life and there are no organizational records available that indicate whether she was or was not ever a formal member of the Communist Party. But the question of Merriam's membership in the Party is not relevant, for, even if she never joined the CP, she was deeply involved in its activities and culture in the decade after World War II. As a consistent participant in courses and forums on the woman question at the Jefferson School of Social Sciences, one of the authors of the musical revue *Singing of Women,* a writer for *Masses and Mainstream,* and the author of frequent letters to the editors of the *Worker* and *Daily Worker* in the late 1940s and 1950s, Merriam was not only a student of the Communist movement's evolving analysis of women's oppression but one of the people who helped to shape it.[8] Until the end of the fifties, Merriam wrote letters to the editor of the *Worker.* In March 1959 she wrote to correct columnist Mike Gold for his puritanical attitudes about sex, insisting that "sexual freedom for women has been a vital part of the emancipation movement" and that "to consider it as totally removed from the main arena [of struggle] is just as incorrect as considering it the be-all and end-all of life."[9]

Communist sensibilities about race and class shaped much of Merriam's work in the 1940s and later. In 1956, for example, she published a volume of poetry entitled *Montgomery, Alabama, Money, Mississippi, and Other Places* that included poems such as "The Carpenter in Alabama," "Miss Lucy," "The Elderly Walking Woman," and "Bus Boycott" that honored the African American working people who were beginning to resist racism and stand up for their civil rights in the South.[10] She was passionate about all the issues that progressives supported in the postwar era, but as one of the women who developed the CP's new position on the woman question, Merriam made writing about women one of her top priorities in the 1950s and later. In 1958 she published a new volume of poetry, *The Double Bed from the Feminine Side,* which included poems about women's bittersweet feelings regarding marriage, childbearing and child rearing, domesticity, and sexuality. The book reflected the Communist movement's analysis of women's oppression as it exposed and condemned the ways that male supremacy in the culture and the family prevented women from living as fully human wives and mothers.[11]

In 1962, Merriam again attempted to popularize the progressive view of women's oppression when she published *After Nora Slammed the Door: American Women in the 1960s, the Unfinished Revolution.* This critique of U.S. women's position in the late twentieth century refuted the myths that women dominate men, that they are naturally submissive and dependent, and that their proper place is in the home. Merriam decried the prevalence of sexism in traditional customs, mass culture, and language patterns. She called for women to demand "radical social changes" including "public babysitter services" and "public houseworkers" in order to "do away with the very real social and economic restrictions that are still set as roadblocks in [their] emancipation path." In other words, even before the publication of Betty Friedan's *The Feminine Mystique* in 1963, Merriam challenged the notion that women could be fulfilled exclusively through their roles as consumers, mothers, and suburban housewives.[12]

Eve Merriam's works never achieved the popularity and recognition that Friedan's did in the early 1960s, but many young feminists of that era read and learned from them. By the early 1970s both Merriam's books and her analysis of the woman question were widely known among supporters of women's liberation because of the efforts of influential feminists such as Lucinda Cisler and others who called Merriam's work "especially worthwhile," praised it for its "incisive critique" and "biting commentary on the present (past? not yet) role and status of women in the United States," and encouraged young women to use Merriam's books to broaden their understanding of women's oppression.[13] As a writer who criticized the status quo for women and proposed radical actions such as the institution of communal living arrangements, the passage of a "GI Bill for mothers," and a "personal strike campaign" against the instruments of mass culture that sold "sex as a commodity and marriage as merchandise," Eve Merriam played a critical role in transmitting the Old Left's materialist analysis of women's oppression and strategies for women's liberation to the second wave of the women's movement.[14]

Unlike Merriam, pioneering women's historian Eleanor Flexner's ties to the Communist movement are well-documented. Flexner joined the Communist Party in 1936, served as secretary of the CAW and as chairman of its Editorial Board in the late 1940s, and taught courses on the woman question at the Jefferson School in the early 1950s.[15] In letters to her friend and former comrade Bertha Reynolds, Flexner wrote about the pain she felt as she left the Party's all-encompassing environment in 1956 and consistently asked to borrow her copies of CP publications such as *Political Affairs* so that she could keep current with Communists' debates and discussions in the years that followed her departure.[16]

As part of the long process of withdrawing from the Communist move-

Billie Jean King, Susan B. Anthony II, Bella Abzug, Sylvia Ortiz, Peggy Kokernot, Michele Cearcy, and Betty Friedan marching at the International Women's Year Conference opening, Houston, 1977. Diana Mara Henry, 1978.

ment Eleanor Flexner moved from New York City to Northampton, Massachusetts. With money she inherited after her mother's death, Flexner occupied herself for the rest of the 1950s by researching and writing *Century of Struggle,* which she published in 1959. In a 1988 interview with Ellen DuBois, Flexner denied that she wrote *Century of Struggle* because of her parents' involvement in the suffrage movement. Nevertheless, she was hardly unaware of the activities that women had undertaken to expand their civil rights between the 1840s and the 1920s.[17] She was actually one of a minority of women of her generation who knew a great deal about the American women's rights tradition because of her involvement in groups such as the Congress of American Women and the Communist Party. Far from having to rediscover or reinvent the feminist tradition on her own, Eleanor Flexner learned about it from the Congress of American Women and the regular women's history features that appeared (and that she sometimes wrote using one of her pseudonyms) in publications such as the *Worker, New Masses,* and *Masses and Mainstream.* After she left the Communist movement, Flexner concentrated on expanding and developing the ideas about the history of women's activism and the uses of women's history that she had learned from Communist writers in the 1940s and early 1950s. The culmination of years of scholarly research and writing, Flexner's *Century of*

*Struggle* successfully legitimized and disseminated the Old Left's work on women's history after the Communist Party was no longer in a position to do so itself.

Eleanor Flexner's analysis of the woman's rights movement in *Century of Struggle* in 1959 was not entirely original. But the book was unusual because, unlike other extant works on the suffrage movement in the 1950s and 1960s, it conceived of women's rights activism broadly and included a whole variety of women's struggles in its chronology. While the standard works on suffrage began with the Seneca Falls Convention of 1848, Flexner's book began with Anne Hutchinson's struggles against the Puritan patriarchy in the 1630s.[18] In keeping with this inclusive view of woman's rights activity that she inherited from the Old Left, Flexner was careful to include white working-class heroines such as the Lowell Mill girls, the women of the Knights of Labor, and the 1909 New York shirtwaist strikers in every chapter of her book. Furthermore, like all progressives who were writing women's history in Communist publications in the 1940s and 1950s, Flexner also wrote a great deal about the links and the conflicts between women's struggles and those waged by African Americans and went to impressive lengths to include the achievements of African American women such as Sojourner Truth, Harriet Tubman, Mary Church Terrell, and Ida B. Wells throughout her narrative. Authors of the major works on the suffrage movement published prior to *Century of Struggle* wrote primarily to applaud their own victories, but Flexner wrote her history of suffrage to honor all the women who participated in the mass movements of the nineteenth and early twentieth centuries. She hoped that her book might someday serve as a guide for women's future struggles to "take part in the political and social life of their time and to stand on a plane of equal human dignity with men in their personal relationships."[19]

Except for a few male reviewers who pronounced *Century of Struggle* "too partisan" and too sympathetic to "feminists' statements on the extent of their oppression," many who read the first edition of the book regarded it as a notable scholarly and analytical achievement.[20] Because Flexner had somehow been able to keep her ties with the Communist movement under wraps, most reviewers evaluated the book on its own merits. Unlike works by the radical historian Herbert Aptheker, which reviewers dismissed out of hand as Communist propaganda in this period, *Century of Struggle* gained significant exposure in the mainstream book market. But although Flexner's work received some critical attention when it first appeared in print in 1959, *Century of Struggle* did not become a powerfully influential work until the later 1960s.

Probably not coincidentally, given her political background, Betty

Friedan relied heavily on Flexner's research for the material on women's history that she included in *The Feminine Mystique*.[21] Calling the book "the definitive history of the woman's rights movement in the United States," Friedan argued that *Century of Struggle* should be "required reading for every girl admitted to a U.S. college."[22] Later, once the women's liberation movement had begun to flourish in the United States, many young feminists who were searching for information about women's movements of the past turned to Flexner's book for information. Soon feminist groups and publications were calling the book "first-rate" and urging everyone to read it. Nearly everyone did.[23]

According to feminist historian Ellen DuBois, "We all read *Century of Struggle*, but so closely did our perspective come to Flexner's that I think, ironically, we simply absorbed her work without fully appreciating how original and innovative it was." In retrospect, however, DuBois also realized that "to the degree that the 'sex/class/race' framework is a feminist commonplace now, Eleanor Flexner's historical vision deserves some of the credit."[24] Indeed, Flexner's inclusive vision of women's rights struggles conveyed the Old Left's emphasis on the intersections of sex, race, and class to young feminists and provided their new movement with black and white working-class heroines as well as educating them about Elizabeth Cady Stanton, Susan B. Anthony, and the other standard-bearers of American feminism.

Flexner's *Century of Struggle* laid much of the important groundwork for the modern discipline of women's history, but several other authors of pioneering works of women's history published in the 1960s before the resurgence of the women's movement also came out of the progressive movement of the 1940s and 1950s. Historian Aileen Kraditor, author of *The Ideas of the Woman Suffrage Movement*, which detailed the racism and classism of many American suffragists, and *Up from the Pedestal: Selected Writings in the History of American Feminism*, which compiled primary sources by early women activists, was a member of the Communist Party from 1947 until 1958, that is, during the time CP women were revolutionizing the way the Party dealt with women's oppression, liberation, and history.[25]

Gerda Lerner, author of *The Grimke Sisters from South Carolina: Rebels against Slavery*, which documented the links between the abolitionist movement and the woman's rights movement, was an active member of the Congress of American Women in the late 1940s. In the acknowledgments of her book Lerner thanked Virginia Brodine, a CAW officer in New York, for "arousing [her] interest in the contribution of women to American history" and for "inspiring the writing of this book."[26]

Even Eve Merriam occasionally stepped outside her usual genre and contributed to the new literature on women's history. In addition to her 1951 collaboration with Lerner on the women's history musical *Singing of Women,* Merriam also wrote a biography of the nineteenth-century woman poet and activist Emma Lazarus, published in 1956, and edited *Growing Up Female in America,* an anthology of primary source material about ten American women, including ex-slave Susie King Taylor, labor organizer "Mother" Mary Jones, and Winnebago Indian Mountain Wolf Woman, published in 1971.[27] As Old Left feminists these women all helped to preserve progressives' work on women in a period when almost no one thought such work was important. During the resurgence of feminism in the late 1960s, their work shaped younger women's thinking about the long tradition of radical women's activism that preceded them and influenced the direction women's activism and women's history would take in the future.

## Direct Influences

When New Left organizations such as SDS burst onto the American political scene in the early 1960s, their members were by-and-large too young to have had their own independent affiliations with the Old Left.[28] It was relatively unusual for adults politicized by the Old Left to become wholehearted supporters of the New Left, but "red-diaper babies," women and men whose parents had been members or supporters of organizations such as the Communist Party between 1930 and 1960, participated in large numbers in the Civil Rights movement, in SDS, and the antiwar movement.[29]

Because red-diaper babies grew up listening to folk music, attending demonstrations with their parents, and talking politics at the dinner table, it is not surprising that so many of them participated in events such as the Berkeley Free Speech movement or activities like the Student Nonviolent Coordinating Committee's 1964 voter registration program, the Mississippi Freedom Summer campaign. Nor is it surprising that the daughters of radical women and men served as one important channel through which elements of the Old Left's work on the woman question could be transmitted across the void of the 1950s. These women grew up in families that challenged the gender norms of the 1950s and they expected to be taken seriously and treated equally in New left politics and culture. Many were central in early discussions about the unfair treatment applied to women within organizations such as SDS. Many also took part in and shaped the movement's early attempts to articulate the nature and sources of women's oppression and, as a result, became key figures in the first women's liberation groups.[30]

Most red-diaper babies had not been formally schooled in the Old Left's analysis of the woman question and most were probably not even aware of the attention that some Communist women and their allies devoted to the issue of women's liberation in the 1940s and 1950s. But unlike their more conventional counterparts in the New Left, red-diaper babies knew that there was a woman question. For the most part they probably had not been exposed to theoretical debates like those that swirled around Mary Inman's contention that housewives performed productive labor or those that accompanied the CP's reckoning with and ultimate rejection of Freud. Like so many of the other battles that distinguished the Old Left experience, these fairly esoteric controversies caused only short-lived ferment before they quickly fell into obscurity. Yet their mothers had been strong female role models and their parents frequently exposed them to discussions about the problems of women's subordination in capitalist society and in the family. By raising their children with an awareness that women were both oppressed and capable of resisting their oppression, progressive women transmitted their work for women's emancipation into the 1960s and 1970s.[31]

Children of Communists who attended the Red Diaper Baby conferences held in New Hampshire in 1982 and 1983 remembered that their activist mothers and other leftist women were the most significant political role models they had. Many also recalled that their parents encouraged them to believe that they could become anything they wanted to be.[32] A large number of these women reported that their parents and other progressive adults talked to them routinely about women's issues. One participant named Kathy remembered "always being told that ideologically [women] were equal to men" and hearing from her father that "the Bible was a book written by men to oppress women." Similarly, other red-diaper daughters report that their parents exposed them frequently to discussions about various aspects of the woman question. Linda Gordon and Rosalyn Baxandall both recall their parents disparaging the actions of various men they knew as male chauvinist, and Norma Allen remembers that her mother attended a Communist women's group in their New Jersey hometown in which they read the Marxist classics on women and discussed them. Like these women, most daughters of the Old Left probably grew up with some awareness of women's oppression and some familiarity with the CP's terms and concepts for discussing the issue including "male chauvinism," "male supremacy," "male superiority," "women's oppression," and "women's liberation."[33]

Red-diaper babies heard their parents talking about the problems of women's oppression and male supremacy. Some of them also watched their parents work to build egalitarian relationships with one another and struggle to achieve their goal of a balanced family life in which women and men, mothers and fathers both contributed equally. Certainly not all Communist families achieved the Party's vision of egalitarian marriage and family life—many probably never even tried to avoid traditional patriarchal assumptions and practices—but more than a few Communist daughters recall that their parents "dealt with the woman question very well in terms of day-to-day task breakdown" and that their mothers and the other women in their circles recognized the inseparability of the personal and the political.[34] Linda Gordon, for example, remembered that her father was a "very feminist man" who "did a tremendous amount of cleaning and a certain amount of cooking" and that she "was certainly never discriminated against in relation to [her] younger brothers." Similarly, Debra, a participant in the Red Diaper Baby conferences, recalled that her father was a "liberated, nonchauvinistic man." Rosalyn Baxandall reports that her mother kept her maiden name and that both her mother and grandmother discussed their past abortions with her and her sisters when they were growing up. Jane Lazarre wrote about Communist fathers teaching their children the need for political discipline and Communist mothers working to create "a consistent personal life." Mothers wanted, she said, to make sure their children valued "what was personal, concrete, and internal along with the essential dialogues of history we were learning at our father's knees."[35]

In this same vein, a Red Diaper Baby Conference participant named Lois concluded that "The women ended up exemplifying the way to behave and—this is may be simplifying it but it sounds like what people are saying—the men passed along the theory. The women presented the [Party's] values and acted on the values and developed relationships and networks."[36] Their parents expressed the view that personal relationships and family life could not be separated from ideology about the necessity of ending exploitation and inequality, so significant numbers of red-diaper babies grew up with the knowledge that housework, motherhood, and sexuality were not just personal matters to be worked out by individuals. These issues, they realized, were political ones that required attention from any activists who were truly committed to reshaping the culture and institutions that dominated capitalist America.

When Communists' daughters became active in the New Left movements of the 1960s, they expected to be treated as equals to men both in personal and political settings. Rosalyn Baxandall indicated, for example, that because of her upbringing she "did expect men not to be male chauvinists." Linda Gordon concurred that because of the relative egalitarianism in her family she did not expect to have to deal with sexism in her adult life. When these women encountered the intense male superiority that characterized much of the New Left many of them were shocked. "In the movement I certainly got a heavy dose of men treating women very poorly," Baxandall recalled. "We were doing most of the organizing . . . we were the ones talking to people, going door to door. Then when it came to talking they were talking, they were writing. So that was a pretty big awakening."[37]

If they were often surprised by the ways that New Left men treated women, however, it did not take these second- and sometimes third-generation radical women long to challenge such dynamics. They had heard women's subordination discussed as they grew up, so red-diaper babies had concepts to identify, words to name, and strategies to confront women's oppression when they experienced it themselves. It is not coincidental that Old Left terms such as "women's oppression," "women's liberation," "women's movement," "male supremacy," "male chauvinism," and "male superiority," all reappear in the first articles about women in *New Left Notes,* in SDS's 1968 "National Resolution on Women," and in early pamphlets and papers from the women's liberation movement.[38] Nor is it coincidental that Communists' debates over the politics of housework, child-rearing, and male-female relationships from the 1940s and 1950s reemerged, albeit in a somewhat revised form, in the New Left and in the women's movement of the 1960s and 1970s. Red-diaper babies such as Rosalyn Baxandall, Kathie (Amatniak) Sarachild, Norma Allen, Anne Froines, Anne Forer, Dinky Romilly —and numerous others who do not openly discuss their ties to the Old Left—served as key feminist leaders in the 1960s and constituted an important link between the Communist movement and the women's movement.[39] These women brought Old Left terms and ideas with them to the New Left and revived them in their own struggles to name the historic patterns of male domination that permeated every aspect of women's lives and to outline the kind of radical, systemic change that was necessary to defeat it.[40]

Finally, even "consciousness raising," the process of "going around the room and rapping" that many second-wave feminists employed to expose the politics of personal experience and build new theories and strategies for ending sexism, came to the women's movement through the medium of red-diaper babies. Anne Forer explains that when she went to an early women's liberation meeting in 1967, she thought about how "In the Old Left . . . they used to say that workers don't know they're oppressed so we have to raise their consciousness." With that in mind she suggested that everyone present give "an example from their own life on how they experienced oppression as a woman" because she needed "to hear it to raise her own consciousness." Kathie Sarachild, sitting behind Forer in the meeting, seized on the term *consciousness raising* and "sort of made it an institution."

Over the next several years Kathie Sarachild offered workshops on con-

sciousness raising (which also had some things in common with the Communists' practice of criticism and self-criticism) and, along with others in
the group Redstockings, mimeographed hundreds of sheets of suggested
consciousness-raising topics that "found their way around the country
where they were used as guidelines for new groups that were forming." By
1972 some chapters of the National Organization for Women had begun to
offer "consciousness-raising nights." The first issue of *Ms.*, published in July
1972, included instructions about how to start a consciousness-raising
group, along with a list of sample topics.

Ultimately, consciousness raising proved an incredibly useful tool for
building the women's movement. Just as some form of consciousness raising had enable progressive workers in the thirties and forties to identify their
collective oppression and recognize their potential power, feminist consciousness raising provided women with a technique for articulating their
collective grievances and formulating their demands. In part through
consciousness raising, feminist language and insights spread into mainstream America and, as Susan Brownmiller has suggested, "many original
perceptions that the pioneer consciousness-raising groups had struggled to
express would become received information, routine and unexceptional,
to a new generation that would wonder what the fuss and excitement was
all about."[41]

Though the threat of anti-Communism and the shame of Stalinism led
many Old Left progressives who later influenced the New Left to conceal
their radical pasts, not everyone whose activism spanned from the Old Left
to the New obscured their political history. Numerous people with ties to
the Communist movement such as Herbert Aptheker, Florence Luscomb,
Marge Franz, Hodee Edwards, and Dorothy Healey sometimes joined in
and supported feminist activities as mentors and as activists while being
quite open about their associations with the Old Left.[42]

Similarly, not all young feminists dismissed Communism as absolutely
outmoded and irrelevant to their concerns. More than a few women who
discovered feminism in the late 1960s and early 1970s sought out Old Left
activists for advice and information, and it was not unusual for young feminists to adopt openly Communist cultural artifacts and traditions as important elements of the women's movement. In 1968, for example, Berkeley feminist Laura X consulted with former Communists William and Tania
Mandel about the American origins of International Women's Day. After
she learned about the history of the holiday from the Mandels and from CP
literature such as Claudia Jones's article "International Women's Day and
the Struggle for Peace," she revived International Women's Day celebrations

in Berkeley in 1969.[43] Later, using her self-published women's history document *Women in World History* and her own feminist newsletter *SPAZM*, Laura X spread the word about International Women's Day to feminists around the country. By 1970 women's liberation groups throughout the nation commemorated the holiday.[44]

In fall 1968, Helen Kritzler, one of the organizers of the Chicago Conference on Women's Liberation, wrote to Mary Inman to ask for copies of her work, and in spring 1969, Susanna Maes, the organizer of a feminist Mother's Day rally in Los Angeles, wrote to Inman to ask if she would be willing to speak about "capitalism and its role in the creation of the woman problem." In the late 1960s also, many young feminists such as Laura X who had contacts with the Old Left rediscovered and revived the 1950s film *Salt of the Earth*.[45] From 1968 into the 1970s women's movement organizations sponsored showings of the film at women's conferences and at many colleges and universities.[46] In all of these ways, early second-wave feminists looked directly to the Old Left's approach to the woman question to help them form their own analysis of women's oppression and their own strategies for women's liberation.

Finally, at least two younger feminists who made critical contributions to the women's movement's thinking about the intersections of race, class, and gender were ideologically rooted in the Old Left even though they also participated, along with their radical contemporaries, in a variety of New Left and civil rights activities. In 1981, Angela Davis, well-known throughout the United States for her prominent role in the CP, her work with the Black Panthers, and her contested appointment to the philosophy faculty at the University of California, published *Women, Race, and Class*. Davis had grown up in Alabama in a middle-class family whose social circle included Communist activists. She won a scholarship to attend the radical Elizabeth Irwin High School in New York City and during the early 1960s she lived with well-known progressives Reverend William Melish and Mary Jane Melish, who had served as an officer of the Brooklyn chapter of the Congress of American Women and a member of the national CAW's advisory council.[47] *Women, Race and Class* developed and expanded upon arguments Communists had long been making about the differences between white and black women's oppressions, the racism of the mainstream women's movement, and the contributions of African American and Communist women to American struggles for women's emancipation.[48] Similarly, in 1982, Bettina Aptheker, daughter of Communist leader Herbert Aptheker and Coordinator of Women's Studies at the University of California–Santa Cruz, published *Woman's Legacy: Essays on Race, Sex, and Class in American History,* which built upon the Old Left's analysis of African American women's "triple oppression" and further documented the links Communists had originally proposed between black liberation and women's liberation struggles.[49] Both Davis's and Aptheker's books, along with Eleanor Flexner's *Century of Struggle,* Aileen Kraditor's *The Ideas of the Woman Suffrage Movement,* and Gerda Lerner's *The Grimke Sisters* and *Black Women in White America,* had tremendous influence on second-wave feminists' thinking about the importance of race and class differences among women. Using the ideas pioneered by Communists such as Claudia Jones in the late 1940s, all these Communist-influenced scholars laid the groundwork for a whole new body of feminist and scholarly literature about African American women and the historical conflicts and connections between racism and sexism, and civil rights and women's rights.[50]

Directly as well as indirectly, then, the Communist movement's political and cultural work on the woman question survived to influence the second wave of the women's movement. Many feminists rejected the Old Left as completely inadequate when it came to the woman question. Certainly, on questions of motherhood, sex, and sexual identity, Old Left feminists did not have very much to offer. When feminist theorists began to consider complex questions about women's relationship to production and Marxist theory's relevance for feminism, they turned to the original nineteenth-century writings of Marx and Engels for answers, not to twentieth-century interpretations of those sources by Mary Inman or Claudia Jones. Nevertheless, not far beneath the surface of second-wave feminists' day-to-day activities and ideas, activists and traditions that emanated from the Communist movement of the forties and fifties continued to shape the direction of the new women's movement in the 1960s and later.

## Conclusions

In November 1977 in Houston, Texas, twenty thousand feminists from around the world came together at a federally funded national conference to celebrate the United Nations International Women's Year. Among the two thousand delegates from the United States there were seven hundred women of color and four hundred women from lower-income households, clearly demonstrating that the women's movement had spread far beyond the relatively small core of white middle-class women who rekindled mass feminist activism in the late 1960s.[51] The conference opened with a march led by a contingent of celebrated feminist leaders including Billie Jean King, Bella Abzug, Sylvia Ortiz, and Betty Friedan. But between King and Abzug marched a less familiar woman with a cross around her neck. That woman was sixty-one-year-old Susan B. Anthony II, identified in the captions that accompanied photographs of the march only as Susan B. Anthony's grandniece.

In 1977 Anthony, who attended the International Women's Year Conference as a delegate from Fort Lauderdale, Florida, was in many ways very different from the young woman who had composed the Congress of American Women's "Report of the Commission on the Status of Women" and allegedly "decorated her apartment with hammers and sickles" thirty years earlier. By the time of the conference she had experienced blacklisting, deportation threats, three divorces, and a dramatic conversion to Roman Catholicism. She had also earned a doctorate in theology from St. Mary's College in South Bend, Indiana, and joined the Prayer Community, a group of Florida women who met regularly for Bible study and prayer. Despite these changes—and despite her many disagreements with second-wave feminists, especially its "sexual freedom aspects"—Anthony still saw herself as a pioneering women's rights activist, and as the author of one of the first modern women's liberation books. She still believed that "the personal just has to come before power, profits, or property, and she remained an ardent advocate for day-care centers, equal pay, birth control, every woman's ability to develop her "inner self" to the fullest.[52] Anthony revealed that she still held the fundamental political views she had formed in the 1940s when she concluded her speech to the 1977 Florida International Women's Year Conference by declaring, "Champions of women, champions of progress seek to form a more perfect union in which we can bring about the radical personal and social change needed for life, liberty and the pursuit of happiness—a society in which that happiness . . . is possible for the largest numbers of women and men."[53]

Participants and journalists at the Houston conference frequently acknowledged Anthony's presence at the history-making event. Her photograph appears alongside many of the articles written about the conference in major publications such as *Time* magazine and the *New York Times*. As these articles indicate, Anthony got this degree of recognition primarily because of her lineage and her name. That she received little or no recognition for her own contributions to the women's movement at the conference illustrates the extent to which the legacy of progressive feminists remained buried. But although very few people knew it at the time Anthony's progressive feminist work influenced Old Left activists such as Bella Abzug and Betty Friedan in the 1940s and 1950s, just as the quiet work of Flexner, Lerner, and Merriam along with Friedan, Abzug, and even Anthony herself ultimately filtered down to younger women such as Sylvia Ortiz. Perhaps as she walked arm-in-arm with her comrades and friends leading a huge and diverse march of feminists with a broad smile on her face, Anthony recognized that, in part because of her efforts, twentieth-century feminism had finally come full circle.

COMMUNIST AND PROGRESSIVE WOMEN refused to associate themselves with the self-proclaimed feminists of the 1940s and 1950s, but they did not forsake or neglect the struggle to improve women's status in these decades. Certainly the gender politics of the Communist Party after World War II were not entirely feminist by our standards today. The Party continued throughout the 1940s and 1950s to follow Soviet policy; this commitment caused American Communists to glorify women's maternal roles and prevented them from supporting birth control and abortion. Their desire to assimilate in working-class culture also led Communists to romanticize the family. Still, Communists' emphasis on the pervasiveness of women's oppression, the importance of race and class differences among women, and the need to politicize personal problems made them more radical than the women's rights–oriented feminists of the time. Communists' work shaped modern feminism. The CP's failure to organize a mass-based women's movement in the wake of World War II stemmed not so much from shortcomings in its ideological and practical treatment of women's issues, but from the anti-Communism and antifeminism that effectively isolated Communists and the progressive left from the masses of American women.

Anti-Communists might have hoped that crippling the Communist movement and silencing a vast number of progressive activists in the 1940s and 1950s could halt the progress that labor, civil rights, and other social justice struggles had made since the 1930s. But they could only obstruct progressives' formal political organizations and activities, not alter individuals' ideas about oppression in U.S. culture and society or eradicate their efforts to live out their politics in their private lives. By the 1960s, when social, economic, and political conditions finally converged to spark a mass women's movement, the Old Left in general and the CP in particular could not influence such a movement openly. But anti-Communism did not stop individual Communists and former Communists from quietly passing on their culture and beliefs as writers and parents. Many Communists and progressives broke their ties with the Communist movement in the 1950s but went on to participate, to varying degrees, in the progressive struggles that dominated the 1960s. The Communist movement's politicization of daily life articulated the cultural and personal politics that quickly became central to social justice struggles in the 1960s and beyond. Second-wave feminism stands as an excellent example of a 1960s movement that blossomed from the seeds that Communist women germinated thirty years earlier.

Second-wave feminists quickly outstripped the older Communist program for women's liberation: once they had adopted the Old Left's language to articulate the ubiquitous effects of male domination, they moved on to challenge institutions Communists regarded as inviolable such as heterosexuality, the nuclear family, and motherhood, and shocked many conventional Old Left activists in the process.[54] But even though the radical women's movement was, by the 1970s, very different from that of the 1940s and 1950s, feminists also incorporated important elements of the Communist Party's program into their agenda for women's liberation. The modern movement's vocabulary for expressing its ideas, its emphasis on the political nature of women's so-called personal problems, its use of women's history to inspire women and to gain support for their ongoing struggles, and its efforts to build feminist unity in the face of women's differences all flowed from the Old Left.

American Communists' answer to the woman question was in many ways incomplete and problematic, but their work in the 1940s and 1950s is a crucial piece of the history of the U.S. women's movement that few have recognized. Because of their importance in creating what we know as modern feminism, Communist feminists are also hugely significant for U.S. history in the last half of the twentieth century. For despite frequent discussions of its irrelevance and speculations about its death, the women's movement—in a broad sense—has revolutionized women's *and* men's lives over the last thirty years. Women and men—those who call themselves feminists and those who do not—still grapple with the questions progressive feminists raised about self-esteem, gender relations, and women's right to participate alongside men in political, economic, social, and cultural life. Their questions and their answers continue to be shaped by Communists' thinking about these issues.

Second-wave feminists rightly take credit for many of these shifts. They did, after all, successfully build a mass movement and inspire the protest that ultimately reshaped social policy and social relations. But they did not do so from scratch; they built upon and expanded feminist frameworks and strategies that Communist and progressive women forged in the 1930s and 1940s and sustained throughout the 1950s and early 1960s. Contemporary feminism could have developed without Communist feminists' influence in the 1960s and 1970s. Liberal feminists such as Dorothy Kenyon, Pauli Murray, Edith Green, and others argued for social reform to promote women's equality throughout the 1950s and supported the President's Commission on the Status of Women and Title VII of the Civil Rights Act in the 1960s. But without the Old Left's legacy of personal politics and race- and class-conscious feminism, current debates about women's status and gender relations would undoubtedly look very different. Communist and progressive women's bequest to modern feminist thought has been almost invisible since the 1940s because of McCarthyism and the Cold War, which characterized the Old Left as both dangerous and irrelevant. But now, at the beginning of the twenty-first century we can see that their struggles to politicize personal life and personalize politics built vital aspects of second-wave feminism and transformed women's and men's lives, women's history, and the social fabric of the United States.

# Notes

Introduction: Old Left Women, the U.S. Women's Movement, and the Legacy of Anti-Communism

1. Susan B. Anthony II, "Report of the Commission on the Status of Women," May 25, 1946, p. 18, in Women's International Democratic Federation Papers, Communism Collection, Sophia Smith Collection, Smith College, Northampton, Mass., box 2, folder 20a.

2. Leila J. Rupp and Verta Taylor, *Survival in the Doldrums: The American Women's Rights Movement, 1945-1960s* (New York: Oxford UP, 1987); and Elaine Tyler May, *Homeward Bound: American Families in the Cold War Era* (New York: Basic Books, 1988).

3. The term *woman question* generally refers to the Left's efforts to formulate an adequate analysis of women's oppression and women's liberation that would be consistent with its primary goals of analyzing the oppression of the working class under capitalism and preparing for class-based revolution.

4. Here I allude to Lois Scharf and Joan Jensen, eds., *Decades of Discontent: The Women's Movement, 1920-1940* (Westport, Conn.: Greenwood P, 1983).

5. I am using the term *McCarthyism* here to refer to the anti-Communist crusade imposed and supported by a variety of groups and individuals including President Harry Truman, the House Un-American Activities Committee (HUAC) and smaller un-American activities committees that existed at the state level, Republican and Democratic politicians including Joseph McCarthy, and many business and labor leaders. See Nora Sayre, *Previous Convictions: A Journey through the 1950s* (New Brunswick, N.J.: Rutgers UP, 1995), and Ellen Schrecker, *Many Are the Crimes: McCarthyism in America* (Princeton, N.J.: Princeton UP, 1998).

6. See, for example, Mari Jo Buhle, *Women and American Socialism, 1870-1920* (Champaign: U of Illinois P, 1983).

7. Nancy Cott, *The Grounding of Modern Feminism* (New Haven: Yale UP, 1988), 74.

8. Buhle, *Women and American Socialism*; Cott, *The Grounding of Modern Feminism*, 74.

9. Elsa Jane Dixler, "The Woman Question: Women and the American Communist Party, 1929-1941" (Ph.D. diss., Yale University, 1974); Robert Shaffer, "Women and the Communist Party USA, 1930-1940," *Socialist Review* 45 (May 1975): 73-118; Ellen Kay Trimberger, "Women in the Old and New Left: The Evolution of the Politics of a Personal Life," *Feminist Studies* 5 (Fall 1979): 432-50; Susan Ware, "Women on the Left: The Communist Party and Its Allies," *American Women in the 1930s: Holding Their Own* (Boston: Twayne Publishers, 1982); Van Gosse, "'To Organize in Every Neighborhood, in Every Home': The Gender Politics of American Communists between the Wars," *Radical History Review* 50 (Spring 1991): 109-41; and Rosalyn Baxandall, "The Question Seldom Asked: Women and the CPUSA," in Michael E. Brown et al., eds., *New Studies in the Politics and Culture of U.S. Communism* (New York: Monthly Review P, 1993).

10. Rupp and Taylor, *Survival in the Doldrums*; Susan Lynn, *Progressive Women*

*in Conservative Times* (New Brunswick, N.J.: Rutgers UP, 1992); Nancy Gabin, *Feminism and the Labor Movement: Women and the United Auto Workers, 1935-1975* (Ithaca: Cornell UP, 1990); Sara Evans, *Personal Politics: The Roots of Women's Liberation in the Civil Rights Movement and the New Left* (New York: Vintage Books, 1978).

11. Maurice Isserman, *If I Had a Hammer: The Death of the Old Left and the Birth of the New Left* (New York: Basic Books, 1989); John D'Emilio, *Sexual Politics, Sexual Communities: The Making of a Homosexual Minority in the United States, 1940-1970* (Chicago: U of Chicago P, 1983).

12. See Cott, *The Grounding of Modern Feminism,* chap. 8; Joan Jensen, "All Pink Sisters," in Scharf and Jensen, eds., *Decades of Discontent;* and J. Stanley Lemons, *The Woman Citizen: Social Feminism in the 1920s* (Champaign: U of Illinois P, 1973).

13. Ferdinand Lundberg and Marynia Farnham, *Modern Woman: The Lost Sex* (New York: Harper Bros., 1947), 237.

14. See Alice Echols, *Daring to Be Bad: Feminism in America, 1967-1975* (Minneapolis: U of Minnesota P, 1989), 8, and Letty Cottin Pogrebin, "The FBI Was Watching You," *Ms.,* June 1977.

15. Rupp and Taylor, *Survival in the Doldrums;* Christine Lunardini, *From Equal Suffrage to Equal Rights: Alice Paul and the National Woman's Party, 1910-1928* (New York: New York UP, 1986); and Cott, *The Grounding of Modern Feminism.*

16. Susan B. Anthony II to Mary Inman, n.d., Mary Inman Papers, Schlesinger Library, Radcliffe College, Cambridge, Mass., box 1.

17. Susan Brownmiller, *In Our Time: A Memoir of Revolution* (New York: Random House, 1999), 46-47.

18. In *The Cultural Front: The Laboring of American Culture in the Twentieth Century* (London and New York: Verso P, 1996), historian Michael Denning calls this movement the "popular front."

19. Harvey Klehr, John Earl Haynes, and Fridrikh Igorevich Firsov, *The Secret World of American Communism* (New Haven: Yale UP, 1995): Klehr, *The Heyday of American Communism: The Depression Decade* (New York: Basic Books, 1984), 415-16.

20. I rely on published and unpublished primary sources generated by both sides of the McCarthy conflict. Archival sources include individual Communist and progressive women's papers including Ella Reeve Bloor and Mary van Kleeck Papers, in the Sophia Smith Collection, Smith College, Northampton, Massachusetts; Eleanor Flexner and Mary Inman Papers, at the Schlesinger Library, Radcliffe College, Cambridge, Massachusetts; Betty Gannett Papers, at the State Historical Society of Wisconsin, at Milwaukee; Dorothy Healey Papers, in the Special Collections at California State University–Long Beach; organizational records of Communist-inspired groups such as the Congress of American Women, in the Sophia Smith Collection at Smith College, and the Women's International Democratic Federation, Communism Collection, Sophia Smith Collection; and the FBI's fragmentary compilation of documents relating to Communist "women's matters," Washington, D.C. Published sources include records compiled by the House Un-American Activities Committee, the U.S. Subversive Activities Control Board, the U.S. Department of Justice, and the FBI, and books, journals, pamphlets, and newspapers published by the Communist Party itself. For further discussion of sources, see the Essay on Sources.

Chapter 1: Building Unity amidst Diversity

1. According to the Communist Party USA entry in Mari Jo Buhle, Paul Buhle, and Dan Georgakas, *Encyclopedia of the American Left* (Champaign: U of Illinois P, 1992), the Bolshevik revolution of 1917 exacerbated existing schisms within the American Socialist Party and ultimately precipitated the factionalization of the group in 1919. Those members of the SP who opposed the organization's emphasis on change through electoral politics formed two opposing groups of Communists. The first, led by Russian Socialists, abandoned the SP in 1919 and named itself the Communist Party. The second, composed primarily of English-speaking socialists, was expelled from the SP in 1919 and formed the Communist Labor Party. The Comintern refused to recognize either group and advised them to unify. Nevertheless, for several more years the two groups continued to fight with one another and with other Left groupings, and each suffered additional schisms. In 1922 the organizational descendants of these two groups finally unified and named themselves the Workers Communist Party. In 1929 that organization became the Communist Party, USA.

2. On the CP's approach to race, see Harry Haywood, *Black Bolshevik: Autobiography of an Afro-American Communist* (Chicago: Liberator P, 1978); Nell Irvin Painter, *The Narrative of Hosea Hudson, His Life as a Negro Communist in the South* (Cambridge: Harvard UP, 1979); Mark Naison, *Communists in Harlem during the Great Depression* (New York: Grove P, 1983); Robin D. G. Kelley, *Hammer and Hoe: Alabama Communists during the Great Depression* (Chapel Hill: U of North Carolina P, 1990); Gerald Horne, "The Red and the Black: The Communist Party and African-Americans in Historical Perspective," in Brown et al., eds., *New Studies in the Politics and Culture of U.S. Communism;* and Mark Solomon, *The Cry Was Unity: Communists and African-Americans, 1917-1936* (Jackson, Miss.: UP of Mississippi, 1998).

3. According to Draper's *The Roots of American Communism,* the Communist Party, founded in 1919, averaged 24,000 dues-paying members. Language federations dominated this organization. The Russian federation had 7,000 members, the Lithuanian federation 4,400, the Ukrainian 4,000, South Slavic 2,200, Polish 1,750, Lettish 1,200, Yiddish 1,000, Hungarian 1,000, German 850, and Estonian 280. There were 1,100 non-English-speaking members not affiliated with a language federation and 1,900 English-speaking members. The Communist Labor Party, founded at the same time, had 10,000 members, fewer than 20 percent of whom were English-speaking.

4. Harvey Klehr and John Earl Haynes, *The American Communist Movement: Storming Heaven Itself* (New York: Twayne Publishers, 1992), 54. These new party units were nominally multiethnic, but, because there was so much ethnic segregation in neighborhoods and workplaces, many of them continued to be dominated by one ethnic group or another.

5. Ibid.

6. Naison, *Communists in Harlem,* 16.

7. Some of these important early African American Communists included Otto Huiswoud, Cyril Briggs, Richard Moore, Grace Campbell, and Lovett Fort-Whiteman, all of whom, according to Mark Naison, entered the movement in 1920. Naison also reports that four of these five were West Indian immigrants and that they were originally attracted to the anticolonialism of the Bolshevik Revolution, not American Communists' organizational accomplishments (ibid., 5).

8. According to Naison, "the most consistent pressure to force the U.S. Party to emphasize black issues came from the Communist International, which was thoroughly dominated by Soviet Party leaders" (ibid., 11). Both Naison and Solomon suggest that this was because national minorities in the Russian Empire had played an important role—even if they were peasants and not workers—in the success of the Soviet Revolution and that Soviet leaders "translated this strategic formula directly to the United States, where blacks represented the largest and most victimized minority group." African American Communists frequently went to the Soviet Union in the 1920s for ideological training. While they were there, these Americans participated in multiracial activities with Asians, non-European Soviet nationals, Europeans, and other Africans, and they found that in those settings their race was actually an advantage rather than a disadvantage. The apparent absence of discrimination in the Soviet Union suggested to African American Communists that racism might dissolve through revolutionary activity. Naison says that black Communists saw the Soviet Union as the one force in the world actively resisting racism and that, for this reason, they were strong supporters of Bolshevization. Furthermore, for these reasons, Bolshevization led to a significant increase in the CPUSA's ability to recruit and retain African American members after 1925.

9. Soviet nationalist experts drafted this resolution with the help of a midwestern black Communist named Harry Haywood. Although Haywood and the other American members of the Comintern's Negro Commission objected to the policy initially because they saw African Americans as a racial minority rather than an oppressed nation, they decided to drop their objections to it once it became clear that it would pass the congress overwhelmingly. See Naison, *Communists in Harlem*, chap. 1.

10. "Resolution of the Communist International," October 26, 1928, in *The Communist Position on the Negro Question* (New York: Workers Library Publishers, 1934), 57–58, quoted in Naison, *Communists in Harlem*, 19.

11. *Daily Worker,* February 19, 1931, quoted in Naison, *Communists in Harlem*, 47.

12. Naison reports that "three black men attending a dance at the Finnish Workers Club in Harlem . . . were shunted off into a corner and threatened by a group of white youths" and also that "the children of two black Party members attending a Workers International Relief camp were harassed and 'called nigger' by other children in spite of the fact that the Party had tried to attract black children to its summer camps" (*Communists in Harlem during the Great Depression,* 43). Naison quotes the *Daily Worker,* December 10, 1930, p. 46.

13. For a more thorough treatment of the African American Communists and the evolution of the Party's approach to white chauvinism, see Solomon, *The Cry Was Unity;* quote on p. 130.

14. *Daily Worker,* December 10, 1930, quoted in Naison, *Communists in Harlem*, 46.

15. Solomon, *The Cry Was Unity,* 132–33.

16. According to Baxandall, "The Question Seldom Asked," in Brown et al., eds., *New Studies in the Politics and Culture of U.S. Communism,* 144–45, and Buhle, *Women and American Socialism,* 319–23, feminist Socialists and suffragists who joined the American CP in the 1920s include Ella Reeve Bloor, Anita Whitney, Maud Malone, Rose Pastor Stokes, and Juliet Stuart Poyntz. Of course others, including Elizabeth Gurley Flynn, Mary Inman, and many more, joined the Party in the 1930s as well. Ac-

cording to Baxandall, women made up only 10 percent of the Party's membership in 1930. I assume that percentage must have been even smaller in the 1920s.

17. See Karl Marx, *The Communist Manifesto* (New York: International Publishers, 1948); Friedrich Engels, *The Origin of the Family, Private Property, and the State* (New York: International Publishers, 1942); August Bebel, *Women and Socialism* (New York: Socialist Literature, 1910); V. I. Lenin, *The Emancipation of Women* (New York: International Publishers, 1972).

18. Baxandall, "The Question Seldom Asked," 144–48.

19. Buhle, Buhle, and Georgakas, *Encyclopedia of the American Left*, 150.

20. Klehr and Haynes, *The American Communist Movement*, 67 and 73.

21. According to Klehr and Haynes, in 1931, 65 percent of all party members had been born abroad and only 50 percent of them were American citizens; by 1935, 40 percent were native-born Americans. That percentage continued to grow as the 1930s progressed (ibid., 73).

22. Ibid., 76; Naison, *Communists in Harlem*, 43–49.

23. Naison, *Communists in Harlem*, chaps. 2 and 3; Kelley, *Hammer and Hoe*. In the Scottsboro trial the International Labor Defense, a Communist-led group of lawyers founded in 1925, vigorously defended the accused in court while the CPUSA conducted an aggressive protest campaign to make the case a symbol of Southern racism and to bring it international attention. The ILD failed to win the defendants' unconditional release in a 1936 trial and in 1937 agreed to a plea bargain that released four defendants and subjected the remaining five to lengthy prison terms rather than the death penalty. The Scottsboro campaign is most significant, however, because of its legal and political ramifications. As a result of the campaign the U.S. Supreme Court ruled in 1935 that the defendants' constitutional rights were violated because blacks were systematically excluded from juries. This decision spurred a long struggle to include more African Americans on jury rolls in the South. The case also exposed many African Americans to Marxist theory and to CP activities for the first time.

24. Buhle, Buhle, and Georgakas, *Encyclopedia of the American Left*, 151.

25. Naison, *Communists in Harlem*, 127.

26. For discussions of this shift, see Baxandall, "The Question Seldom Asked," 148–57, and Gosse, "'To Organize in Every Neighborhood, in Every Home,'" 109–41. The figures on membership come from Robert Shaffer, "Women and the Communist Party USA," 90. For fuller discussions of women's participation in CP political and social activities in the 1930s, see, besides Shaffer, Dixler, "The Woman Question;" Gosse, "'To Organize in Every Neighborhood, in Every Home'"; and Baxandall, "The Question Seldom Asked."

27. Shaffer, "Women and the Communist Party USA."

28. Dixler, "The Woman Question"; Shaffer, "Women and the Communist Party USA"; Ware, *American Women in the 1930s: Holding Their Own*, 131–33; Baxandall, "The Question Seldom Asked."

29. Membership figures come from Nathan Glazer's book *The Social Basis of American Communism* (New York: Harcourt, Brace & World, 1961), 92–93, and Shaffer, "Women and the Communist Party USA," 90. For more detailed discussions of the CP's failure to combat male supremacy in the Party and in U.S. society in the 1930s, see Shaffer, 110.

30. *Daily Worker*, February 19, 1943, quoted in Horne, "The Red and the Black," 215.

31. Maurice Isserman, *Which Side Were You On? The American Communist Party during the Second World War* (Middletown, Conn.: Wesleyan UP, 1979); Baxandall, "The Question Seldom Asked," 156.

32. Following the example of the Soviet Union, which dissolved the Comintern in 1943, Browder dissolved the CP and created the Communist Political Association in 1944 with the hope that the newly structured organization could work within the two-party system and ally with mainstream liberals and the labor movement to support Franklin Delano Roosevelt's New Deal policies and his friendly relationship with Joseph Stalin. At least a few Communists disagreed with Browder's strategy, but after William Z. Foster was disciplined by the former head of the Comintern for his criticism of the new structure, most kept quiet. When French Communist Jacques Duclos denounced Browder's liquidation of the American CP in a French Communist journal in April 1945, Browder's opponents took it as a sign from Moscow and began to orchestrate Browder's downfall. In June 1945 the CPA national committee revoked Browder's executive power and transferred it to a group headed by Foster. In July the delegates at an emergency national convention dissolved the CPA, reconstituted the Communist Party USA, and made Foster the new chairman. For a more thorough discussion of this period of CP history, see Joseph Starobin, *American Communism in Crisis, 1943-1956* (Cambridge: Harvard UP, 1972); Isserman, *Which Side Were You On?* and Klehr and Haynes, *The American Communist Movement*.

33. Evidence for Communists continuing commitment to women's equality can be found in such publications as Elizabeth Gurley Flynn's *Women in the War* (New York: Workers' Library Publishers, 1942) and her *Daughters of America: Ella Reeve Bloor and Anita Whitney* (New York: International Publishers, 1942), and in scores of articles published on the subject in the *Daily Worker* between 1941 and 1945.

34. Kate Weigand, "The Woman Question and the Communist Mystique: Propaganda and Practice in the American Communist Party, 1941–1945" (paper presented at the Twenty-fourth Annual Duquesne History Forum, Pittsburgh, October 24, 1990); Rebecca Hill, "Nothing Personal? Women in the CPUSA, 1940–1956" (senior honors thesis, Wesleyan University, Middletown, Conn., 1991).

Chapter 2: The Mary Inman Controversy and the (Re)Construction of the Woman Question, 1936–1945

1. Mary Inman, *In Woman's Defense* (Los Angeles: Committee to Organize the Advancement of Women, 1940).

2. Mary Inman, "Thirteen Years of CPUSA Misleadership on the Woman Question," mimeographed paper dated 1949, pp. 23–24. Inman's *Woman Power* (Los Angeles: Committee to Organize the Advancement of Women, 1942), "Thirteen Years of CPUSA Misleadership," "Can the Strangling Hand of Browder Revisionism Be Removed from the Throats of Women in These Perilous Times?" (1962), and the rest of Inman's personal and political papers can be found in the Mary Inman Papers, Schlesinger Library, Radcliffe College, Cambridge, Mass., box 3. Documents from this collection will hereafter be cited as Inman Papers, followed by a box number. When I looked at the papers in November 1992, they were in large boxes, in unnumbered

folders, and still being processed. It is likely that the box numbers recorded here are no longer applicable.

3. Letter from Helen Kritzler to Mary Inman, December 22, 1968, Inman Papers, box 2.

4. Mary Inman, "Program for Women" (1946), and "Two Forms of Production under Capitalism" (1964, mimeographed manuscript), Inman Papers, box 3. Inman Papers, box 5, contains a note Inman wrote for herself in the fall of 1978 to keep track of who requested copies of her work.

Correspondence between Inman and Joan Kelly can be found in the Inman Papers, box 2.

Inman's 1973 correspondence with Lorna Hall and Cathy Dreyfuss (Inman Papers, box 1) reveals that she was extremely reluctant to talk in person to people she did not know. Baxandall, in "The Question Seldom Asked," 141–61, also discusses Inman's refusal to grant interviews. In a letter dated August 19, 1991 Sherna Gluck told me that she had interviewed Mary Inman extensively but that Inman had insisted their conversations not be tape-recorded. Gluck has written about Inman in an entry in Buhle, Buhle, and Georgakas, *Encyclopedia of the American Left*, 361–62, and in her article "Socialist Feminism between the Two World Wars: Insights from Oral History," in Scharf and Jensen, eds. *Decades of Discontent*. Baxandall writes about her reliance on Gluck's information about Inman in "The Question Seldom Asked," 161.

4. See esp. Jayne Loader, "Women in the Left, 1906–1941: A Bibliography of Primary Sources," University of Michigan *Papers in Women's Studies* 2 (September 1975): 29–30; Ware, "Women on the Left"; Rosalyn Fraad Baxandall, *Words on Fire: The Life and Writing of Elizabeth Gurley Flynn* (New Brunswick, N.J.: Rutgers UP, 1987), 223–26; and Baxandall, "The Question Seldom Asked," 156–57. For other discussions of Mary Inman's work, see Dixler, "The Woman Question," 131–35, and Shaffer, "Women and the Communist Party USA," 83–87. Cott's *The Grounding of Modern Feminism* also draws on these works and includes a brief reference (282) to Inman's critiques of male chauvinism in the Communist Party as if she were the only one making them.

5. Mary Inman's autobiographical fragment, "part labor history, part problems that still exist, as well as a record of a good life that I would not live different if I could do it over again," was written on July 20, 1978. Inman did not get very far in her attempt to write autobiography, but her efforts, including numerous handwritten autobiographical notes, dated and undated, are in the Inman Papers, box 1.

6. Mary Inman's explanations about their various name changes are found on a Social Security Administration form dated October 18, 1956, Inman Papers, box 1. According to Gluck's "Socialist Feminism between the Two World Wars," later in her life Inman jokingly called herself a "Lucy Stoner," a woman who kept her own name after marriage. In fact, Inman did describe her marriage as egalitarian. In the 1970s she wrote in her autobiographical notes (box 1): "It was the first and only marriage of each and we lived together continuously as husband and wife for forty-two years until his death in Long Beach, Calif., in 1959. There was never any of the so-called 'war between the sexes' in our life together. We had a common political goal and our life together was one of working-class partners."

7. Gluck, "Socialist Feminism between the Two World Wars," 291. Inman Papers, box 1, folder of James F. Inman's personal documents. According to a letter from Eliza-

beth Gurley Flynn to Harrison George, the editor of the *People's Daily World,* dated August 5, 1941, Inman was a Party "friend and sympathizer" before she finally joined the CP officially in late 1939 or so. A copy of Flynn's letter can be found in the Inman Papers, box 3.

8. Dixler, "The Woman Question"; Shaffer, "Women and the Communist Party USA"; Trimberger, "Women in the Old and New Left," 432–450; Ware, "Women on the Left"; Baxandall, "The Question Seldom Asked"; and Gosse, "'To Organize in Every Neighborhood, in Every Home,'" 109–41.

9. Interviews with Rose Kryzak, Mollie Goldstein, Rose Raynes, and other women in the Oral History of the American Left Collection, Tamiment Library, New York University, New York City.

10. Margaret Cowl, *Women and Equality* (New York: International Publishers, 1935). See Louise Mitchell, "Ninety Years of Women's Rights," *Daily Worker,* July 17, 1938, and Ella Reeve Bloor, "The American Woman," *Communist* 18 (September 1939): 829–35, as examples of Communists' assertion that the CP inherited the legacy of the nineteenth-century women's movement. The Party's desire to work in coalition with other women's organizations is clear in a letter from Margaret Cowl, director of the CP National Women's Commission to all state and district women's commissions, July 5, 1938, in the Mary van Kleeck Papers, Sophia Smith Collection, Smith College, Northampton, Mass., box 35, folder 619. Documents from this collection will be cited hereafter as Van Kleeck Papers.

11. Margaret Cowl, "Women's Struggles for Equality," *Political Affairs* 53 (May 1974): 40–44; James Weinstein, *Ambiguous Legacy: The Left in American Politics* (New York: New Viewpoints, 1975), 160–63; Shaffer, "Women and the Communist Party USA," 103; Baxandall, "The Question Seldom Asked," 155; Mary van Kleeck, "The Women's Charter," *Woman Today,* February 1937, p. 3; "A Charter for American Women," n.d., Van Kleeck Papers, box 69, folder 1099.

12. Decisions of the Women's Conference of the Tenth National Party Convention, May 27, 1938, Van Kleeck Papers, box 35, folder 619.

13. *Worker Magazine,* August 5, 1936. See also Shaffer, "Women and the Communist Party USA," 73, and Baxandall, "The Question Seldom Asked," 154–55.

14. *Worker,* September 6, 1935, p. 6, quoted in Shaffer, "Women and the Communist Party USA," 94.

15. *Daily Worker,* February 20, 1934, p. 6 and February 12, 1934, p. 4; *Party Organizer,* October 1936, pp. 16–19; *Working Woman,* September 1936, p. 13.

16. Inman mentions the work of Charlotte Perkins Gilman favorably at several points in *In Woman's Defense.* According to Barbara Garson's entry on Gilman in Buhle, Buhle, and Georgakas, *Encyclopedia of the American Left,* although Gilman never joined the Socialist Party, her work bridged the views of the nineteenth-century woman's movement and Socialist analyses of the "woman question" that were common by the early 1900s. For a thorough discussion of the Socialist view of women's rights, see Mari Jo Buhle, *Women and American Socialism, 1870-1920* (Champaign: U of Illinois P, 1983). In a letter to Lorna Hall (Inman Papers, box 1) in June 1973, Inman wrote, "Did the Party influence me? Of course . . . over and above all, of course, credit should go to Marxist-Leninist theory and practice."

17. Cowl, *Women and Equality,* 3.

18. Inman, *In Woman's Defense*, 37, 8, and 107–11.

19. Ibid., 24–58 and 168–69; see also Marie Pierce, "Some Problems in Our Women's Work," *Party Organizer*, October 1936.

20. Inman, *In Woman's Defense*, 48–52 and 25, 53–56, and 72–75.

21. For a much more detailed discussion of these issues of the economics of domestic labor and their implications for revolutionary theory and practice, see Lise Vogel, *Marxism and the Oppression of Women: Towards a Unitary Theory* (New Brunswick, N.J.: Rutgers UP, 1983); Vogel quotes Marx, pp. 71–72. She also quotes a letter Marx wrote to his friend Dr. Kugelmann, December 12, 1868.

22. Vogel quotes Engels, ibid., 75.

23. *In Woman's Defense*, 136–60 and 166–74.

24. Mercury Printing Company to Barbara Giles, March 25, 1940, Inman Papers, box 4.

25. Elizabeth Gurley Flynn to Harrison George, August 5, 1941, Inman Papers, box 3. Inman quotes the favorable *Daily Worker* review in "Thirteen Years of CPUSA Misleadership," as saying: "The book is of great value as a source of information and as a basis of extending progressive work among women. . . . It is the first work of this worth in the world available to English readers since Bebel's *Woman and Socialism.*"

26. Joan [no last name indicated] to Inman, February 28, 1941, Inman Papers, box 2.

27. Anthony to Inman, December 20, 1940, Inman Papers, box 1. Inman and Anthony conducted extensive correspondence after this time, discussing women's oppression in detail and mulling over plans for a cross-class women's congress that might begin to work toward solutions for women's problems. I will discuss their relationship and Inman's influence on Anthony—which becomes extremely apparent when Susan B. Anthony becomes a central figure in the CP mass organization the Congress of American Women—in greater detail in chapter 3.

28. See Workers' School Materials, Inman Papers, box 3 and her speech, "The Attitude of People's Organizations toward Women and the Role of Women in People's Organizations," given before the Spanish Speaking People's Congress in 1941 in the Inman Papers, "speeches" folder, box 3.

In a letter to Harrison George dated August 5, 1941, Elizabeth Gurley Flynn states that Inman had been in the CP for about a year (box 3).

29. Articles from the 1940–41 debate included Ruth McKenney, "Women Are Human Beings," and "Women Are Human Beings II," *New Masses*, December 10 and December 17, 1940. Responses to McKenney's article include Harrison George, "22,000,000 Housewives Take Notice," *New Masses*, February 11, 1941, pp. 10–11; Elizabeth Gurley Flynn, "What Price Housework?" and Beatrice Blosser's letter in the Readers' Forum, *New Masses*, March 4, 1941.

This issue was also hotly debated in the 1970s and 1980s by Left and feminist scholars. Articles from the more recent debate on the topic include Margaret Benston, "The Political Economy of Women's Liberation," *Monthly Review* 6 (September 1969): 13–27; Peggy Morton, "A Woman's Work Is Never Done, or: The Production and Maintenance and Reproduction of Labor Power," in Edith Altbach, ed., *From Feminism to Liberation* (Cambridge, Mass.: Schenkman Publishing, 1971), 211–27; Eli Zaretsky, "Capitalism, the Family, and Personal Life," *Socialist Revolution*, Part I, 13–14 (January–April 1973): 66–125, and Part II, 15 (May–June 1973): 19–70; Zaretsky, "Socialist Politics and the Family," *Socialist Revolution* 19 (January–March 1974): 83–98; Mariarosa Dalla Costa, "Women and the Subversion of the Community," *The Power of Women and the Subversion of the Community* (Bristol, England: Falling Wall P, 1973); Lise Vogel, "The Earthly Family," *Radical America* 7 (July–October 1973): 9–50; Ira Gerstein, "Domestic Work and Capitalism," *Radical America* 7 (Fall 1973): 101–28; Wally Seccombe, "The Housewife and Her Labour under Capitalism," *New Left Review* 83 (January–February 1974): 3–24; and Margaret Coulson, Branka Magas, and Hilary Wainwright, "'The Housewife and Her Labour under Capitalism': A Critique," *New Left Review* 89 (January–February 1975): 59–71. Lise Vogel devotes a chapter entitled "A Decade of Debate" to this controversy among second-wave feminists in *Marxism and the Oppression of Women.*

In the 1970s and 1980s this debate has been expressed in arguments over the principle of comparable worth and as a question of whether fuller recognition of women's culture and women's work can bring about women's equality or whether sex equality must be achieved by giving women and men equal opportunities. The literature representing both sides of the question is vast and cannot be listed here. The best-known expression of this debate comes from the 1985 sex-discrimination case, EEOC v. Sears Roebuck and Co., in which women's historians Rosalind Rosenberg and Alice Kessler-Harris both testified, one for the prosecution and the other for the defense. The details of the case and its implications for women's history are spelled out in detail in Ruth Milkman, "Women's History and the Sears Case," *Feminist Studies* 12 (Summer 1986): 375–400, and in "Women's History Goes to Trial: EEOC v. Sears Roebuck and Company," *Signs* 11 (Summer 1986): 751–79.

30. Inman's description of Los Angeles Workers' School Teachers Session, March 22, 1941, Inman Papers, box 1.

31. Typewritten copy of letter from Ella Reeve Bloor to Effie M., August 4, 1941, Inman Papers, box 5.

32. Typewritten copy of letter from Elizabeth Gurley Flynn to Harrison George, August 5, 1941, Inman Papers, box 3.

33. Typewritten copy of letter from Bloor to Effie M., August 4, 1941.

34. Flynn to George, August 5, 1941.

35. Mary Inman to Susan B. Anthony II, October 26, 1941, Inman Papers, box 1.

36. Avram Landy, "Two Questions on the Status of Women under Capitalism," *Communist* 20 (September 1941): 818–33.

37. Inman to Anthony, October 26, 1941.

38. See esp. Ware "Women on the Left"; Gluck's entry on Inman in Buhle, Buhle, and Georgakas, *Encyclopedia of the American Left;* Baxandall's "The Question Seldom Asked."

39. Gluck and Baxandall say that Inman was expelled; Ware writes that Inman was forced to leave the Party rather than that she was expelled. During her life Inman was actually infuriated at any suggestion that she had been purged from the Party. In 1944, she wrote letters to the *Daily Worker* and to the Party's national chairman, Earl Browder, asking that they "publish in the *Daily Worker* a retraction of the harmful and untrue statement that [she] had been expelled from the Communist Party." She explained further, "Never at any time was I expelled from the CP. . . . [That] false

statement is derogatory of my character and injurious to my work and should be corrected both in the interest of my work and that of your paper" (reprint of letter from Inman to Browder and *Daily Worker* in *Facts for Women* 2 [August–October 1944]: 4, found in Inman Papers, box 3).

40. Ware, "Women on the Left," 126–27; Gluck, "Socialist Feminism between the Two World Wars," 362; and Baxandall, "The Question Seldom Asked," 156–57.

41. Avram Landy, *Marxism and the Woman Question* (New York: Workers Library, 1943).

42. For a discussion of the Communist Party's rhetoric on women during World War II, see Weigand, "The Woman Question and the Communist Mystique," and Hill, "Nothing Personal?"

43. Elizabeth Gurley Flynn, "A Keen Analysis of Women's Role in Our Changing World," *Daily Worker,* July 30, 1943, p. 7. Party leaders' confusion about what to do in response to *Woman Power* is evident in Bloor's correspondence with California Party leader Anita Whitney when she writes: "I found Elizabeth very indignant about the book by Mary Inman. . . . Her new book contains a bitter attack on Landy, calling him Professor X. Perhaps it would be well to have a notice in the *People's World* that she is not a member of the Party. Of course this is not official and I do not know whether it would be wise or not. You will use your own judgement about it. The book is really worse than the other one. I think notices will be sent to every book store asking them not to handle this book. Certainly not as one of our publications." This letter comes from the Ella Reeve Bloor Papers, Sophia Smith Collection, Smith College, Northampton, Mass., box 13, folder 146.

44. Inman's "Program for Women" can be found in *Facts for Women* 4 (April–May 1946): 1–4. The program is proposed as an alternative to the Communist program, but there are very few differences between the two. Inman, like the CP, calls for day and night nurseries for small children, full maternity and infant care, a national women's congress, equal rights legislation compatible with protective laws for women workers, and defeat of the cultural manifestations of male supremacy. In addition Inman calls for housewives' unions to improve women's working conditions in their homes. "Marxism on Woman Question Outlawed in California in 1941," appears in *Facts for Women* 3 (August–December 1945): 3.

45. Mary Inman to Morris Rubin, editor of the *Progressive,* Carey McWilliams, editor of the *Nation,* Gilbert Hanson, editor of the *New Republic,* and Gus Hall, national chair, CPUSA, February 17, 1972 in the Dorothy Healey Collection, Special Collections Department, California State University–Long Beach Library, Long Beach, Calif., box 125, folder 147.

46. Inman, "Thirteen Years of CPUSA Misleadership."

47. Ibid., 11. The *Daily Worker* during World War II and until about 1948 is filled with stories about Communists' efforts to win state-funded day-care centers for children with working mothers and, after a few centers were established during the war, to keep those centers open in major cities after the war.

48. William Z. Foster, "On Improving the Party's Work among Women," *Political Affairs* 27 (October 1948): 988, quoted in Inman, "Thirteen Years of CPUSA Misleadership," 24.

49. Inman, "Thirteen Years of CPUSA Misleadership," 25 and 34.

50. Inman to Rubin, McWilliams, Hanson, Hall, February 17, 1972.

51. Mary Inman, "Maternity as a Social Function," *Political Affairs* 52 (January 1973): 56–60.

52. See Inman's correspondence files in boxes 1 and 2. In her autobiographical notes (Inman Papers, box 1) Inman lists as her greatest achievement: "When the Supreme Soviet of the USSR wrote into their 'Fundamentals' (comparable to our Constitution), 'We accord the work of the wife in the home as of equal value to that of the husband at his workplace,' a theory which I developed."

53. See, for example, her marked up copy of the summary from the Women's Liberation Conference held in Chicago in November 1968, Inman Papers, box 3; copies of Delores Hayden, "Redesigning the Domestic Workplace," *Chrysalis* 1, no. 1 (1977): 19–29; Gerstein, "Domestic Work and Capitalism," 101–28; Ellen Malos, "Housework and the Politics of Women's Liberation," *Socialist Review* 8 (1978): 41–71, all in box 5.

54. See Inman's correspondence with Hope Busby in 1969, Gertrude Anderson in 1970–71, Arline Flood in 1971, and Cathy Dreyfuss in 1973 in Inman Papers, box 1. See Inman's file "notes on homosexuals" in box 5; Mary Inman to Lorna Hall, June 1, 1973, box 1; Mary Inman to Carl Bloice, n.d., box 5.

Chapter 3: The Congress of American Women

1. Minneapolis *Tribune,* August 25, 1942, quoted in Sara Evans, *Born for Liberty: A History of Women in America* (New York: Free P, 1989), 225.

2. Margaret Bernard Pickel, "How Come No Jobs for Women?" *New York Times Magazine,* January 27, 1946, quoted in Evans, *Born for Liberty,* 231.

3. See Gabin, *Feminism and the Labor Movement,* chap. 3.

4. See Rupp and Taylor, *Survival in the Doldrums,* for a discussion of the National Woman Party's retreat to the margins of politics in the postwar period.

5. Several scholars have begun to challenge the view of the period 1945–60 as uniformly conservative, antifeminist, and hostile to women's activism. See, for example, David J. Garrow, ed., *The Montgomery Bus Boycott and the Women Who Started It: The Memoir of JoAnn Gibson Robinson* (Knoxville: U of Tennessee P, 1987); Gabin, *Feminism and the Labor Movement;* Lynn, *Progressive Women in Conservative Times;* Elizabeth Lapovsky Kennedy and Madeline Davis, *Boots of Leather, Slippers of Gold: The History of a Lesbian Community* (New York: Routledge, 1993); Joanne Meyerowitz, ed., *Not June Cleaver* (Philadelphia: Temple UP, 1994).

6. The sources on the Congress of American Women are, unfortunately, both sparse and scattered. The largest collection of CAW Papers is housed at the Sophia Smith Collection at Smith College as part of the Women's International Democratic Federation Papers in the Communism Collection. These papers will be cited hereafter as WIDF Papers. This chapter relies primarily on documents in that collection, on documents housed in the Van Kleeck Papers and on the *Report on the Congress of American Women* prepared by the U.S. Congress's House Committee on Un-American Activities and released in October 1949. The chapter also makes use of documents in the Mary Inman Papers at the Schlesinger Library and photocopies of CAW documents from the personal collection of historian Katherine Campbell in Acton, Mass.

7. Interview with Harriet Magil, January 12, 1993, New York City.

8. *Daily Worker,* March 9, 1946, p. 12; "Women of America Organize Own PAC,"

*New York Times,* May 26, 1946; House Committee on Un-American Activities, *Report on the Congress of American Women* (Washington, D.C.: Government Printing Office, 1949), 3.

9. See "Original Resolutions of the Women's International Democratic Federation," International Congress of Women in Paris, November–December 1945, in the WIDF Papers, box 2, folder 15; and "Congress of Women Opens in Paris Today," *New York Times,* November 25, 1945. Five hundred women from forty-two countries attended the International Congress of Women, including fifteen American delegates.

10. "Women of America Organize Own PAC," *New York Times,* May 26, 1946.

11. "What Is the Congress of American Women," informational pamphlet from 1946 in WIDF Papers, box 2, folder 20a.

12. The pamphlet "What Is the Congress of American Women" includes the "hundreds of thousands" figure along with a list of the twelve chapters that existed in 1946. This figure is undoubtedly exaggerated, but the CAW's definition of "membership" was very broad. The pamphlet specifies that the organization invites "the membership of all women who, as Citizens, wish to insure peace and further democracy; women who, as Workers, are concerned with an advance in economic and legal status; women who, as Mothers, have a stake in the welfare and education of children" and that "membership can be taken on an individual or group basis. Women's organizations and auxiliaries can affiliate as a body. Membership is open to all women who wish to act together with other women for a secure future and a better world for us all." The organization's 1949 Constitutional Convention Officers Report states on p. 11 that "Dues reports, dues payments are sporadic, and membership has represented in many cases a rather loose form of affiliation with the CAW. . . . During the early years . . . this condition was by no means an unmitigated evil. With both the chapters and the national organization still finding their way, there was a need for a wide latitude in determining what constituted good standing membership. Rigid regulations for membership would possibly have had a stultifying effect."

13. Flexner, who is best known among both feminists and historians for writing *Century of Struggle: The Woman's Rights Movement in the U.S.* (Cambridge: Harvard UP, 1959), wrote these words in her reminiscences found in Flexner Papers, box 1, folder 8, p. II(e). Also in these reminiscences Flexner discusses joining the Communist Party in 1936 and being an active member for seventeen years, until 1953. Flexner was one of the members of the CAW's new editorial board; Betty Millard replaced Flexner on the board in July 1948, probably at the time that the CAW was listed by the attorney general as a subversive organization (*Around the World* 1 [May–June 1948]: 1; *Around the World* 1 [July–August 1948]: 1–2). Although Flexner was apparently a very visible member of the CAW, at least briefly, she somehow escaped inclusion in HUAC's *Report on the Congress of American Women* in 1949.

14. On the CP's treatment of women and women's issues during World War II, see Weigand, "The Woman Question and the Communist Mystique," and Hill, "Nothing Personal?"

15. Amy Swerdlow, "The Congress of American Women: Left-Feminist Peace Politics in the Cold War," in Linda Kerber, Alice Kessler-Harris, and Kathryn Kish Sklar, eds., *U.S. History as Women's History: New Feminist Essays,* (Chapel Hill: U of North Carolina P, 1995), 300.

16. For illustrations of the Communist Party's increasing acceptance of women's struggles for equality at the end of World War II, see, for example, Elizabeth Gurley Flynn, *Women Have a Date with Destiny* (New York: Workers' Library, 1944), which encouraged women to push a "women's program" in the elections of that year. The Communist press and the letters that rank-and-file Communists wrote to the *Worker* and *Daily Worker* in 1946 and 1947 show much more popular support for women's issues than was visible in the 1930s and during the war years.

17. Inman describes her impressions of the newly formed CAW in a letter to Harrison George written on January 20, 1947, in the Inman Papers, box 1. According to that letter Inman attended the first meeting of the CAW in Los Angeles on December 2, 1946, but refused to join and "merely paid [the] ten dollar registration fee required of all attending." Inman details her criticisms of the "Browder revisionism" evident in the CAW in her "Thirteen Years of CPUSA Misleadership," 7–8.

18. See Inman's letter to George, January 20, 1947, and "Thirteen Years of CPUSA Misleadership," 6–11, Inman Papers, box 3.

19. The correspondence that took place between Mary Inman and Susan B. Anthony II, including letters from Anthony to Inman and copies of letters from Inman to Anthony from the period December 1940 to February 1942, are housed in the Inman Papers, box 1.

20. According to Judy Klemesrud, "Another Susan B. Anthony Now Speaks Her Mind" *New York Times*, September 21, 1971, p. 32, Susan B. Anthony II was born in 1916. She became active in progressive circles sometime during the 1930s.

21. Anthony was active in a variety of progressive organizations with close ties to the CP including the Committee for a Democratic Far Eastern Policy, the Voice of Freedom Committee, and the American Peace Mobilization, as well as the Congress of American Women. The full nature of Anthony's relationship with the Communist Party is somewhat unclear. Her husband at the time, Clifford McAvoy, was an open Communist, but she never publicly identified as a member of the Party. If she was an official member of the Party, she probably would have kept it quiet in order to protect her reputation as a journalist writing for mainstream publications such as the *Saturday Evening Post*. In the bizarre manner typical of HUAC, its *Report on the Congress of American Women* states that the committee was in possession of four affidavits showing that "in 1937 and 1938 Susan B. Anthony decorated the walls of her apartment at 1742 P Street NW, Washington, D.C. with hammers and sickles" (p. 102) as evidence to prove her close ties to the Communist Party. At any rate, even if Anthony was not officially a Communist, it is clear from her writing and her affiliations that her political outlook and activities were shaped by the Communist Party.

22. See letters between Anthony and Inman, December 20, 1940, January 11, 1941, and January 30, 1941 in Inman Papers, box 1.

23. Mary Inman's notes from her discussion of the woman's congress with Susan B. Anthony, n.d. (but the context makes it clear that they are from February 1941) in Inman Papers, box 1.

24. Anthony to Inman, August 7, 1941.

25. See letters from Anthony to Inman dated September 3, September 29, November 10, and December 1, 1941.

26. Inman to Anthony, January 12, 1942, and Anthony to Inman, January 15, 1942.

27. Susan Brownell Anthony II, *Out of the Kitchen—Into the War: Woman's Win-*
. *ning Role in the Nation's Drama* (New York: S. Daye, 1943).

28. Anthony and van Kleeck gathered reports about women's contributions to
American life from women in a variety of organizations in order to put together the
delegation's report about American women. According to material in the Van Kleeck
Papers, box 80, folder 1265, the Communist Party contributed information about
women's contributions to the war against fascism, Mary McLeod Bethune wrote the
report about the role of Negro women in American society, Gene Weltfish wrote about
women in the sciences, Mrs. Frederic March on women in U.S. cultural life, and Rose
Schneiderman of the Women's Trade Union League on the activities of that organization. Bethune's "Negro Women in American Life," dated November 11, 1945, is in the
Van Kleeck Papers, box 80, folder 1266.

29. The "Report on the Problems and Status of Women in the United States," by
Elinor Gimbel, Mary van Kleeck, and Susan B. Anthony II, summarized the findings
of the Committee on the U.S. Delegates' Reports. It is located in the Van Kleeck Papers, box 80, folder 1266.

According to the *Report on the Congress of American Women,* pp. 79–82, the American delegates to the First Congress of the Women's International Democratic Federation were Ann Bradford; Charlotte Hawkins Brown, of the National Negro Congress; Henrietta Buckmaster, who had affiliations with numerous Communist/
progressive groups, including the Jefferson School of Social Science, American Youth
for Democracy, and the Civil Rights Congress; Thelma Dale, of the National Negro
Congress; Muriel Draper, of the National Council of American-Soviet Friendship;
Vivian Carter Mason; Dr. Beryl Parker; Cornelia Royce Pinchot, the wife of a former
governor of Pennsylvania; Eleanor Vaughan; Gene Weltfish, an anthropologist at Columbia University; and Communists Elizabeth Gurley Flynn, Jeannette Stern Turner,
and Ruth Young. According to the article, "Congress of Women Opens in Paris Today,"
*New York Times,* November 25, 1945, Elinor Gimbel of the National Association for
Child Welfare was supposed to participate as part of the American delegation, but she
was forced to cancel her trip because she could not obtain return passage from Paris
in time to be present for the start of the New York Political Action Committee Community drive on December 16.

30. See "Women of America Organize Own PAC," *New York Times.* During the
first year of the organization's existence, CAW officers called themselves "chairmen"
of the commissions they led. For the sake of historical accuracy I have retained their
terminology, despite the contemporary preference for gender-neutral titles. It is interesting to note that by 1948 the CAW began to refer to its officers as "president," "vice
president," and the like. Perhaps they were also expressing a preference for gender
neutrality.

31. Anthony, "Report of the Commission on the Status of Women," p. 14, in WIDF
Papers, box 2, folder 20a.

32. Mary Inman's notes for her discussion with Susan B. Anthony II about a
woman's congress, Inman Papers, box 1.

33. For evidence of the CAW's maternalist approach to postwar politics, see the
organization's newsletter, the *Congress of American Women Bulletin,* later called,
*Around the World,* and the Women's International Democratic Federation magazine,

*Women of the Whole World,* in the WIDF Papers. Katherine Campbell discusses this phenomenon in her unpublished paper "The Congress of American Women," and Amy Swerdlow analyzes it in her book *Women Strike for Peace: Traditional Motherhood and Radical Politics in the 1960s* (Chicago: U of Chicago P, 1993) and in her 1995 article "The Congress of American Women."

34. These challenges to arguments about women's nature are evident in documents presented to the WIDF founding congress in November 1945 as well as in later documents prepared by the Commission on the Status of Women. See, for example, Gimbel, van Kleeck, and Anthony, "Report on the Problems and Status of Women in the United States"; anonymous, "The Position of the American Woman Today," n.d., WIDF Papers, box 2, folder 20a; Anthony, "Report of the Commission on the Status of Women."

35. The report's bibliography is three pages long and although it includes books that Inman drew upon, such as Charlotte Perkins Gilman's *Women and Economics* (Boston: Small, Maynard, 1900) and *The Home* (New York: McClure, Phillips, 1903), and Lewis Morgan's *Ancient Society* (Chicago: Charles H. Kerr, 1909), Inman's *In Woman's Defense* is conspicuously absent.

36. See Anthony, "Report of the Commission on the Status of Women," 2–11.

37. Mary Inman, *In Woman's Defense,* 157–58; Anthony, "Report of the Commission on the Status of Women," 10–11.

38. Anthony, "Report of the Commission on the Status of Women," 12–15.

39. See *In Woman's Defense,* 99, and the "Report of the Commission on the Status of Women," 17.

40. See *In Woman's Defense,* chaps. 8–12 passim, and Anthony's "Report of the Commission on the Status of Women," 18–21.

41. See "What Is the Congress of American Women" and Campbell, "The Congress of American Women."

42. "Ten Women Anywhere Can Start Anything."

43. Interview with Harriet Magil by Kate Weigand, New York City, January 12, 1993.

44. I identified black women leaders through photographs in various publications by or about the CAW. See, for example, *Congress of American Women Bulletin* 1 (October 1946): 4; HUAC's *Report on the Congress of American Women,* 6 and 61.

45. Despite its increasing visibility as a Communist-influenced organization, Kenyon also appeared at several of their events in 1947 and attended a CAW reception as late as January 1948. The relevant correspondence between Kenyon and CAW officers is in the Dorothy Kenyon Papers, Series II: General correspondence at Smith College's Sophia Smith Collection. It is interesting that, when Joseph McCarthy publicly charged Kenyon with Communist connections in 1950, she acknowledged that she had supported various Popular Front organizations in the 1930s but denied that she had any memory of an organization called the Congress of American Women. See Kenyon's defense against McCarthy in Kenyon Papers, Series VII: Organizations and activities.

46. An incomplete collection of the CAW's newsletters is housed in the WIDF Papers.

47. *Congress of American Women Bulletin* 1 (October 1946): 4; HUAC's *Report on the Congress of American Women,* 6 and 61.

48. Campbell, "The Congress of American Women," 4.

49. *Congress of American Women Bulletin* 1 (October 1946): 3. On women's efforts to end lynching historically, see Jacquelyn Dowd Hall, *Revolt against Chivalry: Jessie Daniel Ames and the Women's Campaign against Lynching* (New York: Columbia UP, 1979), and Paula Giddings, *When and Where I Enter: The Impact of Black Women on Race and Sex in America* (New York: William Morrow, 1984).

50. *Around the World* 1 (March–April 1948): 4. The group not only argued for Ingram's innocence, but collected money for her defense as well as funds and clothing to help support her other eleven children, circulated a petition to gain her freedom, and visited her and her family in Georgia.

51. See the material relating to the UN Commission on the Status of Women in the Dorothy Kenyon Papers.

52. According to the "Officers' Report" (WIDF Papers, box 2, folder 20a) from the First National Constitutional Convention, held May 6–8, 1949, in New York City, the proposed amendment was "supported by most unions and women's and consumer organizations."

53. In my discussion with Harriet Magil, she said that the CAW regarded the three commissions—Peace, Child Care, and Women's Status—as equally important, but that the rank-and-file members of the organization gravitated more toward the issues of peace and child welfare than toward women's emancipation.

54. *Around the World* 1 (February 1948): 4.

55. *Around the World* 1 (March–April 1948): 4, reports the change in the leadership of the Commission on the Status of Women. Campbell's "Congress of American Women" describes Anthony's reasons for leaving her post (she did remain active as a regular member of the group). The WIDF had Consultative Status B to the Economic and Social Council of the UN. It had great hopes of achieving Status A and thereby gaining the right to speak, the right to suggest items for the agenda, and the right to access the Council's documents, but never achieved that status.

56. Betty Millard, "Report on the Commission on the Status of Women," *Around the World* 1 (May–June 1948): 4.

57. Olive Sutton, "Mrs. Stanton Remembered on Centennial of Women's Vote Fight," *Daily Worker*, July 20, 1948, p. 5.

58. Gerda Lerner is considered by many to be one of the most important figures (along with fellow CAW member Eleanor Flexner) in establishing the discipline of women's history and was an important member of the Los Angeles branch of the CAW. According to the *Worker*, June 19, 1949, p. 2, Lerner was one of the California delegates who attended the CAW national convention in New York in 1949. A photo of the Resolutions Committee of the convention in that article includes Lerner along with Pearl Lawes, Frances Smith, and Helen Wortis from New York, Joan Leib from Ohio, and Anne Jones from Wisconsin. According to the CAW's publication, "American Women in Pictures: Souvenir Journal" (New York: CAW, 1949), 4, Lerner was one of the CAW's delegates to the WIDF convention in Budapest in 1949. For a lengthy discussion, see Eileen Boris, *Voices of Women Historians: The Personal, the Political, the Professional* (Bloomington: Indiana UP, 1999).

59. Interview with Harriet Magil, January 12, 1993, New York City.

60. Anthony's report was serialized on the women's pages of the *Worker* in the fol-

lowing articles: "The Political Status of American Women," July 14, 1946, p. 11; "The Legal Status of Women," August 11, 1946, p. 11; "How Shall Women's Rights Be Protected," August 25, 1946, p. 11; "Economic Status of a Housewife," September 8, 1946, p. 11; and "Jimcrow against Women," October 20, 1946, p. 11. For examples of letters from Communists, see A. E. Hudson, "The Problems of Women in CP Activity," *Worker*, July 28, 1946, p. 11; Hodee Richards, Helen Linia, Jane Renaker, and Anne Taylor, "The Personal Life of the Communist," *Worker*, June 16, 1946, p. 11.

61. See *Around the World* issues from 1948 and 1949; Elizabeth Gurley Flynn's "Life of the Party" columns in the *Daily Worker* on October 22, and October 25, 1948, April 4, 1949, and April 8, 1949; "Women's Rally Gets Grim Idea of Life in U.S.," *New York Herald Tribune*, December 3, 1948.

62. Despite its Soviet and American Communist Party connections, the Congress of American Women had no large financial backers and had never been economically secure. As early as 1947 the group had been forced to borrow money from its wealthier members in order to survive, and by 1949 its financial problems threatened to become overwhelming. In a letter dated April 25, 1947, from CAW member Zelma Brandt to member Thyra Edwards (WIDF Papers, box 2, folder 21), Brandt wrote, "As to the Congress [of American Women], we are coming into very hard times. The financial situation has not straightened out any more than it had been when you were here." In another letter (also in box 2, folder 21) dated September 11, 1947, Acting Executive Secretary Virginia Shull thanked Zelma Brandt for a "loan of $750 to meet our summer nightmare caused by the New Era Letter Company." In the "Officers' Report" for the CAW's First National Constitutional Convention, held on May 6–8, 1949, Gene Weltfish stated that lack of funds was one of the chief causes of the group's crisis.

63. Gene Weltfish et al., "Officers' Report," passim; Campbell, "Congress of American Women," 11.

In her interview with Katherine Campbell in New York in February 1980, Stella Allen, former executive secretary of the CAW described the final days of the CAW as follows: "So CAW became beset with reflections of what was happening on an international level. At the same time things were pretty much closing in nationally, and everything left wing or radical was beginning to be looked into and frowned upon, viewed with suspicion of being under red leadership and guidance. So gradually, the base became narrower and narrower, and we found ourselves near the end with some stalwarts who would stay because they were so much for peace, maybe—or people who were pretty much committed . . . from a leftist point of view."

64. HUAC, *Report on the Congress of American Women*, 1.

65. "D of J Hounding of CAW Called Attack on Peace," *Daily Worker*, January 10, 1950, p. 5.

66. Katherine Campbell interview with Stella Allen, Betty Millard, and Harriet and Abe Magil, New York City, February 17, 1981; Kate Weigand interview with Harriet Magil, New York City, January 12, 1993.

67. The pamphlet "American Women in Pictures: Souvenir Journal," 4, claimed that the group had 250,000 individual and affiliate members at that time, but that figure was clearly exaggerated.

68. Campbell, "The Congress of American Women," 12; Swerdlow, in Buhle, Buhle,

and Georgakas, *Encyclopedia of the American Left*, 161–62; and Swerdlow, "The Congress of American Women."

69. Swerdlow, *Women Strike for Peace* and "The Congress of American Women."

Chapter 4: Women's Work Is Never Done

1. Hodee Richards, Helen Linia, Jane Renaker, Anne Taylor, "The Personal Life of the Communist," *Worker*, June 16, 1946, p. 11.

2. Dixler, "The Woman Question"; Shaffer, "Women and the Communist Party USA"; Gosse, "'To Organize in Every Neighborhood, in Every Home'"; Baxandall, "The Question Seldom Asked."

3. Weigand, "The Woman Question and the Communist Mystique"; Hill, "Nothing Personal?"; articles in most issues of *Daily Worker* and *Worker* in 1945.

4. Flynn, *Women Have a Date with Destiny*; see also Clara Schwartzman, "Role of Women in Fight for Peace," *Daily Worker*, February 19, 1946, p. 6; Flynn, "Why Women Belong in the Communist Party," *Daily Worker*, April 25, 1946, p. 7; and Clara Bodian, "Organizing Women for Progress," *Worker*, June 9, 1946, p. 11.

5. Letter to women's page editor from Joan Garson, "Can a Housewife Be Politically Active," *Worker*, April 21, 1946, p. 11.

6. Flynn, "Why Women Belong in the Communist Party," *Daily Worker*, April 25, 1946, p. 7; "Congress of American Women Asks Equality in All Fields," *Daily Worker*, May 27, 1946, p. 4.

7. Nora Brent, "Housewives Can Be Active," *Worker*, May 19, 1946, p. 11; S.T. letter to editor of the women's page, *Worker*, June 23, 1946, p. 11.

8. A. E. Hudson, "Problems of Women in CP Activity," *Worker*, July 28, 1946, p. 11. I am assuming that A. E. Hudson is a man because, according to his letter, he held a powerful position in the leadership of his district, which was not named, and because he talks about women as "they" and "them" and not as "we" and "us." Nevertheless, because Hudson is identified only by initials, it is possible that the writer is actually a woman.

9. Katrina Mauley, "Woman's Right to a Job," *Worker*, August 4, 1946, p. 11; David Platt, "Film 'Comedy' Attacks Right of Women to Enter Public Life," *Daily Worker*, August 3, 1946, p. 11; Lenore Garrett, "No Women in the Press Box," *Daily Worker*, January 9, 1947, p. 14; Martha Bridger, "Arsenic and Young Lace," *Worker*, September 8, 1946, p. 11.

10. See, for example, "Anita Whitney: Longtime People's Champion Is 79," *Daily Worker*, July 16, 1946, p. 11; "Why Don't You Sign Your Name Too? Seneca Falls Woman Asks Husband," *Daily Worker*, August 10, 1946, p. 5; "How Shall Women's Rights Be Protected," *Worker*, August 25, 1946, p. 11; "Calls for Women's Equal Pay Law," *Daily Worker*, September 2, 1946, p. 5; Anthony, "Economic Status of a Housewife," *Worker*, September 8, 1946, p. 11; "Teas to Register Brooklyn Women," *Daily Worker*, September 25, 1946, p. 5; Anthony, "Jimcrow against Women," *Worker*, October 20, 1946, p. 11; Anna Pennypacker, "Our Heritage, Our Duty," *Daily Worker*, October 28, 1946, p. 1; "Subs Grow in Brooklyn: How They Solve the Problem," *Daily Worker*, December 23, 1946, p. 8.

11. Flynn, *Woman's Place in the Fight for a Better World* (New York: International Publishers, 1947).

12. Claudia Jones, "Pre-convention Discussion—For New Approaches to Our Work among Women," *Political Affairs* 27 (August 1948): 741; Flynn, "International Women's Day, 1947," *Political Affairs* 26 (March 1947): 219.

13. "Family Teamwork—Subs for the Worker," *Worker*, January 5, 1947; "Building the Communist Party," *Daily Worker*, April 2, p. 5, and June 2, 1947, p. 8.

14. Jones's "For New Approaches to Our Work among Women," says that daytime classes for women comrades were held in "practically all major districts" (p. 742). Flynn, "Life of the Party—Kings Highway Women Good Cooks and Good Marxists," *Daily Worker*, January 16, 1948, p. 11.

15. See, for example, memos from National Women's Commission Chairman Elizabeth Gurley Flynn and Secretary Claudia Jones to all CP districts and local women's commissions from March 24, 1947, and August 27, 1947, in the FBI collection of "Women Matters," Bureau file 100-3-78, n.p., section 1.

16. Millard's "Woman against Myth" appeared in *New Masses* on December 30, 1947, pp. 7–10, and January 6, 1948, pp. 7–10. It was reissued in pamphlet form by International Publishers in 1948. It seems likely that the title of Millard's work was a response to the Communist philosopher Barrows Dunham's book *Man against Myth* (Boston: Little, Brown, 1947) published earlier that year. Dunham's book—a series of essays intended to deconstruct and refute a whole series of widely accepted "social superstitions" such as "that the rich are fit and the poor are unfit" and "that there are superior and inferior races"—made no mention of male supremacy.

17. Betty Millard indicated in a conversation with historian Linn Shapiro that she had no recollection of Mary Inman's work. Shapiro conveyed this information to me in personal correspondence in August 1993.

18. Milton Howard's "Male Superiority Debunked in 'Woman against Myth,'" *Daily Worker*, June 20, 1948, p. 11, suggests that some of Millard's work is "too feminist." Margaret Krumbein's "How to Fight for Women's Rights," *Worker*, August 8, 1948, p. 9, argues that she "gives the correct Marxian approach." Harriet Magil, in my interview with her on January 12, 1993, suggested that many women in the CAW and the CP thought Millard had "done a terrific job."

19. Ferdinand Lundberg and Marynia Farnham, *Modern Woman: The Lost Sex.* Various CP sources criticize these works in 1947 and later, including Elizabeth Gurley Flynn, "Hitler's 3 K's for Woman—an American Rehash," *Political Affairs* 26 (April 1947); "Woman against Myth," 1947, p. 10, and Claudia Jones, "We Seek Full Equality for Women," *Worker*, September 4, 1949, p. 11.

20. The Party leadership's recruiting campaign for women is summed up in the "Draft Resolution for the National Convention, CPUSA" submitted by the National Committee and reprinted in *Political Affairs* 27 (March 1948): 497.

21. Flexner interview with Jacquelyn Van Voris, 1982, pp. 68 and 70, Flexner Papers, box 1, folder 6.

22. Elizabeth Gurley Flynn and Claudia Jones, memo to all districts and all women's commissions, January 28, 1948, and National Women's Commission *Monthly Bulletin* 2 (February 1948): 7, both in Federal Bureau of Investigation's "Women Matters," Bureau file 100-3-78-22, section 2.

23. Elizabeth Gurley Flynn, "1948—A Year of Inspiring Anniversaries for Women," *Political Affairs* 27 (March 1948): 265.

24. Gerald Zahavi, "Passionate Commitments: Race, Sex, and Communism at Schenectady General Electric, 1932–1954," *Journal of American History* 83 (September 1996): 514–48.

25. Claudia Jones, "Women Can Decide the Outcome in '48," *Worker*, March 7, 1948, p. 3. Throughout 1948, in articles such as Arnold Sroog's "Women Lead as Two More States Set Up 3rd Parties," *Worker*, April 11, 1948, p. 3, the CP emphasized that the Progressive Party had a firm commitment to women's equality and traditional women's issues. Sroog argued, for example, that

> one of the outstanding features of the rapid development of the 3rd party movement behind Henry Wallace has been the prominent role played by women in all phases of its organization.... [Women's] activity at the meetings, both as leaders and as participants in discussions from the floor was commensurate with their numbers.... First and foremost is the peace plank of the Progressive Party platform, which plays the biggest part in winning women not only to support Wallace, but to actively campaign for him.... The second part of the Wallace campaign that holds special attractions for women is its economic programs, especially for price control to end the inflationary situation at the corner grocers. As the people most concerned with the family budget this national problem is also a personal one for women and thousands of them are looking for the right answer on a political level.

26. Flynn, "Life of the Party—A Women's Meeting of Vital Importance," *Daily Worker*, February 9, 1948, p. 11.

27. Flynn, "Life of the Party—What's Your Mentality as Regards Women? Are Your Prejudices Showing?" *Daily Worker*, March 29, 1948, p. 10.

28. W.O., letter *Worker*, November 10, 1946, p. 11.

29. Letter from "A Communist Woman from NYC," *Daily Worker*, January 28, 1948.

30. Diane Naroff, letter to editor, *Daily Worker*, April 13, 1948, p. 8. Brill's letter appeared under the headline "Can You Help This Wife?" in *Worker*, June 6, 1948, p. 9. Responses appeared in the *Worker*, June 13 and June 20, 1948.

31. J. Gerard's letter appears under the headline, "Married Woman's First Task Is Care of the Home," in *Worker*, June 27, 1948, p. 9.

32. G.P., letter "Two Sided Question," *Worker*, July 4, 1948, p. 9.

33. J. Gingold, "Fight for Equality Begins at Home," *Worker*, June 27, 1948, p. 9.

34. "Few Men Understand Women's Problems," *Worker*, July 4, 1948, p. 9.

35. Lucille Gold, "Afternoon Branches, Sitters' Fund Pays Off," *Worker*, June 27, 1948, p. 9.

36. "Overcome Our Weakness in Our Work among Women," signed by "A Group of Los Angeles Women," in Pre-Convention Discussion Bulletin no. 4 issued by the California Communist Party, July 27, 1948. This document is also reprinted under the headline "Our Work among Women," in *Worker*, August 1, 1948, p. 4; and discussed in the FBI's "Women's Matters" collection, San Francisco Bureau file 100-11889.

37. Unsigned, undated letter to National Women's Commission Secretary Claudia Jones from the microfilmed collection of Betty Gannett Papers, State Historical Society of Wisconsin, reel 13; William Z. Foster, "On Improving the Party's Work

among Women," *Political Affairs* 27 (October 1948): 985. All the information available about the Subcommittee on the Theoretical Aspects of Work among Women comes from these two sources. Although the letter is undated, it is clear from the text that it comes from 1948, when the Subcommittee on the Theoretical Aspects of Work among Women was formed, and that it was written by some member of the subcommittee. It outlines the tasks that lay before the subcommittee, arguing that "our fight is for the complete freedom and equality of woman. We must direct our fire against every form of her subjugation—economic, political, social and sexual" and suggesting ways that Communists could remedy the theoretical deficiencies that had made the fight for women's liberation so difficult in the past. The question of the letter's authorship is an interesting puzzle. The processor's note on the first page indicates that it was "probably by Betty Gannett, although the exact authorship is unclear." In fact, I doubt very much that Betty Gannett wrote the letter. Although she was a woman who worked her way up in the CP national leadership, there is no indication that she ever worked on women's issues: the only other document in her massive collection of papers that concerns women's work is a letter from a group of women in New York City in 1955 and none of her published work deals specifically with women's oppression or women's liberation. This document's recognition that new theory was needed to address issues such as "specific samenesses and . . . differences" between men and women and the role of sexuality in women's oppression indicates to me that it was probably written by someone who dealt with and thought about women's issues on a much more regular basis. It might have been written by Betty Millard and sent to Claudia Jones, who then sent a copy to Betty Gannett, but there is no concrete evidence to support that suspicion. It is also quite possible that some other member of the subcommittee was responsible for writing the letter. Unfortunately, because of the dearth of sources about this subcommittee, there is no record of who its members were.

38. Foster's article, which is adapted from his August 9, 1948, report to the subcommittee, is clearly based on the suggestions put forth in the unsigned letter from the Betty Gannett Papers. Foster cites the same theoretical deficiencies and makes the same suggestions for remedying those deficiencies, often in the same or very similar language as the letter. For example, the letter says about women's intellectual capacities:

> The intellect is one sphere in which the woman and man are not only equal, but almost, if not entirely identical. . . . And here too is one of the major fields where male superiority theories have to be vigorously combatted. There are a host of stubborn and dangerous male chauvinist ideas here, among them being contentions that because of woman's smaller, on the average, brain than man's, therefore she is inferior intellectually to him, that she thinks "intuitively," and does not reason objectively as man is supposed to do.

Foster's article says:

> Male supremacists boldly claim that woman is, by her very make-up, intellectually inferior to man. Her brain is said to average somewhat less in weight than the man's and, therefore, the reactionaries argue that she cannot think as well as he does. They put woman's thinking capacity somewhere between the animal's and man's. That is, the animal is guided by its instincts, the woman thinks "intuitively,"

while the man reasons objectively. Such false arguments, contrary to science and experience but widely current, have done and continue to do grave damage not only to woman's fight for equality, but to society as a whole.

Similarly, the letter says:

We have to pay special attention to the urgent matter of sexual education. Our Party should have very much to say on this crucial question. So far, we have said nothing in our puritanical, hands-off attitude towards sex. . . . Of all the roots of male chauvinism (and these are many) perhaps the most important is the aggressive role played by the man in the sexual act with the woman. It runs like a red thread through the domineering attitude of men towards women in every field of activity.

The article says:

A second weakness is to be found in a pronounced reticence in dealing with questions of sex. . . . Reactionaries contend by inference if not frankly that since man plays the more positive and aggressive role sexually, he also should dominate the woman in her social life. . . . Indeed, in our propaganda and agitational material we hardly deal with the subject at all. . . . Without this it is impossible for us to combat the male supremacy "theory" and to discuss fundamentally the relationship of woman to man in society.

It is not surprising that Foster was not the sole author of this article—he was not known in general for his original thinking on the woman question. Rebecca Hill in "Nothing Personal?" suggested perhaps Claudia Jones was the real voice behind the article, but since the letter was originally sent to her, it is clear that she was not the originator of the ideas the article contained, even if she put it together for Foster in the end. The ideas within the article must have been attributed to Foster in order to insure that they would not be dismissed by sexist CP members as the feminist rantings of misguided CP women.

39. Both the *Worker* and the *Daily Worker* are filled with such photographs before 1949. For examples, see *Daily Worker,* August 18, 1948, p. 4; September 9, 1948, p. 9; November 17, 1948, p. 11.

40. Letter to the editor of the *Daily Worker,* "Against Pictures That Slur Women," from Phyllis and Morty, January 18, 1949, p. 8.

41. Letter to the editor of the *Daily Worker,* "The Cheesecake Question," from A. Kutzik, January 16, 1949, p. 8.

42. A.J.M. to editor, *People's World,* March 23, 1949, quoted in Mary Inman, "Thirteen Years of CPUSA Misleadership."

43. Letter to *Peoples World* from Mary in Oakland, May 3, 1949, quoted in "Thirteen Years of CPUSA Misleadership," 30.

44. For example, Mike and Neil, from New York City, wrote to the editor of the *Daily Worker* "In Defense of the Body Beautiful":

We have just read Phyllis and Morty's letter . . . in which they object to cheesecake. . . . We are two members of the progressive-thinking section of the male population of America. We are for socialism and participate in the struggle to make it possible in our own small way. And yet we still like pictures of the body beautiful (female). Besides the pictures of girls appearing in DW not only show us pretty legs, but those girls look darned intelligent! So, dear editor, take our thanks and encouragement. Keep up the good work, although perhaps for Phyllis's sake (and other females) you should print some shots of the body beautiful (male).

45. See letters to *People's World* from E.C. and S.F., May 19, 1949, and from group of six, May 23, 1949, both in Inman's "Thirteen Years of CPUSA Misleadership," 30–31.

46. Communist Party National Committee, "Speakers Guide on International Women's Day for Club and Group Discussions, Forums, Lectures, Mass Meetings," February 1950, p. 9, in Dorothy Healey Collection, box 125B, item no. 54.

47. See, for example, letter from J.K., "Suggestions on the Woman's Page," *Worker,* February 12, 1950; from L.H., "Another Protest on Fashion Story," *Worker,* February 12, 1950; from E.S., "Wants Different Slant on Cartoons," *Worker,* February 19, 1950.

48. See, for example, Claudia Jones, "Half the World," *Worker,* April 23, 1950, p. 11, and "When Do Girls Grow Up?" *Worker,* August 20, 1950, p. 4; Ethel S., *Worker,* May 7, 1950; E.L., *Worker,* July 9, 1950, p. 4; E.R., *Worker,* May 7, 1950. Many more letters like these appeared in 1950 and 1951 especially, including some by men.

49. See, for example, letter from Randolph C., "Urges All Out Fight on Male Supremacy," *Worker,* June 18, 1950, p. 7; letter from Helen R., *Worker,* September 17, 1950, p. 4; letter from "A Woman Today Reader," *Worker,* April 8, 1951, p. 4; letter from Betty Lewin, *Worker,* April 8, 1951, p. 4.

50. Letter to *Worker* editor from A Housewife, "Male Supremacy," *Worker,* January 11, 1953, p. 10.

51. Betty Feldman [i.e., Eleanor Flexner], "Sports for Women," *Worker,* April 20, 1952, p. 8; Jarrico, "The Campaign in Hollywood Films to Keep Women in Subjection," *Daily Worker,* September 3, 1953, p. 7; Lawson, "Woman: Second Sex," *Worker,* October 24, 1954; letter from Florence S., *Worker,* January 15, 1956, p. 10.

52. Claudia Jones, "International Women's Day and the Struggle for Peace," *Political Affairs* 30 (March 1951): 43.

53. "To Hold Parley on Woman Question," *Daily Worker,* May 27, 1949, p. 5. The Jefferson School was just one of many schools of Marxist studies that the CP sponsored to recruit new members and to educate old ones. According to Shannon *Decline of American Communism* (New York: Harcourt, Brace, 1959), p. 86, other such schools included the George Washington Carver School in Harlem, the Walt Whitman School of Social Science in Newark, the Tom Paine Schools in Westchester and Philadelphia, the Sam Adams School in Boston, the Ohio School of Social Science in Cleveland, the Abraham Lincoln School in Chicago, the Joseph Weydemeyer School of Social Science in St. Louis, the Michigan School in Detroit, the Pacific Northwest Labor School in Seattle, and the California Labor School in San Francisco. In addition to teaching lengthy classes in Marxist theory such schools also offered courses in art and music appreciation, literature, health, American history, and philosophy. Theatre, music, art, poetry and children's dance classes were offered as well. In the 1940s the Jefferson School's faculty included such well-known Marxist scholars as Annette Rubinstein, Philip Foner, and Herbert Aptheker as well as others less well-known. The Party's other Marxist schools, like the Jefferson School, made the humanities, social sciences,

and intellectual debate available to many urban, working-class women and men who did not have access to higher education.

54. "To Hold Parley on the Woman Question," p. 5; Jones, "We Seek Full Equality for Women," p. 11.

55. "Stress 'Woman Question' at Jefferson School Fall Term," *Daily Worker,* September 28, 1949, p. 12. See also the discussion of male supremacy in *Questions and Answers on the Woman Question* (mimeographed; New York: Jefferson School of Social Sciences, 1953), in the Dorothy Healey Collection, box 125b, item no. 53, and in the Bertha Reynolds Papers, Sophia Smith Collection, box 12, folder 151.

56. The copy of this document contained in Eleanor Flexner's papers at the Schlesinger Library (folder 29) is initialed "E.F." In a personal conversation Daniel Horowitz indicated to me that Flexner interviewer Jacqueline Van Voris reported that Flexner used two pseudonyms—Betty Feldman and Irene Epstein.

57. Advertisement for Jefferson School's Lenin Memorial Lectures, *Daily Worker,* January 5, 1951, p. 8; "Eve Merriam, Poet, Tonight at the Jeff School," *Daily Worker,* March 20, 1953, p. 7; "What's On?" *Daily Worker,* March 20, 1953, p. 8; "Forum Sunday on Women's Status," *Daily Worker,* March 5, 1955, p. 4.

58. Jones, "We Seek Full Equality for Women," p. 11. According to David Shannon, *The Decline of American Communism,* 88, "nearly all Communists read the *Worker . . .* but the total circulation of the *Daily* was usually about one-third of the party's membership." He cites the circulation of *Worker* in 1948 as 64,348 and the circulation of the *Daily Worker* as 23,400 in 1949.

59. On white chauvinism, see Shannon, *The Decline of American Communism,* 242–47 and 262–63; Starobin, *American Communism in Crisis, 1943-1956,* 198–201; Klehr and Haynes, *The American Communist Movement,* 125.

60. Lowenfels, "Santa Claus or Comrade X?" *Worker,* December 25, 1949, p. 7.

61. C. and G. Lang, letter to the editor, *Worker,* January 15, 1950, p. 9.

62. Walter Lowenfels's response to the Lang letter, *Worker,* January 15, 1950, p. 9.

63. Rhoda Ashe to editor, "Lowenfels's Point Not Pointed Enough," *Worker,* February 5, 1950.

64. Ruth to editor, *Worker,* March 5, 1950, p. 9.

65. Wendell Addington to editor, "Criticizes Article on Women," *Worker,* March 12, 1950.

66. "Friend Husband" to *Worker* editor, *Worker,* March 19, 1950, p. 9.

67. "Lowenfels Interviewed," *Worker,* April 16, 1950, p. 11.

68. "Male Supremacy Slows Today's Struggle," *Worker,* September 17, 1950, p. 4.

69. Document from FBI's "Women's Matters" collection, Bureau file 100-3-78, Los Angeles 100-1763, November 1, 1955.

70. Ibid.

71. In "The Question Seldom Asked," Baxandall says, "Organizing or discussing women's special oppression proved too threatening for the party to handle. Women would have to wait until 1956 to debate the issues of female liberation."

72. See, for example, the document "Some New Thoughts on the Woman Question," submitted by five unidentified women to *Party Voice,* June 1955, in Betty Gannett Papers, reel 2, and letters in the "Speak Your Piece" column of the *Daily Worker* after the Kruschev revelations of 1956.

73. Claudia Jones, "An End to the Neglect of the Problems of the Negro Woman," *Political Affairs* 28 (June 1949): 51–67.

Chapter 5: Claudia Jones and the Synthesis of Gender, Race, and Class

1. Flexner, *Century of Struggle;* Ellen DuBois, *Feminism and Suffrage: The Emergence of an Independent Women's Movement in America, 1848-1869* (Ithaca: Cornell UP, 1978); Lerner, "Black and White Women in Interaction and Confrontation," *The Majority Finds Its Past: Placing Women in History* (New York: Oxford UP, 1979); Bettina Aptheker, *Woman's Legacy: Essays on Race, Sex, and Class in American History* (Amherst, Mass.: U of Massachusetts P, 1982).

2. Aileen Kraditor, *The Ideas of the Woman Suffrage Movement, 1890-1920* (New York: Columbia UP, 1965); DuBois, *Feminism and Suffrage;* Paula Giddings, *When and Where I Enter: The Impact of Black Women on Race and Sex in America;* Cott, *The Grounding of Modern Feminism.*

3. Susan Becker, *The Origins of the Equal Rights Amendment: American Feminism between the Wars* (Westport, Conn.: Greenwood P, 1981); Rosalyn Terborg-Penn, "Discontented Black Feminists: Prelude and Postscript to the Passage of the Nineteenth Amendment," in Scharf and Jensen, eds., *Decades of Discontent;* Lunardini, *From Equal Suffrage to Equal Rights;* Rupp and Taylor, *Survival in the Doldrums;* Cott, *The Grounding of Modern Feminism;* Cynthia Harrison, *On Account of Sex: The Politics of Women's Issues, 1945-1968* (Berkeley: U of California P, 1988).

4. Earl Conrad, *Harriet Tubman: Negro Soldier and Abolitionist* (New York: International Publishers, 1942). Letters between Catt and Conrad are quoted in Leila Rupp's "Eleanor Flexner's *Century of Struggle:* Women's History and the Women's Movement," *National Women's Studies Association Journal* 4 (Summer 1992): 157–69. This particular quote comes from Catt to Conrad, June 27, 1939.

5. Other organizations, such as the United Auto Workers, the YWCA and the American Friends Service Committee, also had both black and white members and increasingly strong commitments to civil rights in the period after the war. But although they were concerned to some degree with women's rights on the one hand and civil rights for African Americans as a group on the other hand, none of these racially integrated organizations produced any detailed analysis of black women's unique problems that stemmed from their location at the intersection of gender, race, and class. See Gabin, *Feminism and the Labor Movement* and Lynn, *Progressive Women in Conservative Times.*

6. Kelley suggests that many of these African American women became middle-level Party leaders; *Hammer and Hoe*, 21–22, 26.

7. Shaffer, "Women and the Communist Party USA," 101.

8. Naison, *Communists in Harlem*, 137.

9. Flynn, *Women in the War.*

10. Interview with Harriet Magil, January 12, 1993.

11. Flynn, *Woman's Place in the Fight for a Better World*, 16.

12. Jones, "An End to the Neglect" p. 65.

13. Ordinarily the CP's line on African American women was that they were "triply oppressed" by race, class, and gender, but here Betty Millard wrote "doubly oppressed." Since "Woman against Myth" focused on gender, presumably Millard intended the

"doubly" to refer to race and gender. Given Millard's intended progressive audience she probably assumed that everyone would take class oppression for granted. It is also possible that her use of "doubly" instead of "triply" is evidence of her lack of exposure, before 1948, to CP writings about African American women.

14. Claudia Jones, "An End to the Neglect." In an interview with Katherine Campbell in New York City on February 17, 1981, Betty Millard and Harriet Magil discussed Jones's article as a "criticism" of Millard's pamphlet. Jones reiterated many of the points she made in "An End to the Neglect" in a later article, "For the Unity of Women in the Cause of Peace," *Political Affairs* 30 (February 1951): 151–68.

15. Buzz Johnson, *I Think of My Mother: Notes on the Life and Times of Claudia Jones* (London: Karia P, 1985); Fran April, "Civil Rights," *Around the World* 1 (February 1948): 2, Communism Collection, box 2, folder 20a.

16. Johnson, *I Think of My Mother*, 9, 18–19. According to Buhle, Buhle, and Georgakas, *Encyclopedia of the America Left*, the International Labor Defense, founded in 1925, was openly dominated by Communists until the late 1930s. The Scottsboro case was the most significant case in which the ILD participated. It vigorously defended the nine accused men in court while the CPUSA conducted an aggressive protest campaign to make the case a symbol of southern racism and to bring it international recognition. The ILD failed to win the defendants' unconditional release in a 1936 trial and in 1937 agreed to a plea bargain that released four defendants and subjected the remaining five to lengthy prison sentences. The Scottsboro campaign is most significant, however, because of its legal and political ramifications. As a result of the campaign, the U.S. Supreme Court ruled in 1935 that the defendants' constitutional rights were violated because blacks were systematically excluded from juries. This decision spurred a long struggle to include more African Americans on jury rolls in the South. The case also exposed many African Americans—like Claudia Jones—to Marxist theory and CP activities for the first time.

17. Robin D. G. Kelley, "Claudia Jones," in Buhle, Buhle, and Georgakas, *Encyclopedia of the American Left*, 394–95.

18. Zahavi, "Passionate Commitments," 514–48.

19. Dorothy Healey and Maurice Isserman, *Dorothy Healey Remembers: A Life in the American Communist Party* (New York: Oxford UP, 1990), 125.

20. For her discussion of black history Jones relied heavily on the work of Herbert Aptheker, the Communist historian of slavery and of black life and struggles in the United States. Articles in journals such as *Political Affairs* did not usually make use of scholarly citations, and Jones was no exception to this trend. But it is very clear that Jones paraphrased her discussion of black women's history (and indeed other parts of her argument as well) from Herbert Aptheker's article "The Negro Woman" that appeared in the Communist intellectual journal *Masses and Mainstream* 2 (January 1949): 10–17.

21. See, for example, Elizabeth Gurley Flynn, "International Women's Day," *Political Affairs* 26 (March 1947): 216–20; Clara Bodian, "How Will She Vote," *Worker*, March 14, 1948, p. 4; Consuelo Saez, "Puerto Rican Women Still Seek Emancipation," *Worker*, April 11, 1948; "On Work among Women," *Worker*, August 1, 1948, p. 4; Herbert Aptheker "The Negro Woman," pp. 10–17; and numerous other articles in the mainstream Party press between 1945 and 1948.

22. Magil interview, January 12, 1993; Betty Millard discussed her feelings about Claudia Jones with Katherine Campbell in New York on February 17, 1981.

23. Flexner's memoir on her life and writings, 1988, p. II (e), Flexner Papers, box 1, folder 8.

24. "Green Testifies on Women's Rights," *Daily Worker*, June 30, 1949, p. 9.

25. See, for example, Eugene Feldman, "If They Oppress Nations They Also Abuse Women," *Worker*, October 30, 1949, p. 11; Jo Willard, "Upgrading, Equal Pay for Women Protects Conditions for Men," *Worker*, August 7, 1949, p. 7; Elizabeth Gurley Flynn, "A Better World," *Daily Worker*, June 5, 1951, p. 8; Dora Johnson, "For Equality on the Job," *Worker Magazine*, March 7, 1952; and also John Hudson Jones, "Negro Women—Vanguard Fighters," *Worker*, February 12, 1950, p. 15; Irene Epstein [Eleanor Flexner], "Woman under the Double Standard," *Jewish Life* 4 (October 1950): 8–12; Peggy Dennis, "A Salute to Negro Women," *Worker*, February 11, 1951, p. 8; Lillian Brody, "Women's Job in Union Leadership," *Worker*, August 10, 1952, p. 8.

26. Self-congratulatory writing by women's page editors includes "We're One Year Old," *Worker*, March 25, 1951, p. 4 and "Your Page . . . Your Help Needed," *Worker*, November 30, 1952. For examples of letters requesting more coverage of Negro women, see letters from E.L. in *Worker*, July 9, 1950, p. 4, and from Helen Alison Winter and "Local 65er," *Worker*, April 8, 1951, p. 4.

27. See, for example, Feldman, "If They Oppress Nations They Also Abuse Women," p. 11; "Women Victims of Empire," *Worker*, December 1, 1950, p. 8; "As Women, Workers, Mexicans—They're Triply Oppressed," *Worker*, July 15, 1951, p. 8; Helen Vasquez, "Among the Most Militant," *Worker*, April–June 1952, p. 8; "Puerto Rican Women Have Played a Patriotic Role," *Worker*, March 11, 1956, p. 11.

28. Conrad, *Harriet Tubman*; Aptheker, "The Negro Woman," pp. 10–17.

29. See, for example, "Mrs. Mary Church Terrell Dies," *Worker*, April 3, 1955, p. 14; Clara Bodian, "Workers of Carolina Looked to Moranda Smith," *Worker*, April 24, 1955, p. 12; "Words That Will Live," *Worker*, July 24, 1955, p. 10; Peggy Dennis, "World Labor's Debt to American Women," *Daily Worker*, March 8, 1954, p. 4; Charlotte Williams, "Sojourner Truth Traveled the Land Fighting Slavery," *Daily Worker*, February 15, 1952, p. 7; Charlotte Williams, "Sojourner Truth—Michigan Heroine: She Travelled the Land and Fought Slavery," *Worker*, February 10, 1952, p. 8; John Hudson Jones, "Negro Women—Vanguard Fighters," *Worker*, February 12, 1950, p. 15; "Harriet Tubman," *Worker*, May 28, 1950, p. 11. At the beginning of February, then known as Negro History Month, the *Worker* usually featured a lot of coverage of black women's contributions to U.S. history. In 1951, for example, the *Worker* women's pages included an article by Claudia Jones about black women's struggles that began with Harriet Tubman and ended with Rosa Ingram and Ada Jackson. That issue of the paper also included an article about Frederick Douglass's contributions to the woman's rights movement condensed from Philip Foner's book on Frederick Douglass. The International Women's Day issue of the women's pages of the *Worker* on March 11, 1956, included articles about Ida Wells Barnett, Harriet Tubman, and Sojourner Truth.

30. "Peace Festival Tonight to Hear 'Ballad for Sojourner Truth,'" *Daily Worker*, June 15, 1951, p. 11.

31. Shirley Graham was the wife of W. E. B. DuBois and a writer and activist in

her own right. Moranda Smith was a leader in the Food and Tobacco Workers Union. Samuel Sillen, *Women against Slavery* (New York: Masses and Mainstream, 1955).

32. "Letters from Negro Women: 1827–1950," *Masses and Mainstream* 4 (February 1951): 24–33.

33. Dennis, "World Labor's Debt to American Women."

34. See, for example, announcement for Claudia Jones's lecture "Negro Women in the Struggle for Peace and Democracy," in *Daily Worker*, February 15, 1952, p. 8; "Jeff School Maps Active Week on Negro History," *Daily Worker*, February–June 1953, p. 6; advertisement for Jefferson School, *Daily Worker*, October 13, 1953, p. 8; Eleanor Flexner's syllabus for her Jefferson School course on the woman question, 1953–1954, Flexner Papers, box 1, folder 29.

35. Irene Epstein, "A Bibliography on the Negro Woman in the United States." This mimeographed document, self-published by the Jefferson School of Social Science in 1951, is located in the Bertha Reynolds Collection, box 12, folder 151.

36. Herbert Aptheker, ed., *Documentary History of the Negro People* (New York: Citadel P, 1951); Carter Woodson, "The Negro Slave Family," *Journal of Negro History* (October 1918); Alexander Crummell, "The Black Woman of the South: Her Neglects and Needs," *Africa and America: Addresses and Discourses* (Springfield, Mass.: Willey Publishers, 1891); Elizabeth Davis, *Lifting as We Climb* (Washington, D.C.: National Association of Colored Women, 1936).

37. In this bibliography Flexner refers readers to Harriet Jacobs's *Incidents in the Life of a Slave Girl* (Boston, 1861) and to "Maggie Lena Walker," *Journal of Negro History* 20 (1935): 610–33. Jacobs's work, with an introduction by Jean Fagan Yellin, was published in 1987 by Harvard University Press. Maggie Lena Walker was the subject of Elsa Barkley Brown's recent article "Womanist Consciousness: Maggie Lena Walker and the Independent Order of St. Luke," originally published in *Signs* 14 (Spring 1989): 610–33, and reprinted in Ellen Carol DuBois and Vicki L. Ruiz, *Unequal Sisters: A Multi-Cultural Reader in U.S. Women's History* (New York: Routledge, 1990): 208–23.

38. See, for example, Claudia Jones, "Peace Is a Woman's Business," *Worker*, June 19, 1949, p. 2; John Pittman, "Negro Women Take Lead at Union Conference," *Worker*, July 2, 1950, p. 4; Claudia Jones, "Women's Organizations in the Struggle for Peace," *Daily Worker*, February 13, 1951, pp. 7–8; "Open Drive for Jobs in Industry for Negro Women," *Daily Worker*, May 31, 1951, p. 4; "Aim to End Job Bias for Negro Women," *Daily Worker*, June 5, 1951, p. 4; Dora Johnson, "For Equality on the Job," *Worker*, March 7, 1952; "Rally March 16 for Job Rights of Negro Women," *Daily Worker*, March 11, 1952, p. 8; Pat Richards, "Open Fight on Firms Which Won't Employ Negro Women Workers," *Daily Worker*, March 22, 1953, p. 8; Michael Singer, "Mrs. Bass Fights 'For the Things I Know Are Right,'" *Daily Worker*, July 14, 1952, p. 2.

39. "Household Helpers Find It's Time to Help Themselves," *Worker*, June 12, 1949, p. 5.

40. Quotes come from "Call Negro Women to 'Sojourn for Justice,'" *Daily Worker*, September 20, 1951, p. 5; Claudia Jones, "Sojourners for Truth and Justice," *Worker*, February 10, 1952, p. 8. This group could justifiably be called a Communist front organization. The leadership of the group consisted entirely of Communist women and progressive allies of the Party. In fall 1951, when the group formed, the leaders were Beulah Richardson, Charlotta Bass, Alice Childress, Shirley Graham, Josephine

Grayson, Dorothy Hunton, Sonora Lawson, Amy Mallard, Rosalie McGee, Bessie Mitchell, Louise Patterson, Eslanda Robeson, Pauline Taylor, and Frances Williams. Grayson, Hunton, and Mallard were the wives of lynch victims or political prisoners. The others were all women whose names were associated with other Communist-influenced organizations such as the Congress of American Women and American Women for Peace. In October 1951 Sojourners for Truth and Justice traveled as a group to Washington and held a picket line and prayer meeting in front of the White House to protest segregation, lynching, and the Smith Act and to present flowers to Mary Church Terrell, Emma Richards, and Sally Peek. See also "Negro Women Bring Story of Persecution to U.S. Officials," *Daily Worker,* October 3, 1951, p. 8; "Sojourners for Our Rights," *Worker,* October 14, 1951, p. 8; and "Sojourners for Truth Hold Brooklyn Meeting," *Daily Worker,* June 29, 1952, p. 8.

See numerous articles about the Ingram case in CP publications in the late 1940s and 1950s and Clara Bodian, "Women's Groups Alert to Issues," *Worker,* March 11, 1956.

41. Jones, "For the Unity of Women in the Cause of Peace," 168; Elizabeth Gurley Flynn, "The Feminine Ferment," *Worker,* January 3, 1960, p. 9.

Chapter 6: Communist Culture and the Politicization of Personal Life

1. Flexner's review "'Singing of Women,' Important Achievement in People's Theatre," (written under the name Betty Feldman, one of her regular pseudonyms) appeared in the *Daily Worker,* April 5, 1951, p. 11.

2. Flexner, "History of American Women 'Living Newspaper' Drama," *Daily Worker,* March 5, 1951, p. 11.

3. Marvin Gettleman's essay "The New York Workers School, 1923–1944: Communist Education in American Society," in Brown et al., *New Studies in the Politics and Culture of American Communism,* argues that the American CP's recognition of the importance of workers' education shows that the Party was aware of the importance of cultural hegemony even before Gramsci's ideas were assimilated by the U.S. left in the late 1950s. Paul Mishler's "The Littlest Proletariat: American Communists and Their Children, 1922–1950" (Ph.D. diss., Boston University, 1988) makes a very similar argument. These ideas, and especially Gettleman's and Mishler's discussion of Gramsci, were particularly useful as I clarified and articulated my ideas for this chapter. Isserman suggests in *If I Had a Hammer* that it was not Communists but disillusioned Marxist intellectuals such as Dwight Macdonald, Irving Howe, and Clement Greenberg who drew on the theories of Theodor Adorno and others from the Frankfurt school in the 1950s as they formulated their own critiques of mass culture. Communists in this period, though they criticized some aspects of mass culture, still romanticized "the masses" and therefore would not have embraced the ideas of the Frankfurt school even if they had been familiar with them.

4. Even the FBI was aware of the Communist Party's efforts to create an alternative culture and way of life. In 1958, in "Communist Propaganda in the U.S., Part VII, Art, Entertainment, and Misc. Vehicles," the FBI observed that "Communists have always attempted to combine propaganda with art and entertainment. As a consequence, various forms of art and entertainment have been used extensively, persistently and effectively as a media of communist propaganda and agitation in the U.S. These include paintings, cartoons, songs, dances, motion pictures, plays, radio, tele-

vision and phonograph records. Other channels which have been widely and successfully employed to serve communist propaganda ends are schools, camps, visual aids, awards, prizes, flags, emblems, and sports." See Mark Naison and Maurice Isserman, eds., *The Communist Party USA and Radical Organizations, 1953-1960: FBI Reports from the Eisenhower Library* (Bethesda, Md.: University Publications of America, 1990), reel 2.

5. Sociologist Wini Breines coined the term, "prefigurative politics," in her book *Community and Organization in the New Left, 1962-1968: The Great Refusal* (New York: Praeger, 1982). She uses it to discuss SDS's attempts to practice the "participatory democracy" it hoped to establish at all levels of American society.

6. "Communist Party Convention Discussion—The Individual Communist and Life within the Party," *Daily Worker*, July 27, 1948.

7. According to Benjamin Harris in "'Don't Be Unconscious, Join Our Ranks': Psychology, Politics and Communist Education," *Rethinking Marxism* 6 (Spring 1993): 44-76, cultural politics became increasingly important during the Cold War because (1) they addressed "practical problems in home life faced by leftists . . . such as civil defense drills and anti-Communism at school, male chauvinism at home, sexual promiscuity, and racism among the children of party members" and (2) Communist leaders thought it an important part of Communists' "defense against what it considered to be the imminent ascendance of a fascist government."

8. Vivian Gornick, *The Romance of American Communism* (New York: Basic Books, 1977), 53-59.

9. Paul Mishler, *Raising Reds: The Young Pioneers, Radical Summer Camps, and Communist Political Culture in the United States* (New York: Columbia UP, 1999).

10. Jessica Mitford, *A Fine Old Conflict* (New York: Knopf, 1977); Martin Bauml Duberman, *Paul Robeson: A Biography* (New York: Ballantine Books, 1989); Annette T. Rubinstein, "The Cultural World of the Communist Party: An Historical Overview," and Alan Wald, "Culture and Commitment: U.S. Communist Writers Reconsidered," in Brown et al., *New Studies in the Politics and Culture of U.S. Communism.*

11. See, for example, Robbie Lieberman, *My Song Is My Weapon: People's Songs, American Communism, and the Politics of Culture, 1930-1950* (Champaign: U of Illinois P, 1989); Charlotte Nekola and Paula Rabinowitz, eds., *Writing Red: An Anthology of American Women Writers, 1930-1940* (New York: Feminist P, 1987); Rubinstein, "The Cultural World of the Communist Party: An Historical Overview," and Wald, "Culture and Commitment: U.S. Communist Writers Reconsidered."

12. Susan B. Anthony II, "Jimcrow against Women," *Worker*, October 20, 1946, p. 11.

13. David Platt, "Film 'Comedy' Attacks Right of Women to Enter Public Life," *Daily Worker*, August 3, 1946, p. 11; Martha Bridger, "Arsenic and Young Lace," p. 11.

14. See, for example, Lloyd L. Brown, "Words and White Chauvinism," *Masses and Mainstream* 3 (February 1950): 3-11; "When Do 'Girls' Grow Up?" p. 4, and Claudia Jones's response to the letter printed on the same page; Harry Lee to the editor, "Chauvinist Term," *Daily Worker*, January 31, 1951; Detroit auto worker to the editor, "Condemns Use of Word 'Yellow,'" *Daily Worker*, January 26, 1951, p. 6; Marvin S., Brooklyn, to editor, "Critical of Chauvinist Word," *Daily Worker*, January 11, 1951, p. 6; Claudia Jones, "Beware of Lady Nicotine," *Worker*, January 19, 1954, p. 12.

15. The best example of a Communist's critique of the ways women were depicted in literature is Margrit Reiner's article, "The Fictional American Woman," *Masses and Mainstream* 5 (June 1952): 1–10. See also Robert Friedman, "Three Books on Women, The Novel, and Chekhov," *Daily Worker,* July 31, 1950, p. 11. Others continued to complain about the misrepresentation and lack of representation of women in magazines and even in Communist Party literature. See, for example, Will Parry, "Sex, Sadism and Slaughter Is the Magazine Menu at Newsstands," *Daily Worker,* June 5, 1953, p. 7; Leila Haber, "A Look at the Big 3 in Women's Magazines," *Worker,* December 27, 1953, p. 8; Elizabeth Lawson, "Critical of Article on Women in Chess," *Daily Worker,* July 7, 1955, p. 7.

16. N.E. to editor, "Children Misused on Television Program," *Daily Worker,* October 25, 1950, p. 6; Vic Miller, "Looking at TV Shows Featuring Women," *Daily Worker,* December 1, 1955, p. 7. The FBI also kept careful track of the CP's assessment of the portrayal of women in television. See "The Communist Party Line," in Naison and Isserman, eds., *The Communist Party USA and Radical Organizations,* reel 6.

17. Elizabeth Gurley Flynn, "Women's Rebellion: There's Another Grassroots Movement Rising—And the Fashion Dictators Had Better Beware," *Worker,* October 26, 1947, p. 9; "High Heels and Health," *Worker,* June 12, 1949, p. 11, and L.H. to the editor, "Another Protest on Fashion Story," *Worker,* February 12, 1950.

18. Ted Tinsley's column in the *Daily Worker,* was called "Ted Tinsley Says." This particular column, entitled, "Gene and Jean," appeared on January 16, 1951, p. 11. Flynn's attack on conventional beauty standards appeared in her regular column "Life of the Party" in the *Daily Worker,* on September 20, 1948.

19. David Carpenter's review of *The Woman Question: Selections from the Writings of Karl Marx, V. I. Lenin, J. V. Stalin and Frederick Engels* appeared in *Worker,* on July 8, 1951, p. 7.

20. Merriam and LeSueur wrote frequently for *Masses and Mainstream,* the successor to the Communist publication *New Masses.* Merriam's "Birthday," *Masses and Mainstream* 2 (July 1949): 34–35, and LeSueur's "Eroded Woman," *Masses and Mainstream* 1 (September 1948): 32–39, are just two examples of their work. Less-well-known writers also wrote pieces praising women for the CP press. In April 1952, for example, the *Daily Worker,* published Sadie Van Veen's poem "Symphony of Women" that praised women's bravery and their desire to "save the youth, to save mankind from terror and war." These writers were continuing an older trend of Communist women's authorship of proletarian novels, poems, and short stories that aimed to portray women, especially those from the working class, in a more favorable and realistic light. Some of the books, stories, and poems published before and during World War II include Agnes Smedley, *Daughter of Earth* (New York: Coward-McCann, 1929); Meridel LeSueur, "Women on the Breadlines," *New Masses* 7 (January 1932): 00, and "The Fetish of Being Outside," *New Masses* 10 (February 1935): 00; Ruth McKenney, *My Sister Eileen* (1938), *Industrial Valley* (1939), and *Jake Home* (1943); Josephine Herbst, *Rope of Gold* (1939); Tillie (Lerner) Olsen, "The Strike," *Partisan Review* 1 (September–October 1934) and "I Want You Women Up North to Know," *Partisan* (March 1934); Myra Page, *The Gathering Storm* (1932). For critical discussions of these authors and their works, see Deborah Rosenfelt, "From the Thirties: Tillie Olsen and the Radical Tradition," *Feminist Studies* 7 (Fall 1981): 370–406; Elinor Langer, *Josephine Herbst:*

*The Story She Could Never Tell* (Boston: Little, Brown, 1984); Charlotte Nekola and Paula Rabinowitz, eds., *Writing Red: An Anthology of American Women Writers, 1930-1940;* Constance Coiner, "Literature of Resistance: The Intersection of Feminism and the Communist Left in Meridel LeSueur and Tillie Olsen," in Lennard J. Davis and M. Bella Mirabella, eds., *Left Politics and the Literary Profession* (New York: Columbia UP, 1990) and Constance Coiner, *Better Red* (New York: Oxford UP, 1995).

21. Virginia Warner's "Battle for Women's Rights Began in 1848," *Worker,* December 1, 1946, p. 11, outlines the history of the Seneca Falls Convention of 1848 and discusses the "Declaration of Sentiments" in some detail.

22. Samuel Sillen, "'Go Home, Ladies, Go home,'" *Daily Worker,* September 13, 1946, p. 11 and "The Feminine Ferment," *Worker,* October 13, 1946, p. 8; Virginia Warner, "How Women Helped Fight against Slavery," *Worker,* November 24, 1946, p. 11.

23. Philip Foner, "Sarah Bagley and the Lowell Factory Girls Who Pioneered," *Worker,* September 22, 1946, p. 11; Virginia Gardner, "Women Waged Bitter Strike for the Vote," *Worker,* December 15, 1946, p. 11.

24. E.R. to editor, "Liked Article on Women in Abolitionist Movement," *Daily Worker,* October 17, 1946, p. 7; E.L. to editor, *Worker,* January 19, 1947, p. 10.

25. See, for example, articles from the *Worker:* Mother Bloor, "Great American Women," January 19, 1947, p. 9; on Kaethe Kollwitz, February 15, 1948, pp. 6–7; Mary Southard, "Southern Women Who Pioneered," June 20, 1948, p. 5; on Prudence Crandall, April 6, 1950; on Harriet Tubman, May 28, 1950, p. 11; "Woman Fighter for Negro Rights," July 1, 1951, p. 8; Charlotte Williams, "Sojourner Truth—Michigan Heroine: She Travelled the Land and Fought Slavery," February 10, 1952, p. 8; Joseph Morton, "From Suffragette to Peace Partisan," March 7, 1952; Steve Murdock, "Labor Heroine," May 2, 1952; "200th Anniversary of the Birth of Phillis Wheatley, Negro Woman Poet," March 6, 1953; Walter Lowenfels, "Woman of Her People," July 12, 1953, p. 9; Betty Feldman, "Jim Crow's Number One Foe," July 12, 1953, p. 11; Betty Feldman, "Socialist Women's Leader and Fighter for Amnesty," August 23, 1953, p. 12; "'Impatient Crusader' for Women's Rights," November 29, 1953, p. 8; Samuel Sillen, "Slaveholders Raged at Sarah and Angelina," March 6, 1955, p. 8; Clara Bodian, "Mrs. Mary Church Terrell," April 3, 1955, p. 14; Clara Bodian, "Workers of Carolina Looked to Moranda Smith," April 24, 1955, p. 12; Barbara Jones, "Brave, Gifted, Ernestine Jones," April 10, 1955, p. 12; Lena Gold, "Rose Wortis—Garment Leader," July 10, 1955, p. 11; Clara Bodian, "She Fought the Sweatshops," July 17, 1955, p. 11; and Elizabeth Lawson, "Milestones in the Struggle for Women's Rights," March 11, 1956, p. 11; and from the *Daily Worker:* Flynn, "Life of the Party," October 15, 1947, p. 11, and June 2, 1948, p. 10; "Maud Malone Dies at 78; Fought for Women's Rights," February 8, 1951, p. 9.

During my research I read some of these articles about women's history and was struck by the similarities between some of them and parts of Flexner's book *Century of Struggle.* It appeared that Flexner had plagiarized *Worker* articles when she wrote her book, but in fact Flexner wrote for the CP press using pseudonyms. Flexner actually wrote the articles that listed Betty Feldman as the author, and she probably wrote the ones without a byline as well. Later when she wrote *Century of Struggle,* she must have incorporated bits of writing she had done earlier for the *Worker.*

26. Flynn, "1948—A Year of Inspiring Anniversaries for Women," *Political Affairs*

27 (March 1948): 259–65; Flynn, "'Petticoat Revolt' They Sneered," *Worker Magazine,* July 18, 1948, p. 1; Dennis, "World Labor's Debt to American Women." For other examples of such articles, see Robert Friedman, "Women Early Found the ABC of Struggle," *Worker,* September 5, 1948, p. 3; Peggy Dennis, "Comradely Yours," *Worker,* April 29, 1951, p. 8; Harry Raymond, "Heroes of the Civil War," *Worker Magazine,* March 6, 1953; "'May My Right Hand Wither If I Turn Traitor,'" *Worker,* December 5, 1954, p. 12; and Margaret Cowl, "Our Women Pioneers," undated clipping from *Worker Magazine,* in the Dorothy Healey Collection, box 125, folder 147.

27. Herbert Aptheker, "The Political Prisoners in the Woman Suffrage Movement," *Daily Worker,* July 8, 1954, p. 5. The other two articles in the series were: Aptheker, "How Women Opened Prison Doors and Won the Right to Vote," *Daily Worker,* July 10, 1953, p. 4, and "Woman's Fight for the Right to Vote," *Worker,* August 7, 1953.

28. Herbert Aptheker, "Woman's Fight for the Right to Vote"; Dennis, "World Labor's Debt to American Women"; and FBI, "The Communist Party Line, January–April 1954," p. 53 in Naison and Isserman, eds., *The Communist Party and Radical Organizations,* reel 6.

29. "History of American Women 'Living Newspaper' Drama," *Daily Worker,* March 5, 1951, p. 11.

30. Betty Feldman [Flexner], "'Singing of Women,' Important Achievement in People's Theatre." According to this review, Virginia Warner also contributed to three of the numbers in the production and Florence Greenberg wrote the music. Will Lee directed the play, Becky Lee choreographed it, and a "full regalia of radio and Broadway talent" participated in making "'Singing of Women' the kind of entertainment both women and men sing about!"

31. S.T., of New York City, to *Worker,* June 23, 1946, p. 11.

32. W.O. to *Worker,* November 10, 1946, p. 11.

33. See, for example, S.H.A., from New York, to the *Daily Worker,* "Closer Attention Needed to Personal Problems," March 5, 1946, p. 6, and letter to the editor, *Daily Worker,* from "A Communist Woman," January 28, 1948.

34. Many of these letters appeared in response to Margaret Brill's letter to the *Worker,* published on June 6, 1948, asking for advice about how to deal with her husband's insistence that it was her job to take care of the house and children so he could go out to meetings.

35. Joseph Gingold, "The Fight for Equality Begins at Home," *Worker,* June 27, 1948, p. 9; E.E., from Long Island City, "Expel Male Chauvinists," *Worker,* June 20, 1948, p. 9.

36. M.L., from the Bronx, to the editor, *Worker,* June 13, 1948, p. 9.

37. Harris, "'Don't be Unconscious,'" passim.

38. Joseph Wortis, "The Psychoanalytical Tradition," *New Masses,* October 2, 1945, and "New Paths for Psychoanalysis," *New Masses,* October 9, 1945. On Wortis and his role in changing Communist educators' approaches to psychology, see Harris, "'Don't be Unconscious,'" 61–65.

39. David Carpenter, review of *The Woman Question, Worker,* July 8, 1951, p. 7. Krumbein, "How to Fight for Women's Rights," and Jones, "We Seek Full Equality for Women," are two more examples of Communist writers who present this analysis of the negative effects of male supremacist culture on men.

40. Jones, "We Seek Full Equality for Women"; Jean Vermeersch, "Fight for Women's Rights Concern of All Communists," *Worker*, July 11, 1948, p. 9.

41. Krumbein, "How to Fight for Women's Rights." Margaret Krumbein is the married name of 1930s CP women's leader Margaret Cowl.

42. *Daily Worker*, April 27, 1948, p. 5.

43. *Worker*, April 3, 1949.

44. M.S., to editor, *Worker*, September 17, 1950, p. 4. For examples of other articles and letters, see Elizabeth Gurley Flynn's "Life of the Party" columns in the *Daily Worker*, in the late 1940s and early 1950s; letter to the editor from "Friend Husband," "Is Washing Dishes Enough?" *Worker*, March 19, 1950, p. 9; Randolph C., letter to the editor, "Urges All Out Fight on Male Supremacy," *Worker*, June 18, 1950, p. 7; anonymous letter to the editor, *Worker*, February 22, 1953; letter to the editor, "Making Time for Political Work," *Worker*, March 1, 1953, p. 12; letter to the editor, "Getting Time for Activity," *Worker*, March 15, 1953, p. 12.

45. Jean Josephs, "Double Burden," *Worker*, February 14, 1954, p. 12.

46. Elizabeth Lawson, "Woman: Second Sex," review of Simone DeBeauvoir's *Second Sex*, in *Worker*, October 24, 1954, p. 12.

47. Naison and Isserman, eds., *The Communist Party and Radical Organizations*, reel 6, "The Educational Program of the Communist Party, USA, Part I: Communist Front Schools," May 1954, pp. 47–48; "Post-Election Courses at Jeff School," *Daily Worker*, November 17, 1954, p. 4.

48. Epstein and Wilkerson, *Questions and Answers on the Woman Question.*

49. Naison and Isserman, eds., *The Communist Party and Radical Organizations*, reel 6, "The Educational Program of the Communist Party, USA, Part I: Communist Front Schools," May 1954, pp. 47–48; "Post-Election Courses at Jeff School," p. 4; Eleanor Flexner's syllabus for her Jefferson School course, "The Woman Question," 1953–54, Flexner Papers, box 1, folder 29.

50. Epstein and Wilkerson, *Questions and Answers on the Woman Question*, 12–13.

51. Steve Nelson, Rob Ruck, and James Barrett, *Steve Nelson: American Radical* (Pittsburgh, U of Pittsburgh P, 1981), 267–68.

52. Gannett's notes from these lectures and others are available in Gannett Papers, reel 5.

53. Betty Gannett, "Morality in Marriage," n.d., Gannett Papers reel 5.

54. Peggy Dennis's book *The Autobiography of an American Communist: A Personal View of a Political Life, 1925-1975* (Westport, Conn.: Lawrence Hill, 1977), clearly demonstrates that not all families made efforts to live according to nonsexist practices. Her experiences cannot be used to generalize about all Communists' and progressives' experiences, however. In fact, that she was the wife of a nationally visible and prominent Party leader probably makes her experiences quite different from those who were involved in Communist politics at the state and local levels.

55. Nelson, Ruck, and Barrett, *Steve Nelson: American Radical*, 267.

56. Weigand, telephone interview with Joan Acker, June 29, 1993; Ruth Prago, interview with Rose Kryzak, New York City, January 4, 1982, Oral History of the American Left, Series I, Tamiment Library, New York University; Weigand, author's interview with Ann Fagan Ginger, Cleveland, Ohio, May 1, 1989.

57. Weigand, interview with Dorothy Healey, December 30, 1992, Washington,

D.C.; FBI's "Women's Matters," Bureau file 100-3-78, Los Angeles 100-1763, October 14, 1955, pp. 57–58.

58. "Male Supremacy Slows Today's Struggle," *Worker*, September 17, 1950, p. 4.

59. Lillian Brody, "Painless Childbirth," *Worker*, June 15, 1952, p. 8; Larry Collins, "How Paris Adopted Painless Childbirth," *Daily Worker*, January 11, 1956, p. 2; "How Chinese Doctors Aid in Painless Childbirth," *Worker*, January 22, 1956, p. 11; "These Parents Plan Painless Childbirth," *Worker*, February 12, 1956, p. 11.

60. "Family Relations Are Changing in People's Democracies," *Worker*, August 24, 1952, p. 8; "Children Should Be Free to Challenge and Question," *Worker*, May 31, 1953, p. 12; Jean Josephs, "Fighting Prejudices," *Worker*, July 12, 1953.

61. Jane Lazarre, "The Lessons of Radical Women," *Village Voice*, December 2–8, 1981; Jane Lazarre, "Growing Up Red: Remembering a Communist Childhood in New York," in Geoffrey Stokes, ed., *Village Voice Anthology, 1956–1980: Twenty-five Years of Writing from the Village Voice* (New York: William Morrow, 1982), 249–55; Barbara Melosh with Linn Shapiro and Judy Kaplan, "Growing Up Red: Children of the Left Meet and Remember," *Radical History Review* 31 (December 1984): 72–84; Judy Kaplan and Linn Shapiro, eds., *Red Diaper Babies: Children of the Left* (Washington, D.C.: Red Diaper Productions, 1985).

62. In her commentary that appears in Michael Wilson, *Salt of the Earth* (New York: Feminist P, 1978), Deborah Rosenfelt discusses the radical backgrounds of those who participated in the making of *Salt of the Earth* and suggests that they all had significant contacts with the Communist Party, either as members or as participants in the organization's front groups and radical subculture. See esp. 100–102.

63. This discussion relies heavily on Schrecker's *Many Are the Crimes*, 316–40.

64. Wilson, *Salt of the Earth*, 90.

65. Schrecker, *Many Are the Crimes*, 333.

66. Ibid., p. 334.

67. Wilson, *Salt of the Earth*, 90.

68. Ibid., 95 and 187. Advertisements for *Salt of the Earth* ran in the *Worker*, continuously in March 1954.

69. David Platt, "'Salt of the Earth'—A Great American Movie," *Daily Worker*, March 15, 1954, p. 7; Elizabeth Gurley Flynn, "What 'Salt of the Earth' Means to Me," *Political Affairs* 33 (June 1954): 63–65; Betty Millard, "A Visit with the Actors Who Made One of Our Great Movies," *Daily Worker*, May 11, 1955, p. 6; Betty Millard, "'Salt of the Earth': A Postscript," *Daily Worker*, April 27, 1955, p. 6.

70. David Platt, "Housewives, Teachers, Office, Shops, Mill Workers Hail 'Salt of the Earth,'" *Daily Worker*, March 24, 1954, p. 7.

71. Saul Gross to the editor, "Salt of the Earth," *Daily Worker*, May 14, 1954, p. 7.

72. Platt, "Housewives, Teachers, Office, Shops, Mill Workers Hail 'Salt of the Earth,'" p. 7.

73. Rosenfelt in Wilson, *Salt of the Earth*, 93 and 96.

74. E.R.R., "Needed: Still Newer Look at Women's Problems," Sixteenth National Convention Discussion Bulletin, no. 2, November 27, 1956, p. 2.

75. See, for example, Florence S. to the editor, *Worker*, January 15, 1956, p. 10; women's pages, *Worker*, March 18, 1956; Archie Johnstone, "Women 'Man the Cranes' But the Process Can Be Speeded," *Worker*, April 8, 1956; letter to the editor from "A

Continuing Reader on Women's Status," *Daily Worker*, April 18, 1956, p. 4; Elizabeth Lawson, "Abolition of Housework Seen Possible with Public Planning," *Worker*, May 6, 1956, p. 11; Ruth Simon to the editor, *Worker*, May 27, 1956, p. 11; Elizabeth Lawson, "What Can Be Done about the Burden of Housework," *Worker*, May 13, 1956, p. 10; letter to the editor, "Says We Do Poorly by the Women," *Worker*, June 3, 1956; letter to the editor, "Second Look at the Woman Question," *Worker*, June 10, 1956; letter to the editor, "More Understanding Needed at Home," *Worker*, June 10, 1956; letter to the editor, "Two Can Lighten Burdens of Wife," *Worker*, June 24, 1956; "Housewife Wonders: Can Marriage Be a 50-50 Deal with Progressives?" *Worker*, October 14, 1956, p. 11.

76. E.R.R., "Needed: Still Newer Look at Women's Problems."

## Chapter 7: Old Left Feminism, the Second Wave, and Beyond

1. Ann Shanahan, "Northampton Author Eleanor Flexner: Works Quietly at Her Craft," *Daily Hampshire Gazette*, December 7, 1972, p. 2.

2. Van Voris interview, January 8, 1977, p. 1, in Flexner Papers, box 1, folder 6; transcript of conversation between Eleanor Flexner and Jacqueline Van Voris, Northampton, 16 October 1982, in Flexner Papers, box 1, folder 6. See esp. pp. 60–61 and 67–71. Ellen DuBois, "Eleanor Flexner and the History of American Feminism," *Gender and History* 3 (Spring 1991): 81–90; Leila Rupp, "Eleanor Flexner's *Century of Struggle*: Women's History and the Women's Movement," *NWSA Journal* 4 (Summer 1992): 157–69. According to the obituary in the *Daily Hampshire Gazette*, Flexner died at age eighty-six in a nursing home in Westboro, Mass., in March 1995, and the Schlesinger Library opened her papers shortly afterwards. Since her death historians Ellen Fitzpatrick and Daniel Horowitz have made use of the papers. Fitzpatrick wrote about Flexner's CP membership in the introduction for the latest edition of *Century of Struggle* (Cambridge: Harvard UP, 1996), and Horowitz writes about Flexner's Communist ties in *Betty Friedan and the Making of "The Feminine Mystique": The American Left, the Cold War, and Modern Feminism* (Amherst: U of Massachusetts P, 1998).

3. Gerda Lerner does discuss her political history in Eileen Boris and Nurpur Chaudhuri, eds., *Voices of Women Historians: The Personal, the Political, the Professional* (Bloomington: Indiana UP, 1999).

4. Evans, *Personal Politics*; Echols, *Daring to Be Bad*.

5. Judith Hole and Ellen Levine, *The Rebirth of Feminism* (Chicago: Quadrangle Books, 1971); Jo Freeman, *The Politics of Women's Liberation* (New York: David McKay Co., 1975); Flora Davis, *Moving the Mountain: The Women's Movement in America Since 1960* (New York: Simon & Schuster, 1991).

6. O'Brien, "The Development of a New Left in the United States, 1960–1965"; Kirkpatrick Sale, *S.D.S.* (New York: Random House, 1973); James Miller, *Democracy in the Streets: From Port Huron to the Siege of Chicago* (New York: Touchstone, 1987); Todd Gitlin, *The Sixties: Years of Hope, Days of Rage* (New York: Bantam Books, 1987).

7. See Horowitz, *Betty Friedan and the Making of "The Feminine Mystique."*

8. See, for example, Eve Merriam, "Birthday" in *Masses and Mainstream* 2 (July 1949): 34–35; "History of American Women 'Living Newspaper' Drama," *Daily Worker*, March 5, 1951, p. 11; "Eve Merriam, Poet, Tonight at Jeff School," *Daily Worker*, March 20, 1953, p. 7.

9. Eve Merriam, "Sex and Sensibility," *Worker*, March 29, 1959, p. 11.

10. Eve Merriam, *Montgomery, Alabama, Money, Mississippi, and Other Places* (New York: Cameron Associates, 1956).

11. Eve Merriam, *The Double Bed from the Feminine Side* (New York: Cameron Associates, 1956).

12. Eve Merriam, *After Nora Slammed the Door: American Women in the 1960s, the Unfinished Revolution* (Cleveland: World Publishing Co., 1962), 233, 235–36. Betty Friedan, *The Feminine Mystique* (New York: W. W. Norton, 1963).

13. Lucinda Cisler, "Women: A Bibliography," Women's Liberation Papers, Sophia Smith Collection; "Feminine Focus VII," in *Newsletter of the International Association of Personnel Women,* March 1971; Pat Schuman and Gay Detlefsen, "Sisterhood Is Serious: An Annotated Bibliography," *Library Journal,* September 1, 1971; all in the Women's Liberation Papers, Sophia Smith Collection, box 3, folder 24.

14. Merriam proposes these radical solutions to the problem of women's oppression in the last chapter of her book *After Nora Slammed the Door.* It is interesting that in this book Merriam actually makes many of the same arguments about women's problems that Friedan became so famous for only one year later. She argues that middle-class women who have been educated, who have lost their function in the home, and who have not yet gained a respected function in the world, are in a unique position to question their purpose and to initiate the changes that might complete women's "unfinished revolution." Like Friedan, Merriam also details suburban housewives' frustration with their role and alienation from the real world, criticizes social scientists such as Margaret Mead, Marynia Farnham, and Ferdinand Lundberg for essentializing gender differences and blaming women for their own problems, and attacks the U.S. educational system and mass culture for "brainwashing" women into accepting a rigid classification of what is properly masculine and what is properly feminine behavior and convincing them that marriage and motherhood were the most natural aspirations for them.

15. See Flexner's typed memoir on her life and writings, Flexner Papers, box 1, folder 8.

16. See especially Flexner's and Reynolds's correspondence from early 1961 in the Bertha Reynolds Papers, Sophia Smith Collection, box 1, folder 7, and box 2, folder 28. According to Flexner, her disillusionment with Marxism began in 1953, when she realized that very few of her comrades could think or talk critically about their political assumptions, and culminated in 1956, after she heard Kruschev's revelations about Stalin's crimes. She writes that her departure from the movement and her isolation from her former comrades "baffled" her and caused her to suffer incurable migraine headaches that ultimately led her to seek help from a therapist. While in therapy, Flexner wrote to Reynolds, she decided that she could find the fellowship she missed from the Communist Party in the church, and so she decided to convert to Catholicism in 1961. But Flexner did not abandon her social conscience after she became religious. Rather, she continued to engage in political work of various kinds including educating her Northampton parish about poverty. In July 1970, she wrote to Reynolds to say, "My energies are devoted almost entirely to our parish religious education program. I call it working with Mr. Nixon's silent majority! But we are having no difficulty in using texts and films on poverty and discrimination, just as long as we stay away from any suggestion of the radical new politics!"

17. Ellen DuBois discusses her 1988 interview with Flexner in "Eleanor Flexner and the History of American Feminism."

18. Both DuBois's "Eleanor Flexner and the History of American Feminism" and Leila Rupp's "Eleanor Flexner's *Century of Struggle*" also discuss the ways in which Flexner's work was unusual for its time.

19. Flexner, xi.

20. DuBois, "Eleanor Flexner and the History of American Feminism," 86.

21. Friedan's chapter four, "The Passionate Journey," is essentially a summary of Flexner's history of the woman's rights movement. It is not surprising that Friedan was familiar with Flexner's arguments since she herself had ties to the Old Left. See Horowitz, "Rethinking Betty Friedan and *The Feminine Mystique:* Labor Union Radicalism and Feminism in Cold War America," *American Quarterly* 48 (March 1996): 1–42; and *Betty Friedan and the Making of "The Feminine Mystique."*

22. Friedan, *The Feminine Mystique*, 382.

23. See, for example, *Notes from the First Year*, by New York Radical Women, June 1968, pp. 3–5; Cisler, "Women: A Bibliography," 1969; syllabus from early women's studies course at Cornell University, 1970; Schuman and Detlefsen, "Sisterhood Is Serious: An Annotated Bibliography"; Mary Mays, "The New Feminism: A Basic Booklist" (Cleveland Heights–University Heights Public Library, 1972); Ellen Stoll Isaly, "KNOW Bibliography," compiled December 1972; "The Women's Equal Rights Movement," a bibliography compiled by the Women's Equity Action League, n.d.; all in the Women's Liberation Papers, Sophia Smith Collection, box 3, folder 24; *SPAZM,* published by Laura X, June 15, 1969, reel 21, and "Pandora's Box" from San Diego, April 1970, reel 20, *Herstory* microfilm collection; Women's History Research Center, "Towards an Annotated Book Bibliography," n.d., and "Library Catalog," 1969, Women's Liberation Papers, Sophia Smith Collection, box 21, folder 220; Connie Brown and Jane Seitz, "You've Come a Long Way Baby," in Robin Morgan, ed., *Sisterhood Is Powerful: An Anthology of Writings from the Women's Liberation Movement* (New York: Vintage Books, 1970); Judith Hole and Ellen Levine, "The First Feminists" in Anne Koedt, Ellen Levine, and Anita Rapone, eds., *Radical Feminism* (New York: Quadrangle Books, 1973).

24. DuBois, "Eleanor Flexner and the History of American Feminism," 89.

25. Aileen Kraditor, *The Ideas of the Woman's Suffrage Movement, 1890-1920* (New York: Columbia UP, 1965) and Kraditor, *Up from the Pedestal: Selected Writings in the History of American Feminism* (Chicago: Quadrangle Books, 1968). On Kraditor's associations with the Communist Party, see her article "Unbecoming a Communist" in *Continuity* 12 (1988): 97–102.

26. Gerda Lerner, *The Grimke Sisters from South Carolina: Rebels against Slavery* (Boston: Houghton Mifflin, 1967), ix and x. According to the *Worker,* June 19, 1949, p. 2, Gerda Lerner was one of the California delegates who attended the CAW national convention in New York in 1949. A photo of the Resolutions Committee of the convention in that article includes Lerner along with Pearl Lawes, Frances Smith, and Helen Wortis, from New York, Joan Leib, from Ohio, and Anne Jones, from Milwaukee. According the CAW's publication, "American Women in Pictures: Souvenir Journal" (1949), p. 4, Lerner was one of the CAW's delegates to the WIDF convention in Budapest in 1949.

27. Merriam, *Emma Lazarus* (New York: Emma Lazarus Federation of Jewish Women, 1956); Merriam, *Growing Up Female in America: Ten Lives* (New York: Doubleday, 1971).

28. There were a few significant exceptions to this generalization: former socialists Michael Harrington and Mildred Jeffrey served as advisers to the Port Huron Conference, *Studies on the Left* editor James Weinstein had been a member of the Communist Party in New York in the late 1940s and 1950s, and Barbara (Easton) Epstein belonged to the Communist Party and the Harvard chapter of SDS simultaneously in the early 1960s. For more thorough discussions of Old Leftists who participated in New Left organizations, see Evans, *Personal Politics;* Isserman, *If I Had a Hammer;* and Paul Buhle, ed., *History and the New Left: Madison, Wisconsin, 1950-1970* (Philadelphia: Temple UP, 1990).

29. Many writers on both the Old Left and the New Left comment on the importance of red-diaper babies to 1960s movements. See, for example, Evans, *Personal Politics;* Lyons, *Philadelphia Communists;* Isserman, *If I Had a Hammer;* Miller, *Democracy in the Streets;* Barbara Melosh, Linn Shapiro, and Judy Kaplan, "Growing Up Red: Children of the Left Meet and Remember," *Radical History Review* 31 (1984): 72–83; Judy Kaplan and Linn Shapiro, eds., *Red Diaper Babies: Children of the Left* (Washington, D.C.: Red Diaper Productions, 1985); Mishler, "The Littlest Proletariat" and *Raising Reds;* Epstein, *Political Protest and Cultural Revolution.* Political commentators in the early 1960s, especially those writing from a conservative point of view, were also very much aware that Communists' children championed New Left causes. In September 1965, for example, *New Guard* magazine printed an article entitled "The Red Diaper Babies Grow Up," listing Communists' children who had participated in the New Left and student movement demonstrations and activities. Similarly, in 1969 *U.S. News and World Report* published the book *Communism and the New Left* allegedly documenting the links between the Old and the New Left.

30. Evans, *Personal Politics,* Lyons, *Philadelphia Communists,* and Baxandall, *Words on Fire* have also made this point.

31. In "Women in the Old and New Left," Trimberger implies that most New Leftists, especially after 1965, grew up in the suburbs in upwardly mobile middle-class families in which neither parents nor communities "transmitted a political tradition of dissent." For more thorough discussions of typical white middle-class American family life in the Cold War era, see Friedan, *The Feminine Mystique;* May, *Homeward Bound;* Wini Breines, *Young, White, and Miserable: Growing Up Female in the Fifties* (Boston: Beacon Press, 1992); Brett Harvey, *The Fifties: A Women's Oral History* (New York: Harper Collins, 1993); David Halberstam, *The Fifties* (New York: Villard Books, 1993).

32. Kaplan and Shapiro, eds., *Red Diaper Babies,* 75–86. These edited transcripts of the Red Diaper Baby conferences held in Conway, New Hampshire, on July 31–August 1, 1982, and July 9–10, 1983, are an extremely useful compilation of the experiences of the approximately 150 red-diaper babies who attended the gatherings. Melosh, Shapiro, and Kaplan also summarize the main themes of the conferences in "Growing Up Red," 72–83. Kaplan and Shapiro's *Red Diaper Babies* grew out of the conference as well. Red-diaper babies I interviewed also shared this sense that their mothers, and sometimes their grandmothers as well, were important political role models

and remembered their parents encouraging them to aspire to adult lives that incorporated political activities and careers as well as marriage and children. Interviews
with Rosalyn Baxandall, New York City, January 14, 1993; with Norma Allen via telephone to Bethesda, Md., July 19, 1993, and with Linda Gordon via telephone to Madison, Wis., July 20, 1993. Jane Lazarre discusses similar memories in her articles "The
Lessons of Radical Women" and "Growing Up Red."

33. Kaplan and Shapiro, eds., *Red Diaper Babies,* 76–77; interviews with Gordon,
Baxandall, and Allen; Evans makes this point about red-diaper babies' awareness of
women's oppression in *Personal Politics,* 120.

34. Several of the participants at the Red Diaper Baby Conferences remember that
their households and families were characterized by traditional male-female roles and
behaviors. Despite the Party's emphasis on the need to share housework and child care,
for example, numerous red-diaper babies reported that even if both parents worked
outside the home, their mothers were still in charge of cooking and housework. In my
interview with her, Norma Allen also suggested that her mother "cooked . . . cleaned,
she did everything" and that her father "was a traditional man" who "couldn't cook to
save his life and didn't even try." The quote in the text comes from Kaplan and Shapiro,
eds., *Red Diaper Babies,* 77.

35. Author's interview with Gordon, July 20, 1993; Kaplan and Shapiro, eds., *Red
Diaper Babies,* 77; Baxandall interview, January 14, 1993; Lazarre, "The Lessons of Radical Women."

36. Kaplan and Shapiro, eds., *Red Diaper Babies,* 78.

37. Baxandall interview, January 14, 1993.

38. See, for example, "Liberation of Women," *New Left Notes,* July 10, 1967, p. 4;
"SDS National Resolution on Women," reprinted by New England Free Press, 1968
in the Women's Liberation Papers, Sophia Smith Collection, box 27, folder 259; Lynn
O'Connor, "Male Supremacy," n.d., Women's Liberation Papers, Sophia Smith Collection, box 2, folder 22.

39. Evans's *Personal Politics* was the first analysis of the women's movement to discuss the important connections between the Old Left and feminism. She quotes
daughters of feminists at length but, because of the continuing fears among Communists sparked by McCarthyism, she did not reveal the names of her red diaper baby
respondents. Evans does say that in her research she did not seek red-diaper babies
out. Rather, she says she "pursued women and men who had participated in specific
new left activities and in particular the women who provided the links between the
new left and the early leadership of the women's liberation movement. Again and
again I was surprised to discover a radical family background" (p. 120 n.). Since the
mid-1970s, when Evans was completing her book, however, more of these women have
begun to talk openly about their parents' political histories. Baxandall is very straight-
forward about her political heritage in both *Words on Fire* and "The Question Seldom
Asked." In her memoir *A Fine Old Conflict,* Mitford writes at length about her daughter Constancia (Dinky) Romilly's Communist childhood and participation in the
early feminist movement. Kathie Sarachild was somewhat more cautious in her re-
marks "The Civil Rights Movement: Lessons for Women's Liberation," given at The
Sixties Speak to the Eighties: A Conference on Activism and Social Change at the University of Massachusetts–Amherst in October 1983, but still said that she "considered

[herself] a radical before going South" to participate in Freedom Summer in 1964 and identified herself as someone who "came from a left-leaning middle- to lower-middle-class family in which I had grown up in the silent fifties loving Pete Seeger and Paul Robeson renditions of folk songs and freedom songs." Susan Brownmiller identifies Sarachild as a red-diaper baby in *In Our Time: History of a Revolution* (New York: Dial P, 1999), 20.

40. Some men who grew up in Communist families also had some of these same sensitivities to issues about women's equality. In a 1994 talk at Smith College about her experiences in the Old Left and the New, historian Barbara Epstein told a story about how she and a male friend (both red-diaper babies and active Communists) served on the steering committee of SDS at Harvard in the mid-1960s. She said that she woke up one morning to find out that she had been excluded from a meeting about a demonstration taking place on the campus later that day because she was a woman. She complained about the exclusion at an SDS meeting and got nowhere, but when she brought it up in a CP meeting the man was accused of male chauvinism and admitted that he had male chauvinist tendencies. The CP's concept of male chauvinism, she explained, gave her the ability to bring up the problem and also made it possible for CP men to take the problem seriously.

41. This discussion of consciousness raising relies heavily on Brownmiller, *In Our Time*, 20–21, 78–80.

42. Historian Herbert Aptheker was a very visible Communist in the 1960s and 1970s well known for his associations with the younger generation of activists. In 1966, for example, he visited Hanoi along with New Left activists Tom Hayden and Staughton Lynd. According to Leila Rupp, in the late 1960s, when he was a visiting professor at Bryn Mawr College, Aptheker led the first discussion of women's liberation on the campus because the women students asked him to do it.

Florence Luscomb was an old suffragist and progressive whose 1957 memoir "Progressive Movements and What They Did to Me: Some Informal Recollections" (photocopied document in the Bertha Reynolds Collection, box 12, folder 142) indicates that she had been close to the Communist Party in the 1930s and 1940s, frequently participated in feminist activities in Boston in the early 1970s. An article in *Time Magazine* (April 26, 1971) called Luscomb an "ardent women's liberationist," one who made "frequent speaking appearances at high schools and colleges arguing for abortion on demand and job equality." According to a flyer for an International Women's Day event sponsored by the MIT Socialist Club (Women's Liberation Papers, Sophia Smith Collection, box 3, folder 24), Luscomb led a seminar called the Struggle for Women's Rights and Suffrage at MIT in 1970; in 1972 she spoke along with Florynce Kennedy and Maryanne Weathers at Women's Liberation Day in Boston (flyer for Women's Liberation Day, New England Women's Coalition in the Women's Liberation Papers, Sophia Smith Collection, box 27, folder 255). For other material on Luscomb's seven decades of political activity, see Ellen Cantarow, Susan Gushee O'Malley, and Sharon Hartmann Strom, "Florence Luscomb for Suffrage, Labor, and Peace," *Moving the Mountain: Women Working for Social Change* (Old Westbury, N.Y.: Feminist P, 1980).

Robin Kelley writes about Marge Franz's Communist activism in the deep South in the 1930s in *Hammer and Hoe* and Jessica Mitford about Franz's participation in the California CP in the 1940s and 1950s in *A Fine Old Conflict*. Since the 1970s Franz, now a historian at the University of California–Santa Cruz, has been active in feminist causes and in the discipline of women's studies. Hodee Edwards Richards, one of the authors of the 1946 letters to the editor of the *Worker* that helped to spark the CP's revision of its approach to the woman question contributed an article entitled "Housework and Exploitation: A Marxist Analysis" to the journal *No More Fun and Games: A Journal of Female Liberation* 5 (July 1971): 92–100. In my interview with Dorothy Healey she said that she "was always involved with the young movements" and that she had "very good relations with all these young women." She suggested that young feminists saw her as a role model and that they regularly invited her to their events.

43. In June 1993, I wrote to Laura X to inquire about how she learned about International Women's Day and other Communist traditions and activists. She forwarded my letter to William and Tania Mandel, the sources of her information, in Berkeley, Calif. I interviewed the Mandels by telephone on June 27, 1993. Laura X was familiar with all of Claudia Jones's writing on the woman question from the 1940s and 1950s. Her Women's History Research Center "Library Catalog" from March 1971 (in the Women's Liberation Papers, Sophia Smith Collection, box 21, folder 220) lists not only Jones's "International Women's Day and the Struggle for Peace," but also "For New Approaches to Our Work among Women," "An End to the Neglect," "Foster's Political and Theoretical Guidance to Our Work among Women," *Political Affairs* 30 (March 1951): 68–78, and "The Struggle for Peace in the United States," *Political Affairs* 31 (February 1952): 1–20.

44. Laura X details her rediscovery of International Women's Day and her work to revive the holiday throughout the country in several sources. See "Laura X and the SPAZM Society," *Women in World History*, Women's Liberation Papers, Sophia Smith Collection, box 22, folder 226; pamphlet describing the Women's History Research Center Library, Women's Liberation Papers, Sophia Smith Collection, box 21, folder 220; *SPAZM* newsletter published by Laura X, n.d., *Herstory* microfilm collection, reel 21. Later feminists attributed the revival of International Women's Day to Laura X. See, for example, "Everywoman" (Los Angeles), March 26, 1971, p. 4, in the *Herstory* microfilm collection, reel 1; the "Women's Press" (Eugene, Ore.), March 1971, *Herstory* microfilm collection, reel 4; and Seattle Women's Liberation newsletter *And Ain't I a Woman*, 1 (February 1970): 14, *Herstory* microfilm collection, reel 13.

45. Correspondence between Kritzler and Inman and between Maes and Inman are in the Inman Papers, box 2.

Laura X discussed *Salt of the Earth* in an early but undated issue of *SPAZM*. She also reviewed the film in *SPAZM*, October 21, 1969, *Herstory* microfilm collection, reel 22.

46. In 1968, Chicago Women's Liberation chapters sponsored *Salt of the Earth* at an all-movement party; in 1969, Berkeley Women's Liberation and the Radical Student Union showed the movie in honor of Mrs. Albert Parsons, the wife of one of the Haymarket Square martyrs. In 1970 and 1971 it was shown in Seattle, Austin, Northampton, San Francisco, and Providence. In its "Internal Education Packet on Sexism," Part I, n.d., the Women's Caucus of the New University Conference urged all its chapters to "make a special effort to obtain the film *Salt of the Earth*" to further educate their members about how women might go about obtaining equality and about the "Mexican national minority."

47. Angela Davis, *Angela Davis: An Autobiography* (New York: International Publishers, 1974). Mary Jane Melish is listed among CAW members in HUAC's *Report on the Congress of American Women*, p. 84.

48. Angela Davis, *Women, Race, and Class* (New York: Random House, 1981). Davis joined the Communist Party in California in the summer of 1968. She quickly rose in the Party's ranks and, after she was acquitted of murder, kidnapping, and conspiracy charges in her famous 1972 case, she became a nationally recognized CP leader. In addition to teaching women's studies and black studies at San Francisco State University in the late 1970s, she ran for Vice President on a ticket with CP National Chairman Gus Hall in 1980.

49. Bettina Aptheker, *Woman's Legacy: Essays on Race, Sex, and Class in American History* (Amherst: U of Massachusetts P, 1982).

50. Gerda Lerner, *Black Women in White America: A Documentary History* (New York: Random House, 1972).

51. For a more thorough discussion of the Houston conference, see Evans, *Born for Liberty*, 306–7.

52. Klemesrud, "Another Susan B. Anthony Now Speaks Her Mind," p. 32.

53. Susan B. Anthony, speech to Florida Women's Conference in Orlando, July 15, 1977, Women's Rights Collection, box 9a, Sophia Smith Collection, Smith College, Northampton, Mass.

54. In December 1970, for example, Eleanor Flexner's companion Helen Terry wrote to Bertha Reynolds: "Eleanor's *Century of Struggle* may be the basic book for women's libbers, but it doesn't seem as if many of them are much interested in anything pre-1970! She was invited to speak at Smith (by the students) and at Skidmore (a 'name' lecture) but all the discussion periods dealt with was abortion, on which she is not an authority. It is a way to make a living, she says in disgust, but she thinks she'll stick to the typewriter!" In an interview with a *New York Times* reporter Judy Klemesrud on September 21, 1971, Susan B. Anthony II said not only that the original Susan B. Anthony would not have approved of women's liberation, but that she thought "liberated women are buying these values of the male-created society."

# Essay on Sources

## Primary Sources

Researching and writing about Communists and Communism in the post–Cold War but still anti-Communist environment of the 1990s presents numerous challenges and difficulties. First, the Communist Party USA has been on the defensive since its very beginnings. Consequently, the group has not always kept the most reliable records, and it is very protective of any organizational records it has maintained over its seventy-year history. Unlike those who research the YWCA or the United Auto Workers' Union, for example, historians of American Communism cannot go to an archive or a microfilm collection and gain access to decades worth of organizational history. Without minutes of meetings, membership lists, budgets, internal memos, and other such documents, historians must rely instead on scattered and often fragmentary evidence, much of which has been compiled by individuals or groups that were hostile to Communism, such as the U.S. Subversive Activities Control Board or the FBI. Evidence that has not been tainted by anti-Communism often bears the mark of intense Communist partisanship. In the fight between Communists and anti-Communists, everyone took one side or the other and available sources certainly reflect both extremes; it is always a challenge to sort out the biases and exaggerations—both positive and negative—and to determine what is useful and what is not.

For historians of Communist women the problems are perhaps even more difficult. Despite Communist women's efforts to reform it, the Communist Party continued to be a male-dominated organization throughout the 1940s, and later, and women's issues often remained submerged within the Party's larger discussions of oppression and liberation. Women's activities on their own behalf usually occurred at the grassroots level and did not get very much attention at the top levels of Party hierarchy or in the Party press. Furthermore, the sparse material on Communist women that does exist is often buried in larger manuscript collections and completely hidden in the finding aids associated with those collections. Many of the manuscript collections that do clearly contain information about progressive women's activities are closed to researchers until the women whose lives they detail can no longer be hurt by the revelation of their associations with the Communist Party. And Communist and progressive women who are still alive to tell the tales of their work for women's issues in the postwar period are, because of the caution that was necessarily instilled in them during the McCarthy period, still extremely hesitant to talk to outsiders about their experiences.

Despite these difficulties I did find the evidence I needed to begin to piece together the history of women's activism in the CP in the 1940s and 1950s and to show how their activities helped to change the Communist Party's position on the woman question in those years. First, I made use of archival collections of individual Communist and progressive women, including Ella Reeve Bloor (Sophia Smith Collection, Smith College, Northampton, Mass.), Eleanor Flexner (Schlesinger Library, Cambridge, Mass.), Betty Gannett (microfilm edition, State Historical Society of Wisconsin, Milwaukee), Dorothy Healey (Special Collections, California State University–Long Beach Library, Long Beach, Calif.), Mary Inman (Schlesinger Library, Cambridge, Mass.), and Mary van Kleeck (Sophia Smith Collection, Smith College, Northampton, Mass.), Dorothy Kenyon (Sophia Smith Collection, Smith College, Northampton, Mass.); organizational records of Communist-inspired groups such as the Congress of American Women (personal collection of Katherine Campbell, Acton, Mass.) and the Women's International Democratic Federation (Communism Collection, Sophia Smith Collection, Smith College, Northampton, Mass.), Bertha Reynolds (Sophia Smith Collection, Smith College, Northampton, Mass.); and the FBI's fragmentary compilation of documents relating to Communist "women's matters" (Federal Bureau of Investigation, Washington, D.C.). These collections included miscellaneous pieces of correspondence with Party leaders and other internal Party documents not otherwise available in addition to personal papers. They proved most useful for uncovering the origins of the radical critique of male supremacy that progressive women formulated in the 1930s, for documenting the ways women sustained those ideas through World War II and reintroduced them within the more receptive Communist Party of 1945–46, and for making sense of the process through which rank-and-file women's demands were at least partially incorporated into official Party policy by the late 1940s.

Second, I used published sources, including records compiled by the House Un-American Activities Committee, the U.S. Subversive Activities Control Board, the U.S. Department of Justice, and the FBI, and books, journals, pamphlets, and newspapers published by the Communist Party itself. The letters to the editors in the Communist newspapers, the *Worker,* the *Daily Worker,* and the *People's World,* which served as forums for rank-and-file Communists to express their opinions about many aspects of CP life, proved surprisingly useful for revealing rank-and-file women's dissatisfactions with the Party line. Articles and advertisements in those publications described the activities women undertook to solve their gender-related problems within the Party. All of these sources, especially the Communist newspapers, journals, and pamphlets, provided the evidence necessary to trace the evolution of the Communist Party's official policy on the woman question and to show how women successfully transformed the CP's approach to women's issues between 1946 and 1956. Such texts do not usually reveal the complicated processes by which CP leaders decided to change the Party's official position on women, but because they are the best source available, I have used them as the basis for my discussions about how such changes took place. CP publications are also probably not always reliable indicators of the extent to which Party policies and positions actually affected the day-to-day activities of Communists, but they do show that at least some Communist women were thinking and writing about the issues of women's oppression and women's liberation and that the Party came to endorse their ideas. The articles Communist women published in CP publications such as the *Worker* and *Political Affairs* in this period undoubtedly exposed thousands of Communist and progressive readers to a radical critique of male supremacy that they would not have encountered elsewhere. According to David Shannon's *The Decline of American Communism* (pp. 88–91), the *Worker* had a circulation of 64,348 in 1948 and the Party's theoretical journal, *Political Affairs* had a circulation of 12,500. The two publishing houses the CP used to publish its books and pamphlets, International Publishers and New Century Publishers, were, according to Shannon, "very busy." In 1946 they published over two million copies of CP publications. Halfway through 1947 they were running ahead of 1946. Of course these figures dropped dramatically by the 1950s as the Cold War and McCarthyism did their damage to the Party. According to an FBI estimate published in Glazer's *The Social Basis of American Communism* (pp. 92–93), the Party's membership had decreased from approximately 65,000 in 1945 to 22,663 by 1955. Nevertheless, also according to the FBI's report on the Communist Party Press (in the FBI's *Reports on the Communist Party and Radical Organizations, 1953-60*, reel 6) the circulation of the *Worker* was down to 28,822 in 1954 whereas the circulation of *Political Affairs* had increased to 17,000. Such exposure was important even if many of those readers did not ultimately resolve to fight male chauvinism in their own personal and political lives.

Finally personal interviews with Old Left women about their attitudes and experiences in the 1940s and 1950s proved to be an important source of evidence about the real lives of Communists in this period. I conducted nine semistructured, opened-ended interviews myself, six with women who were active in the Communist Party in the post–World War II period (one woman's husband also participated in the interview along with her), and three with daughters of Communists who were later involved in the women's liberation movement. I also made use of four oral history interviews with Communist women that had been recorded by the Oral History of the American Left project at New York University, and one interview with three Communist women that was conducted by historian Katherine Campbell in 1981. Locating potential interview subjects was difficult and the advanced ages of many of the women I interviewed meant that they did not always remember as much about their activist lives as I would have hoped. Nevertheless, despite their problems these women's recollections supplied information about the rationale behind some Party decisions that would have been impossible to know otherwise. They also yielded information about the impact of CP policies on individuals' personal beliefs and family lives that was difficult if not impossible to detect in printed sources.

In contrast, examining the 1960s and 1970s women's movement for evidence of Old Left influence was relatively unproblematic. The women's movement, like the New Left, was extremely prolific and created a large body of writings that laid out its analyses of women's oppression and strategies for women's liberation. Many such unpublished writings are readily available in archival collections. In addition to well-known published sources by women's movement participants I made extensive use of the Women's Liberation Papers, Sophia Smith Collection, Smith College, which contains hundreds of pamphlets, manifestos, and mimeographed documents from early women's liberation organizations, and the microfilmed edition of the International Women's History Periodical archive known as the *Herstory* Collection, which contains mission statements and newsletters from local women's liberation groups all around the United States. These sources, in addition to the interviews I conducted with feminist daughters of Communists provided abundant evidence that, despite the power of McCarthyism, various elements of the Old Left's thinking about women's oppression and women's liberation filtered down, in a variety of ways, to a younger generation of feminists who were educated and politicized in the distinctly antifeminist and anti-Communist 1950s.

## Secondary Sources

Considering the difficulties of writing Communist history, the Communist Party has been the subject of numerous studies and interpretations since the 1950s. The Cold War and anti-Communism dominated scholarly interpretations of the Communist Party from the 1950s until the mid-1970s. Good examples of works that frame the Communist Party as the American arm of the Comintern include Daniel Bell, "The Background and Development of Marxian Socialism in the United States," in Donald Drew Egbert and Stow Parsons, eds., *Socialism and American Life* (Princeton: Princeton UP, 1952); Theodore Draper, *The Roots of American Communism* (New York: Viking P, 1957) and *American Communism and Soviet Russia* (New York: Viking P, 1960); Irving Howe and Lewis Coser, *The American Communist Party: A Critical History, 1919-1957* (Cambridge: Harvard UP, 1957); Joseph Starobin, *Communism in Crisis, 1947-1957* (Cambridge: Harvard UP, 1972). Some historians have continued to write about the CP from this perspective in the 1980s and 1990s. These works include Harvey Klehr, *The Heyday of American Communism: The Depression Decade* (New York: Basic Books, 1984); Harvey Klehr and John Earl Haynes, *The American Communist Movement: Storming Heaven Itself* (New York: Twayne Publishers, 1992); Harvey Klehr, John Earl Haynes, and Fridrikh Igorevich Firsov, *The Secret World of American Communism* (New Haven: Yale UP, 1995); Haynes, *Red Scare or Red Menace? American Communism and Anti-Communism in the Cold War Era* (Chicago, 1996); Klehr, Haynes, and Kyrill Anderson, *The Soviet World of American Communism* (New Haven: Yale UP, 1998). These authors rely on recently released Soviet documents showing that some Communists participated in Soviet espionage. They emphasize the American CP's subservience to Soviet Communists, argue that the Communist leaders' activities embody the history of the Communist Party, and conclude that the Cold War view of the CP stands as the correct one.

Beginning in the 1970s some historians began to reappraise the history of the Communist movement in the U.S. Their work acknowledges the problems with Soviet Communism and American CP leaders but also emphasizes the ways in which Communist activists contributed to important and influential movements for social justice in the United States. They tend to conceive of the Communist Party as the center of a broad progressive movement that encompassed numerous struggles for social change. These works include Vivian Gornick, *The Romance of American Communism* (New York: Basic Books, 1977); Nell Irvin Painter, *The Narrative of Hosea Hudson: His Life as a Negro Communist in the South* (Cambridge: Harvard UP, 1979); Roger Keeran, *The Communist Party and the Auto Workers' Unions* (Indianapolis: Indiana UP, 1980); Paul Buhle, "Historians and American Communism: An Agenda," *International Labor and Working Class History* 20 (Fall 1981): 38–45; Maurice Isserman, *Which Side Were You On?* (Middletown, Conn.: Wesleyan UP, 1982); Paul Lyons, *Philadelphia Communists, 1936-1956* (Philadelphia: Temple UP, 1982); Ronald Schatz, *The Electrical Workers: A History of Labor at General Electric and Westinghouse* (Urbana: U of Illinois P, 1983); Melosh, Kaplan, and Shapiro, "Growing Up Red: Children of the Left Meet and Remember," *Radical History Review* 31 (December 1984):

72–84; Mark Naison, *Communists in Harlem during the Great Depression* (New York: Grove P, 1984); Ellen Schrecker, *No Ivory Tower: McCarthyism and the Universities* (New York: Oxford UP, 1986); Isserman, *If I Had a Hammer: The Death of the Old Left and the Birth of the New Left* (New York: Basic Books, 1987); Nelson Lichtenstein, "Opportunities Found and Lost: Labor Radicals and the Early Civil Rights Movement," *Journal of American History* 75 (December 1988): 786–811; Bruce Nelson, *Workers on the Waterfront: Seamen, Longshoremen, and Unionism in the 1930s* (Urbana: U of Illinois P, 1988); Robbie Lieberman, *"My Song Is My Weapon": People's Songs, American Communism, and the Politics of Culture, 1930-1956* (Urbana: U of Illinois P, 1989); Joshua Freeman, *In Transit: The Transportation Workers Union in New York City* (New York: Oxford UP, 1990); Robin D. G. Kelley, *Hammer and Hoe: Alabama Communists during the Great Depression* (Chapel Hill: U of North Carolina P, 1990); Dorothy Healey and Maurice Isserman, *Dorothy Healey Remembers: A Life in the American Communist Party* (New York: Oxford UP, 1990); Fraser Ottanelli, *The Communist Party of the United States from the Depression to World War II* (New Brunswick, N.J.: Rutgers UP, 1991; Barbara Epstein, *Political Protest and Cultural Revolution: Non-violent Direct Action in the 1970s and 1980s* (Berkeley: U of California P, 1991); Leo Ribuffo, "The Complexity of American Communism," *Right Center Left: Essays in American History* (New Brunswick, N.J.: Rutgers UP, 1992); Michael E. Brown et al., eds., *New Studies in the Politics and Culture of U.S. Communism* (New York: Monthly Review P, 1993); Robert Cohen, *When the Old Left Was Young: Student Radicals and America's First Mass Student Movement, 1929-1941* (New York: Oxford UP, 1993); Michael Denning, *The Cultural Front: The Laboring of American Culture in the Twentieth Century* (London and New York: Verso P, 1996); Ellen Schrecker, *Many Are the Crimes: McCarthyism in America* (Boston: Little, Brown, 1998); Paul Mishler, *Raising Reds: The Young Pioneers, Radical Summer Camps and Communist Political Culture in the United States* (New York: Columbia UP, 1999); Linn Shapiro and Judy Kaplan, *Red Diapers: Growing Up in the Communist Left* (Urbana: U of Illinois P, 1999). Most of these authors agree that the CP's local activities and influence were ultimately more significant than its relationship to the Communist International. For the impact of the Old Left on the gay and lesbian movement, see John D'Emilio, *Sexual Politics, Sexual Communities: The Making of a Homosexual Minority in the United States, 1940-1970* (Chicago: U of Chicago P, 1983); Stuart Timmons, *The Trouble with Harry Hay: Founder of the Modern Gay Movement* (Boston: Alyson Publications, 1990), esp. chaps. 5–8; and Eric Marcus, "The Organizer— Chuck Rowland," in *Making History: The Struggle for Lesbian and Gay Equal Rights, 1945-1990: an Oral History* (New York: Harper Collins, 1992).

In addition to these works, memoirs of former Communists such as Peggy Dennis's, *The Autobiography of an American Communist: A Personal View of a Political Life, 1925-1975* (Westport, Conn.: Lawrence Hill, 1977) and Jessica Mitford's, *A Fine Old Conflict* (New York: Knopf, 1977), also support the notion that the American Communists worked to aid a wide variety of progressive movements and causes. Vivian Gornick's *The Romance of American Communism* (New York: Basic Books, 1977), a compilation of her interviews with current and former American Communists, also fits into this category.

For a more thorough discussion and analysis of these historiographical issues, see Maurice Isserman's "Three Generations: Historians View American Communism," *Labor History* 26, 4 (1985): 517–45, and Michael E. Brown's introduction to *New Studies in the Politics and Culture of U.S. Communism*; Michael Kazin, "The Agony and Romance of the American Left," *Journal of American History* 83 (1996): 1503–9.

On the broad history of McCarthyism, see Michael Belknap, *Cold War Political Justice: The Smith Act, the Communist Party, and American Civil Liberties* (Westport, Conn.: Greenwood P, 1984); Peter Steinberg, *The Great "Red Menace": United States Prosecution of American Communists, 1947-1952* (Westport, Conn.: Greenwood P, 1984); Ellen Schrecker, "McCarthyism and the Decline of American Communism, 1945–1960," in Brown et al., eds., *New Studies in the Politics and Culture of Communism*; and Schrecker, *Many Are the Crimes.*

The primary studies of women in and around the Communist Party focus on the decade of the 1930s. These studies include Elsa Jane Dixler, "The Woman Question: Women and the American Communist Party, 1929–1941" (Ph.D. diss., Yale University, 1974); Robert Shaffer, "Women and the Communist Party USA, 1930–1940," *Socialist Review* 45 (May 1975): 73–118; Ellen Kay Trimberger, "Women in the Old and New Left: The Evolution of the Politics of a Personal Life," *Feminist Studies* 5 (Fall 1979): 432–50; Susan Ware, "Women on the Left: The Communist Party and Its Allies," in *American Women in the 1930s: Holding Their Own* (Boston: Twayne Publishers, 1982); Van Gosse, "'To Organize in Every Neighborhood, in Every Home': The Gender Politics of American Communists between the Wars," *Radical History Review* 50 (Spring 1991): 109–41; and Rosalyn Baxandall, "The Question Seldom Asked: Women and the CPUSA," in Michael E. Brown et al., eds., *New Studies in the Politics and Culture of U.S. Communism.* Buhle's *Women and American Socialism* (Champaign-Urbana: U of Illinois P, 1993), and Nancy Cott's *The Grounding of Modern Feminism* (New Haven: Yale UP, 1987) also contribute to this view.

In the last few years this view has begun to change as some scholars have recognized that even this traditionally female work had important political components. See Norah Chase, "Cookies and Communism," in Linn Shapiro and Judy Kaplan, eds., *Red Diapers: Growing up in the Communist Left* (Champaign-Urbana: U of Illinois P, 1998); Deborah Gerson "'Is Family Devotion Now Subversive?': Familialism against McCarthyism," in Joanne Meyerowitz, ed., *Not June Cleaver: Women and Gender in the Postwar U.S., 1945-1960* (Philadelphia: Temple UP, 1995). See Joyce Antler, "Between Culture and Politics: The Emma Lazarus Federation of Jewish Women's Clubs and the Promulgation of Women's History, 1944–1989," and Amy Swerdlow, "The Congress of American Women: Left-Feminist Peace Politics in the Cold War," in Linda Kerber, Alice Kessler-Harris, and Kathryn Kish Sklar, eds., *U.S. History as Women's History: New Feminist Essays*, (Chapel Hill: U of North Carolina P, 1995); Constance Coiner, *Better Red* (New York: Oxford UP, 1995); Daniel Horowitz, "Demystifying Betty Friedan and *The Feminine Mystique:* Labor Union Radicalism and Feminism in Cold War America," *American Quarterly* 48 (March 1996): 1–42, and *Betty Friedan and the Making of "The Feminine Mystique": The American Left, the Cold War and Modern Feminism* (Amherst: U of Massachusetts P, 1998). After this book went to press I discovered that Linn Shapiro's dissertation on women activists in the Communist Party (American University, 1997) is also titled "Red Feminism." Shapiro analyzes the links between CP feminists and first wave feminism.

It is well known that the years between 1945 and the early 1960s were not particularly conducive to struggles for women's equality. Americans' desire to return to some kind of "normal" life after years of Depression and war, combined with widespread efforts to push women back into the home after World War II and influential neo-Freudian arguments that equated feminism with neurosis, effectively thwarted the development of any mass-based women's movement in the late 1940s and 1950s. On the antifeminism of the period, see Ferdinand Lundberg and Marynia Farnham, *Modern Woman: The Lost Sex* (New York: Harper Bros., 1947); Marty Jezer, *The Dark Ages: Life in the United States, 1945-1960* (Boston: South End P, 1982); Eugenia Kaledin, *American Women in the 1950s: Mothers and More* (Boston: Twayne, 1984); Leila J. Rupp and Verta Taylor, *Survival in the Doldrums: The American Women's Rights Movement, 1945-1960s* (New York: Oxford UP, 1987); and Elaine Tyler May, *Homeward Bound: American Families in the Cold War Era* (New York: Basic Books, 1988).

Despite the hostile climate of the Cold War era, numerous scholars have written about how individual women and women's organizations sustained elements of a women's movement for equal rights in the 1950s. See Cynthia Harrison, *On Account of Sex: The Politics of Women's Issues, 1945-1968*

(Berkeley: U of California P, 1988); Nancy Gabin, *Feminism and the Labor Movement: Women and the United Auto Workers, 1935-1975* (Ithaca, N.Y.: Cornell UP, 1990); Susan Lynn, *Progressive Women in Conservative Times: Women in the YWCA and AFSC* (New Brunswick, N.J.: Rutgers UP, 1992) on the persistence of feminism in the period 1945–60. Sara Evans's *Personal Politics: The Roots of Women's Liberation in the Civil Rights Movement and in the New Left* (New York: Vintage Books, 1980) is the definitive study of the origins of the women's movement in the New Left. Other useful discussions of this question include Mary King, *Freedom Song: A Personal History of the 1960s Civil Rights Movement* (New York: William Morrow, 1987); Alice Echols, *Daring to Be Bad: Radical Feminism in America, 1967-1975* (Minneapolis: U of Minnesota P, 1989); and Flora Davis, *Moving the Mountain: The Women's Movement in America Since 1960* (New York: Simon & Schuster, 1991).

On the evolution and growth of the second-wave women's movement in the 1970s, see Alice Echols, *Daring to Be Bad;* Steven Buechler, *Women's Movements in the United States: Woman Suffrage, Equal Rights, and Beyond* (New Brunswick, N.J.: Rutgers UP, 1990); Flora Davis, *Moving the Mountain: The Women's Movement in America Since 1960;* Nancy E. Whittier, *Feminist Generations: The Persistence of the Radical Women's Movement* (Philadelphia: Temple UP, 1995).

# Index